STUDIES OF THE AMERICAS

edited by

James Dunkerley

Institute for the Study of the Americas
University of London
School of Advanced Study

Titles in this series are multi-disciplinary studies of aspects of the societies of the hemisphere, particularly in the areas of politics, economics, history, anthropology, sociology and the environment. The series covers a comparative perspective across the Americas, including Canada and the Caribbean as well as the USA and Latin America.

Titles in this series published by Palgrave Macmillan:

Cuba's Military 1990–2005: Revolutionary Soldiers during Counter-Revolutionary Times
   By Hal Klepak

The Judicialization of Politics in Latin America
   Edited by Rachel Sieder, Line Schjolden, and Alan Angell

Latin America: A New Interpretation
   By Laurence Whitehead

Appropriation as Practice: Art and Identity in Argentina
   By Arnd Schneider

America and Enlightenment Constitutionalism
   Edited by Gary L. McDowell and Johnathan O'Neill

Vargas and Brazil: New Perspectives
   Edited by Jens R. Hentschke

When Was Latin America Modern?
   Edited by Nicola Miller and Stephen Hart

Debating Cuban Exceptionalism
   Edited by Laurence Whitehead and Bert Hoffman

Caribbean Land and Development Revisited
   Edited by Jean Besson and Janet Momsen

Cultures of the Lusophone Black Atlantic
   Edited by Nancy Naro, Roger Sansi-Roca, and David Treece

Democratization, Development, and Legality: Chile, 1831–1973
   By Julio Faundez

The Hispanic World and American Intellectual Life, 1820–1880
   By Iván Jaksić

The Role of Mexico's Plural in Latin American Literary and Political Culture: From Tlatelolco to the "Philanthropic Ogre"
   By John King

The Political Economy of Hemispheric Integration

Responding to Globalization in the Americas

Edited by

Diego Sánchez-Ancochea

and

Kenneth C. Shadlen

THE POLITICAL ECONOMY OF HEMISPHERIC INTEGRATION
Copyright © Diego Sánchez-Ancochea and Kenneth C. Shadlen, 2008.

First published in 2008 by
PALGRAVE MACMILLAN™
175 Fifth Avenue, New York, N.Y. 10010 and
Houndmills, Basingstoke, Hampshire, England RG21 6XS
Companies and representatives throughout the world.

PALGRAVE MACMILLAN is the global academic imprint of the Palgrave
Macmillan division of St. Martin's Press, LLC and of Palgrave Macmillan Ltd.
Macmillan® is a registered trademark in the United States, United Kingdom
and other countries. Palgrave is a registered trademark in the European
Union and other countries.

ISBN-13: 978–0–230–60657–9
ISBN-10: 0–230–60657–1

Library of Congress Cataloging-in-Publication Data

The political economy of hemispheric integration: responding to
globalization in the Americas / edited by Kenneth C. Shadlen and
Diego Sánchez-Ancochea.
p. cm.—(Studies of the Americas series)
Papers presented at a conference held in London June 1–2, 2006.
Includes bibliographical references and index.
ISBN 0–230–60657–1
1. America—Foreign economic relations—Congresses. 2. America—
Economic integration—Congresses. 3. Free trade—America. I. Sánchez-
Ancochea, Diego. II. Shadlen, Kenneth C.

HC94.P65 2008
337.1'7—dc22   2007047111

A catalogue record for this book is available from the British Library.

Design by Newgen Imaging Systems (P) Ltd., Chennai, India.

First edition: July 2008

10 9 8 7 6 5 4 3 2 1

Printed in the United States of America.

Contents

Figures

Tables

x   TABLES

Acknowledgments

The contributions to this book were first presented at the conference "Responding to Globalization in the Americas: The Political Economy of Hemispheric Integration," which took place in London on June 1–2, 2006. The conference was hosted by the Institute for the Study of the Americas (ISA) of the University of London and the Development Studies Institute (DESTIN) of the London School of Economics. Neither the June 2006 conference nor this subsequent volume would have been possible without the support of ISA and the Inter-American Development Bank (IADB). We thank both institutions for their generous financial backing, and we wish to thank the staff at ISA for providing invaluable administrative, organizational, and academic support. In particular, Olga Jimenez was as charming, efficient, and patient as ever; her tireless work in liaising with the participants, the organizers, travel agencies, caterers, and everyone else involved is one of the principal reasons for the conference being so successful. Thanks to the London School of Economics for making the facilities available. Within DESTIN, we thank Jo Beall for her encouragement and backing, Elisa Nelson for her assistance with organizational matters on the southern end of the Kingsway, and Emily Verellen for formatting the chapters in preparation of submitting the manuscript to Palgrave.

The success of an edited volume depends on the quality of the contributions. We would like to thank the authors for their effort and professionalism—submitting strong papers prior to the conference, responding to comments and suggestions, and promptly returning revised versions of their chapters. We also acknowledge the few authors who, regrettably, we could not include in the final version of the manuscript, and thank them for their participation. We thank Rhys Jenkins, Dirk Willem te Velde, and Kevin Middlebrook for serving as panel discussants at the conference and providing the authors with insightful and constructive comments. Likewise, we are grateful to Palgrave's external reviewer, whose suggestions helped strengthen the individual chapters and the volume as a whole, and to Joanna Mericle from Palgrave for all her help and guidance in preparing the manuscript.

Lastly, we express our profound thanks to Professor James Dunkerley, for his decisive support from beginning to end. He welcomed our initial proposal for a conference, helped to raise funds to make it happen, and made possible the rapid publication of the book in this series *Studies of the Americas*. We are grateful to James for his encouragement and unshakable enthusiasm for our project.

Abbreviations

AAGR	Average Annual Growth Rate
ARENA	Alianza Republicana Nacionalista, Republic Nationalistic Alliance
ASCM	WTO Agreement on Subsidies and Countervailing Measures
BITs	Bilateral Investment Treaties
CANACINTRA	Cámara Nacional de la Industria de Transformación
CARICOM	Caribbean Community and Common Market
CBI	Caribbean Basin Initiative
CBRA	Caribbean Basin Recoverty Act
CEPAL	Comisión Económica para América Latina y el Caribe, Economic Commission for Latin America and the Caribbean
CODESA	Costa Rican Corporation for Development
CUSFTA	Canada-U.S. Free Trade Agreement
DESTIN	Development Studies Institute
DR-CAFTA	Dominican Republic-Central America Free Trade Agreement
ECLAC	Economic Commission for Latin America and the Caribbean
EOI	Export-Oriented Industrialization
EPA	Economic Partnership Agreements
EPZ	Export Processing Zones
FMLN	Frente Farabundo Martí de Liberación Nacional, Farabundo Martí Nacional Liberation Front
FOCAL	Canadian Foundation for the Americas
FTA	Free Trade Agreement/Area

FTAA	Free Trade Area of the Americas
GAO	General Accounting Office
GATS	General Agreement on Trade in Services
GATT	General Agreement on Tariffs and Trade
GCI	Global Competitiveness Index
GDP	Gross Domestic Product
IADB	Inter-American Development Bank
ICSID	International Center for the Settlement of Investment Disputes
ICT	Information and Communication Technology
IP	Intellectual Property
ISA	Institute for the Study of the Americas
ISI	Import-Substituting Industrialization
ITAM	Instituto Tecnológico Autónomo de México
LACs	Latin American and Caribbean Countries
LATN	Latin American Trade Network
MAs	Mergers and Acquisitions
Mercosur	Mercado Común del Sur South American Common Market
NAFTA	North American Free Trade Agreement
NEM	New Economic Model
NGOs	Nongovernmental Organizations
NICs	Newly Industrialized Countries
OAS	Organization of American States
OEM	Original Equipment Manufacture
PAC	Partido de Acción Nacional, Citizen's Action Party
PTA	Preferential Trade Agreements
RBTAs	Regional and Bilateral Trade Agreements
SDT	Special and Differential Treatment
SEZs	Special Economic Zones
SITC-2	Two-digit Standard International Trade Classification
SOEs	State-Owned Enterprises
SPP	Security and Prosperity Partnership of North America
TNCDB	Trade Negotiations and Commercial Diplomacy Branch
TNCs	Transnational Corporations
TRIMs	World Trade Organization's Agreement on Trade-Related Investment Measures

TRIPs	World Trade Organization's Agreement on Trade-Related Aspects of Intellectual Property Rights
UNAM	Universidad Nacional Autónoma de México
UNCTAD	United Nations Commission for Trade and Development
USAID	U.S. Agency of International Development
USTR	Office of the United States Trade Representative
WTO	World Trade Organization

Chapter 1

Introduction: Globalization, Integration, and Economic Development in the Americas

Diego Sánchez-Ancochea and
Kenneth C. Shadlen

The 1990s and the early years of the twenty-first century witnessed important changes in patterns of regional integration, namely the emergence of formal "trade" agreements between developed and developing countries. These agreements typically liberalize trade in most goods and services, and they also coordinate measures on a broad range of economic policy areas that go beyond "trade" per se. The first and most prominent of these agreements, of course, is the North American Free Trade Agreement (NAFTA), which the United States, Canada, and Mexico signed in the early 1990s. In subsequent years, the United States has concluded agreements (or, at least, has either begun negotiations or undertaken preliminary discussions on such agreements) with more than half the countries of Latin America and the Caribbean.[1] And, of course, since 1994 discussions have continued for the Free Trade Area of the Americas (FTAA), a hemispheric that would include all thirty-four countries in the region (except Cuba).

The new agreements that we are witnessing mark a considerable break with the types of integration schemes that have historically been prevalent. In the first regard, they stand out for their "North-South" dimensions. Although integration among developed countries and among developing countries has considerable precedent, these agreements transcend the previous divide and bind developed and developing countries in new ways. The second aspect of the new agreements that stands out is their breadth, in that they cover not just trade but also a broader set of regulatory issues, such as rules on managing investment and intellectual property (IP).

Of course, countries approach negotiation of these agreements with markedly different objectives. At the most general level, the primary objective for developing countries is to secure better market access to the developed world and increase inward flows of foreign investment. For developed countries, in contrast, a primary objective is to secure stable business environments that facilitate cross-border expansion of their firms' activities. The ensuing approach to constructing regional and bilateral economic governance, thus, has been to increase market access while also expanding more developed countries' economic rules and regulatory systems. Indeed, regional and bilateral trade agreements (RBTAs) between the United States and developing countries are based on a bargain of market access in exchange for regulatory harmonization (Shadlen 2005; 2006).

In this book we aim to systematically evaluate the economics and politics of the new pattern of North-South integration in the Americas. Two overarching issues orient our analysis. First, we consider the developmental implications of this new pattern of integration. Are RBTAs appropriate mechanisms to promote economic development? To be sure, such agreements provide Latin American and Caribbean (LAC) countries with significantly improved access to the U.S. market: both the breadth of sectoral coverage and the depth of import liberalization promised by the United States are greater under agreements of this type than that available under either the World Trade Organization (WTO) or the Generalized System of Preferences. Yet purchasing such preferential access via negotiation of RBTAs with the United States obliges countries to adopt U.S.-style practices in areas such as the management of inward foreign investment and IP. In assessing the complex trade-offs embodied in regional integration, many of the contributors in this volume conclude that the price of market access may be too high. The prevailing concern, quite simply, is that RBTAs, which dramatically restrict countries' opportunities for policy innovation, may lock in strategies of economic development that have thus-far failed to spur economic development. The first half of the volume addresses these issues, focusing on the challenges derived from new patterns of foreign investment (Mortimore), the rise of China as an exporting power (Dussel Peters), the emergence of a new regime for investment protection (Van Harten), and the multiplicity of intrusive forms of economic governance embodied in regional and global trade regimes (Abugattas and Paus).

Why, then, are these agreements so popular? Explaining the pattern of formal integration in the region is the second overarching issue that orients our analysis. Here we focus on both the proliferation of RBTAs, and, critically, the limits to their spread. The authors consider the interests in integration and strategies for negotiating RBTAs from the perspective of a variety of actors, deploying a range of analytic approaches. We consider, for example, the capacities of the U.S. to fulfill ambitions for integration (Phillips), and the strategy of Canada to both maintain close relations with the United States and counterbalance its neighbor's preponderant influence throughout the region (Macdonald). We also analyze the response of smaller countries in Central America and the Caribbean (Sánchez-Ancochea), and the reactions toward integration and strategies vis-à-vis the FTAA of the larger South American countries in Mercosur (Bahadian and Carvalho Lyrio). And we examine the broader question of how developing countries form coalitions and design collective bargaining strategies to participate in international trade politics (Tussie).

In the remainder of the introduction, we present the logic and research undergirding the book's two principal themes, the economics and politics of RBTAs in the Americas. As a way of providing a point of departure for the subsequent chapters, we begin by presenting an overview of broad changes in the global economic environment, paying particular attention to their effects in Latin America and the Caribbean. In doing so, we offer an assessment of the region's recent economic performance. We then consider how changes in global economic governance affect the options for responding to these changes, explaining, in particular, how RBTAs with the United States can circumscribe the array of policy tools available to developing countries. In the subsequent section we concentrate on the political dynamics of integration in the Americas and explain the diversity of responses. We conclude the chapter with reflections on the policy agenda for the future.

Latin America in the New Global Economy

Economic integration must be understood within the context of broader changes in the global economy. Central to any analysis of the global economy are the emerging strategies of transnational corporations (TNCs). In the pursuit of higher profits, many international firms have gradually shifted labor-intensive production processes to developing countries. This has resulted in an expansion of foreign trade and foreign investment, as well as the emergence of new suppliers in the developing world. Importantly, TNCs have also entered into new sectors of the economy, becoming increasingly active in energy, telecommunications, transportation, utilities, and other services.

The fragmentation of production and the expansion of TNCs' activities create new opportunities and constraints for developing countries. Following a long history of cross-regional forms of interaction with the global economy (Gereffi and Wyman, 1990), Latin American and Asian countries have responded differently to the new global environment. Most generally, Latin American countries embraced neoliberal reforms enthusiastically during the 1990s and performed relatively poorly. In contrast, China and other Asian countries adopted a more managed approach to globalization. We now examine the changes in the behavior of TNCs, and then review the Latin American response.

Globalization and the Reorganization of Global Production

Two distinct waves of transnationalization are evident in the post–World War II period. During the late 1950s and the 1960s, large industrial corporations began expanding to developing countries. These corporations tended to establish local subsidiaries to produce for domestic markets (Evans, 1998; Maxfield and Nolt, 1990). In doing so these firms received the support of many governments, especially in Latin America, that relied on foreign investment to deepen local industrial structures.

From the early 1970s TNCs gradually shifted their productive strategies. Instead of creating subsidiaries that would produce and market their goods locally within many countries, they began organizing production and distribution on global and regional bases. Exploiting opportunities created by new communication technologies and reduced transportation costs, and relying on a range of business practices (including direct investment, subcontracting, and licensing), TNCs have been able to place various stages of their operations (e.g., design, production, assembly, and marketing) in different geographical locations (ECLAC, 2002; Gereffi, 2005). A result of modularization has been the establishment of integrated production networks, typically constructed around "strategic alliances" among TNCs and including entrepreneurial groups from developing countries, in which an increasing number of tasks in the production of goods and services moves to new locations (Evans, 1998).

A significant component of the second wave of transnationalization has been the expansion of TNCs into new sectors of the economy. In the context of rapidly changing technologies, the privatization of state-owned enterprises, which occurred on a massive scale throughout developing and transition economies in the 1980s and 1990s, has facilitated the entry of foreign firms into utilities, energy, telecom, and other sectors that historically had been reserved for local (and at times public) owners. Data on mergers and acquisitions (MAs) provide indicators of the spread of TNCs: cross-border MAs increased from US$75 billion in 1987 to US$720 billion in 1999, with concentration in telecommunications, finance, and business services (UNCTAD, 2000; 2005). In the developing world, Latin America was the most active region in terms of MAs, with major service-sector, utility, and natural resource firms coming to dominate new markets in the region (Mortimore, this volume).

The spread of TNCs and their supply networks is behind the significant expansion of foreign direct investment (FDI) and foreign trade in the global economy. Table 1.1 provides data on FDI inflows for the global economy for 1990 and 2005, as well as the average annual rates of growth for the fifteen years. The stock of inward FDI in the global economy experienced a nearly sixfold expansion over this period, with an average rate of growth of 10.4 percent each year. Although FDI remains concentrated in developed countries, the relative importance of developing countries and transition economies has expanded rapidly. Table 1.2 presents data on FDI inflows for developed, developing, and transition economies 1990, 1995, and 2005. The stock of FDI in developed countries still accounted for 71.3 percent of the world total in 2005, yet, the share of

Table 1.1 Global FDI Stock and Net Inflows, 1990–2005

	US$ billions		Annual Average
	1990	2005	Rate of Growth
FDI Inflows	201	916	10.64
FDI Outflows	230	779	8.47
FDI Inward Stock	1,789	10,130	12.25
FDI Outward Stock	1,791	10,672	12.64

Source: UNCTAD electronic database of FDI (accessed October 15, 2007).

Table 1.2 FDI Inflows by Type of Economy, 1990–2005

	1990		1995		2005	
	US$ billions	%	US$ billions	%	US$ billions	%
Developed Economies	1,433	80.1	209	75.6	7,219	71.3
Developing Economies	356	19.9	667	24.1	2,655	26.2
Transition Economies	0.1	0.0	7.9	0.3	256	2.5
World Total	1,789	100.0	2,766.1	100.0	10,130	100.0

Source: UNCTAD electronic database of FDI (accessed October 10, 2007).

developing countries increased by nearly a third over the period covered, growing from 19.9 percent in 1990 to 26.2 percent in 2005. In the same period the share of FDI in transition economies increased from virtually nil to 2.5 percent. Within developing countries, the expansion of FDI in labor-intensive manufacturing sectors has been particularly significant.

Total exports have also expanded steadily during this period, outpacing the expansion of gross domestic product (GDP). As figure 1.1 shows, the internationalization of production began in 1988 and accelerated at the end of the 1990s. Developing countries have been active participants in this process and have succeeded in expanding their participation in international trade. As table 1.3 indicates, low-income and middle-income countries' share of global exports increased by 60 percent in the period 1990–2005, rising from 16.5 percent to 26.3 percent. This expansion was primarily the result of the increasing fragmentation of global production, which allowed these countries to export manufactures. Manufacturing exports as percentage of total exports in low and middle-income countries doubled over twenty years, increasing from 31 percent in 1984 to 65 percent in 2004 (table 1.4).[2]

Table 1.3 World Exports and GDP by Type of Economy (% of Total), 1980–2004

	1980[a]		1990		2000		2004	
	GDP	Exports	GDP	Exports	GDP	Exports	GDP	Exports
High Income	77.2	78.9	82.3	83.1	81.0	77.5	79.6	73.8
Low and Middle Income	2.9	19.7	17.7	16.5	19.0	22.5	20.4	26.2

Note:
[a] Exports of low and middle-income countries refer to 1982.
Source: World Bank. World Development Indicators electronic database (last accessed October 15, 2007).

Table 1.4 Manufactures Exports (% of Merchandise Exports), 1984–2004

	1984	1990	2000	2004
High Income	73	77	80	81
Low and Middle Income	31	51	63	64
World	65	73	76	77

Source: World Bank. World Development Indicators electronic database (accessed October 14, 2007).

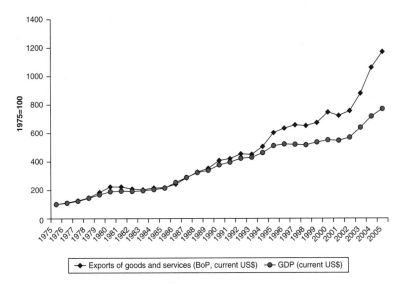

Figure 1.1 Expansion of Global Economy, 1975–2005: Exports and GDP in Current US$ (1975=100)

Source: World Bank, World Development Indicators database (accessed October 10, 2007).

Table 1.5 Selected Developing Countries. Stock of FDI (Millions of US$ and Percentage of Total), 1990 and 2005

Countries	1990		2005	
	US$ millions	%	US$ millions	%
South Africa	9,207	2.6	69,372	2.6
British Virgin Islands	126	0.0	67,359	2.5
Mexico	22,424	6.3	209,564	7.9
Argentina	8,778	2.5	55,245	2.1
Brazil	37,243	10.4	201,183	7.6
Chile	10,067	2.8	73,620	2.8
China	20,691	5.8	317,873	12.0
Hong Kong	45,073	12.6	532,956	20.1
Republic of Korea	5,186	1.5	63,199	2.4
Singapore	30,468	8.5	186,926	7.0
Thailand	8,242	2.3	56,542	2.1
Total eleven countries	197,505	55.4	1,833,839	69.1

Source: UNCTAD electronic database of FDI (accessed October 10, 2007).

Of course, developing countries' participation in the global expansion of investment and trade has been geographically uneven. As table 1.5 shows, the stock of FDI in the ten leading developing countries represents nearly 70 percent of all FDI to developing countries in 2005, with five East Asian countries alone accounting for more than 40 percent. Meanwhile, Latin American countries' share declined slightly during this period. Of the four countries presented in table 1.5, Brazil constitutes the most extreme case, with its share in the stock of FDI to developing countries decreasing from 10.4 percent in 1990 to 7.6 percent in 2005. The East Asian success and Latin American poor performance in relative terms extends to other areas, including manufacturing exports and economic growth.

Different Responses to the Reorganization of Global Production

The changes at the level of global investment and trade flows have been accompanied by significant changes in developing countries' orientation toward the global economy. Since the mid-1980s, and especially during the 1990s, most developing countries have made concerted efforts to expand exports and attract new foreign investors. Yet there are significant differences in the way countries went about increasing exports and FDI, something that Dussel Peters (this volume) highlights well with his comparison of the approaches adopted by China and Mexico. Most generally, China (and Vietnam and other Asian countries), following the lessons from the earlier wave of Asian industrializers such as Korea and Taiwan, adopted managed and pragmatic strategies of integration. These countries combined degrees of liberalization and privatization with the maintenance of an active role for the state to correct for market failures and to build productive capacities in strategic sectors. Liberalization was gradual, and executed with the twin goals of expanding domestic markets and reducing social costs. Most Latin American countries, in contrast, adopted more orthodox and open-ended strategies integration. Liberalization and privatization were more widespread, the state's role systematically de-emphasized, and the achievement of macroeconomic stability (and the attraction of capital inflows, of all sorts) was of paramount importance.

The difference in economic performance between these two sets of countries during the 1990s and early 2000s is striking. Table 1.6 compares the rates of economic growth between 1990 and 2004. In Latin America GDP per capita grew at an annual average rate of only 1.3 percent, lower than both the world average (1.4%) and that of high-income countries (1.7%). In South Asia and East Asia, GDP per capita grew at an annual average of 3.5 percent and 6.7 percent respectively. China's

Table 1.6 Various Regions. Annual Average Rate of Growth of GDP and GDP per Capita (Constant 2000 Dollars), 1990–2004

Region	GDP	GDP per capita
Sub-Saharan Africa	2.7	0.2
Latin America and the Caribbean	*2.9*	*1.3*
East Asia and Pacific	7.9	6.7
South Asia	5.4	3.5
OECD Countries (High Income)	2.4	1.7
World Total	2.7	1.4
China	9.7	8.6
India	5.7	3.9
Singapore	6.2	3.6

Source: Author's calculations from World Bank. World Development Indicators electronic database (accessed October 15, 2007).

progress was particularly impressive: between 1990 and 2004 Chinese GDP per capita grew by an annual average of 9.6 percent, more than three times higher the world average (see Dussel Peters, this volume).

The evolution of economic activity in Latin America was also disappointing when compared to the much-criticized era of import-substituting industrialization. As table 1.7 indicates, in the 1960s per capital GDP in Latin America and the Caribbean grew faster than any region of the developing world. And the per capita growth rates were even higher in the 1970s (though in this decade surpassed by East Asia). The turning point was the debt crisis of the early 1980s, after growth rates in Latin America (and other highly indebted regions, such as sub-Saharan Africa) ground to a halt, while less debt-burdened Asian economies continued to experience remarkably high rates of per capita growth. Even more significant for the discussion of responses to globalization and trade policy choices has been Latin America's mixed record in terms of exports. Trade liberalization and targeted export incentives contributed to strong rates of export growth (see table 1.8). Between 1990 and 2004, the exports grew by an annual average of 7.2 percent—above the world average for the first time in the past half century. Yet here too Latin America's performance was significantly behind that of East Asian countries, which grew by an annual average of 12.6 percent during this period.[3]

Lackluster economic performance was accompanied by increases in unemployment, informality and income inequality. Taylor and Vos

Table 1.7 Various Regions. Annual Average Rate of Growth of GDP (Constant 2000 Dollars), 1960–2004

Region	1960–1970	1970–1980	1980–1990	1990–2004
Sub-Saharan Africa	4.9	3.6	1.8	2.7
Latin America and the Caribbean	*5.3*	*5.6*	*1.2*	*2.9*
East Asia and Pacific	4.5	6.6	7.5	7.9
South Asia	4.4	3.0	5.6	5.4
OECD Countries (high income)	5.3	3.4	3.1	2.4
World Total	5.3	3.7	3.1	2.7
China	3.6	6.2	9.3	9.7
India	4.1	3.0	5.8	5.7
Singapore	9.8	8.9	7.4	6.2

Source: Author's calculations from World Bank. World Development Indicators electronic database (accessed October 15, 2007).

Table 1.8 Annual Average Rate of Growth of Exports per Decade (Constant 2000 Dollars), 1960–2004

Region	1960–1970	1970–1980	1980–1990	1990–2004
Sub-Saharan Africa	6.4	3.4	0.8	4.2
Latin America and the Caribbean	*5.1*	*4.5*	*4.9*	*7.2*
East Asia and Pacific	—	—	5.7	12.6
South Asia	—	6.2	5.9	14.1
OECD Countries (High Income)	8.1	6.1	4.9	5.6
World Total	7.6	6.0	5.0	6.3
China	—	—	5.7	16.6
India	—	8.5	5.3	10.8

Source: Author's calculations from World Bank. World Development Indicators electronic database (accessed October 15, 2007).

(2003) found that inequality increased in seventeen of twenty-four episodes of reform identified in sixteen different Latin American countries. In a study published in 2004, the World Bank collected data on income distribution for sixteen countries for the 1990s and shows that inequality only decreased in Brazil and Honduras (World Bank, 2004). Berry's (2005) review of a large number of studies on income distribution during the neoliberal era also concluded that inequality increased in a significant number of cases. Growing asymmetries between wages received by skilled and unskilled labor and the expansion of the informal market have both contributed to this expansion in inequality (Portes and Hoffman, 2003; Taylor and Vos, 2003).

How to Integrate? Policy Choice in the Global Economy

This brief review of Latin America's poor economic performance prompts a reconsideration of prevailing development strategies. One of our over-arching concerns is that the new patterns of integration discussed at the start of this chapter may lock-in the current policy trajectories that have been demonstrably unsuccessful. To make this point more clearly, it is worth taking a step back and considering how political choices over integration strategy are affected by the range of policy choices available to developing country governments.

The processes of economic globalization that we have discussed transpire in the context of significant changes in international economic governance that, in turn, place constraints on national governments. The Uruguay Round of multilateral trade negotiations went further in the promotion of multilateral trade liberalization than previous rounds. More types of goods and more types of measures to manage trade (e.g., subsidies) became subject to international trade rules. And the Uruguay Round also incorporated new areas on the international trade agenda, such as investment, IP, and services.[4] The introduction of these new accords significantly widened the scope of international economic governance. And, of course, from the Uruguay Round emerged the WTO, which consolidated the emerging regulatory regimes, established a new system for dispute settlement, and opened a new arena for more flexible and on-going trade negotiations (Narlikar, 2005).

For all its importance as a major international organization with near-universal membership, however, the WTO has been just one of several mechanisms to organize and expand the deep integration of the global economy. The regulation of investment and IP, for example, has advanced further at the bilateral and regional level than in the WTO (Shadlen, 2005). With regard to investment, hundreds of bilateral investment treaties (BITs) have been signed since the late 1980s. As Van Harten (this volume) explains, the proliferation of BITs has created a de facto international investment regime by which TNCs can use international arbitration, based on a hybrid of commercial and public law, to challenge public policies that may affect their operations. By shifting judicial review of public policy from domestic courts to international arbiters, BITs can limit the ability of states to regulate TNCs. This type of regulation of investment rights has recently been incorporated into several recent agreements, beginning with NAFTA. Despite the controversial nature of NAFTA's investment provisions, the United States has demanded that similar provisions be included in all subsequent RBTAs.[5]

Likewise, in the case of IP, RBTAs with the United States invariably include provisions that go far beyond the TRIPS Agreement. Indeed, the contrast between TRIPS and the IP provisions in most RBTAs is striking (Shadlen, 2005). To illustrate, consider the case of patents, which confer *limited* monopoly rights to the owners of new, non-obvious, and industrially useful ideas. Patent holders' rights are limited in three ways: (1) the rights are nonautomatic, in that the owner must apply for a patent and the state must formally grant private ownership rights; (2) the rights are nonabsolute, in that the third parties have some automatic rights of use and the state has rights to regulate how the patentee uses her private rights; and (3) the rights are temporally bounded, in that when patents expire what is treated as private property enters into the public domain. IP agreements establish obligations for how countries set the boundaries of these limitations: how easy or difficult countries make it for private actors to obtain patents, the extent to which the patent holders can exclude others from freely using their ideas and operate independently of state regulations, and how long the exclusive rights last. Comparing the WTO with RBTAs, the IP provisions in the latter place significantly tighter restrictions on how countries establish these boundaries: establishing private rights becomes more automatic (states have limited ability to declare certain types of inventions "non-patentable"), the private rights are more absolute (third-party use and the state's regulatory discretion are both significantly diminished), and the private rights are longer (patent terms are more easily renewable and extensions at times automatic).[6]

The promotion and protection of more—and stronger—rights to investors and owners of IP are just two of the many areas in which regional agreements have allowed some countries to superimpose new governance structures above and beyond those of the WTO. Indeed, these agreements typically exceed WTO obligations in *all* areas, including use of tariffs and subsidies, services, and so on. Moreover, by negotiating with individual or small groups of developing countries (i.e., bilaterally or regionally), developed countries have also been able to push the agenda of international economic governance into areas not (yet) addressed by the WTO, such as competition policy, government procurement, and trade facilitation. Of course, developing countries also acquire economic concessions in exchange for the extensive commitments they make as parties to RBTAs, in the form of increased market access for both traditional and nontraditional exports.[7]

The relative merits of these arrangements have been the subject of extensive analysis. On the one hand, regionalism is regarded by some as a coping strategy: as global economic governance becomes more complex and intrusive, regional negotiations promise policymakers greater control over the "pace, sequence, and direction" of economic policy (Lengyel and Ventura-Dias, 2004: 12). Advocates of RBTAs also maintain that RBTAs with the United States can lead to efficiency gains and the consolidation of business-friendly political environments, both preconditions for higher economic growth. The World Bank (2006: 1) in its review of the impact of the Dominican Republic-Central America Free Trade Agreement (DR-CAFTA) in Central America, for example, argues that this agreement "is likely to improve growth levels for the participating countries in Central America and the DR, due to the expected positive effects on trade and investment levels." Likewise, Estevadeordal et al. (2004: 5), while acknowledging the existence of risks, highlight the benefits these agreements promise to bring, "in the form of technological transfer, FDI creation, scale economies in shipping and potentially large increases in trade volumes."

On the other hand, many analysts, including most contributors to this volume, question the net economic benefits of RBTAs with the United States. More market access is certainly desirable, but more steps toward regulatory harmonization and further retiring of key policy instruments may be worrisome.[8] Abugattas and Paus (this volume) synthesize much of the research along these lines, defending the need to adopt "capability-centered" development strategies based on the following four components: (1) trade, investment, and IP policies that facilitate learning and innovation; (2) expansion of tax revenues to support increased expenditures in infrastructure, health, and education; (3) macroeconomic policies aimed at minimizing financial instability and securing high capacity utilization (see Ffrench-Davis, 2005); (4) pro-poor policies that explicitly target poverty reduction and compensate for social dislocations. Their chapter raises red flags by pointing to the serious constraints that RBTAs create for implementing these sorts of policies.

Whatever the "correct" economic assessment of RBTAs, the proliferation of these agreements throughout the Americas demands explanation. What factors drive the spread of RBTAs? At the most basic level, RBTAs may be regarded as a response to the emergence of abundant low-cost manufacturing capacity in Asia. As discussed above, China has become a global factory and a major importer to the U.S. market. The Chinese threat is particularly acute for those countries whose export profiles depend on a narrow range of labor-intensive manufactures. Faced with such competition, many LAC countries search to gain preferential access to the U.S. market. Indeed, some of the countries that most actively sought RBTAs with the United States are those whose export profiles demonstrate the highest degree of concentration. Take, for example, El Salvador, Honduras, Guatemala, Nicaragua, and the Dominican Republic: for each of these countries, three types of commodities account for greater than 60 percent of their exports to the United States over the period 1996–2003, with apparel alone accounting for more than half.[9]

In contrast, Brazil, which has a significantly more diversified export profile, has demonstrated minimal interest in negotiating an RBTA with the United States.[10] In short, the deal offered by the United States is unattractive, and the structure of the Brazilian economy does not leave policy-makers with a sense of urgency to accept integration on these terms. In fact, as Bahadian and Carvalho Lyrio (this volume) show, the principal concern of Brazilian economic diplomats with regard to the U.S. economy is to improve market access for agricultural exports, and this is not part of the contemporary regional trade agenda.

Though export profiles serve as a useful starting point, they provide insufficient explanation for the full pattern of integration with the United States. After all, countries with similar export profiles have shown different degrees of interest in this new form of integration: the Dominican Republic, for example, did not show any enthusiasm for an RBTA with the United States until El Salvador, Guatemala, Honduras, and Nicaragua began formal negotiations for what would eventually become DR-CAFTA. And we also observe the converse relationship: Costa Rica's export profile is dissimilar to its fellow participants in DR-CAFTA.

Beyond export profiles, an important factor explaining the apparent enthusiasm for such agreements is a "fear of exclusion." Some countries may embrace the RBTA agenda as a way to make sure they are not left alone while their neighbors strike deals with the United States that—arguably—increase market access and foreign investment. The fear of exclusion has been driven by the U.S. strategy of "competitive" or "serial" liberalization of step-ladder negotiations with "can do" countries, which has the goal of generating a "dynamic in which countries compete to become fuller members of the trading system and better partners of the United States" (former USTR Robert Zoellick, as quoted in Shadlen (2008: 12). Indeed, the U.S. strategy is designed to make the broader hemispheric project appear more attractive by instilling a fear of marginalization in non-participating countries. LAC officials know they are not choosing between agreeing an RBTA or retaining the status quo (no RBTA), but that there is a strong likelihood that neighboring countries will agree RBTAs with the United States and they will be left out (Shadlen, 2008).

Fear of exclusion complements and reinforces domestic political processes that also contribute to the proliferation of RBTAs, namely the asymmetric information, resources, and capacities for political mobilization of distinct actors (Shadlen, 2008). Notably, the actors within developing countries who stand to benefit directly from the new form of integration with the United States tend to be better positioned politically than those who stand to lose. In contrast to standard models of trade politics, where the beneficiaries are expected to be unaware of their potential gains, geographically diffuse, and unorganized, while those who stand to lose are expected to be keenly aware of their likely fate, concentrated, and organized (Destler, 1995; Haggard, 1995; Salazar-Xirinachs, 2004; Wise, 2004), the politics of trade and integration in Latin America generally features well-organized winners who are well aware of how they stand to gain from the proposed policy change and diffuse and disorganized losers. Quite simply, exporting firms already exporting to the United States are likely to be better informed, better organized, and more politically influential than firms that might benefit from regulating inward FDI or technology transfer via alternative arrangements for managing IP (Thacker, 2000; Shadlen, 2004; 2008).

As Sánchez-Ancochea's chapter shows, the politics of regional integration in the Caribbean Basin demonstrate the importance of both fear of exclusion and the disproportionate power of exporters. The Dominican Republic's interest in an RBTA with the United States was driven in no small part by DR-CAFTA negotiations between the United States and the five Central American countries, which, it was feared, would lock in the others' preferential access to the United States and leave the Dominican Republic in an unacceptably disadvantageous position.[11] And throughout Central America and the Caribbean, an emphasis on exports since the 1980s has greatly increased the economic and political influence of those actors who are oriented to global markets and have built ties with TNCs. In particular, new exporters from the export processing zones (EPZs) have become extraordinarily influential, reshaping the patterns of interactions between the state and the business elite. This is clear in the Dominican case, where the active support and increasing economic power of local firms operating in the EPZs was pivotal in securing the passage of DR-CAFTA. And it is also evident in the case of Costa Rica, where exporters were key supporters of DR-CAFTA and, more generally, the broader set of neoliberal economic reforms that have been introduced in that country.

Indeed, for Sánchez-Ancochea, Costa Rica, the last country to pass the agreement domestically and the country where domestic ratification faced the greatest opposition, provides the most vivid example of how the current era of trade politics is accompanied by a fundamental restructuring of state-society relations. Here, the existence of other social actors (mainly trade unions in the public sector and other social movements) with long traditions of political participation and influence in the process of policy design helps to explain the protracted and contentious debate over DR-CAFTA in Costa Rica. These alternative actors were still able to mobilize social opposition in the streets and to contribute to a healthy public debate. Yet it is a debate that they too lost, as DR-CAFTA was passed by national referendum in October 2007.

However useful fear of exclusion and exporters power may be in understanding patterns of integration, the undeniable fact is that RBTAs have spread in a remarkably halting and uneven fashion. While some authors regard the strategy of "competitive liberalization" as a key to the United States' ability to achieve regional integration on its own terms (Shadlen, 2008), an alternative interpretation is that the gradual and step-by-step pattern of liberalization is indicative of the *inability* of the United States to advance its ambitious trade agenda. This logic is at the heart of Phillips's chapter, who suggests that the United States' promotion of bilateral and subregional agreements is a function of its internal and external weaknesses.

Phillips asks why the United States has not succeeded in using its high degree of structural power to secure the approval of the FTAA within the Americas, and attributes this failure to a combination of external and internal constraints that have weakened the capacity of the United States to transform its goals into actual policy. The first of these constraints derives from the internal structure of policymaking in the United States, where bureaucratic and institutional fragmentation leads to reduced coherence. That is, trade policy in the United States is designed and implemented by the Trade Policy Review Group and the Trade Policy Staff Committee, both of which have members from different agencies. In particular, these committees include participants from the Office of the United States Trade Representative (USTR) and the Departments of the State, the Treasury and Commerce, each of which follows a different agenda when promoting trade agreements. As a result, Phillips argues, the United States has adopted an approach of "ad hoc reactivism" by which it usually responses to the demands and desires of other countries. Phillips also highlights the opposition from several Latin American countries to the creation of a hemispheric trade agreement. Hugo Chavez's anti-American rhetoric, Brazil's desire for policy autonomy and geopolitical influence, and widespread regional opposition to U.S. foreign policy (economic and otherwise) have all combined to undermine the United States' capacity to achieve integration on its desired terms. Negotiating the occasional agreement here and there with smaller "can do" countries is easier to manage bureaucratically and more likely to gain the necessary public support from a skeptical U.S. public.

While the chapters by Bahadian and Carvalho Lyrio, Sánchez-Ancochea, and Phillips all focus principally on trade politics between the United States and Latin America, the final two chapters focus on different aspects of regional integration. Macdonald analyzes the politics of regional integration in the other "developed" country of the region, namely Canada. Macdonald analyzes Canada's approach toward regional integration since the 1980s, tracing the path traveled from the controversial signing of a trade agreement with the United States (Canada-U.S. Free Trade Agreement, CUSFTA) in 1988, membership in the Organization of American States (OAS) in 1990, extension of CUSFTA to include Mexico in 1994, and the active role that Canada has since taken in promoting the FTAA. In contrast to Mexico, which only supported the FTAA tepidly, out of fear of diluting the preferential market access delivered by NAFTA, Canada has been the region's most dedicated advocate and leader throughout the process. Indeed, for Macdonald, this unbridled enthusiasm—"fervor and frenzy"—for hemispheric integration and not just acquiescence to hemispheric integration is the central analytic puzzle to be explained. While most of the contributors to the volume emphasize structural and material factors, Macdonald's analysis places greater emphasis on the changing perceptions of Canada's national identity, as the definition of "American" is constantly updated to respond to challenges presented by the evolving relationship with the United States, the broader economic trends discussed throughout this volume, and, critically, the rise of Brazil as subregional hegemon.

The final chapter, by Tussie, supplements our analysis of "North-South" relations by considering how developing countries interact among themselves to improve their negotiating capacity in international trade politics. Tussie shows how simultaneous negotiations at the multilateral and regional level also present Latin American countries with additional complexities and dilemmas. Since the late 1980s, regional projects of integration have evolved side-by-side with multilateral trade negotiations, sometimes creating positive interactions but also severe contradictions. She analyzes Latin America's use of negotiations at different levels to improve their insertion in the global economy. On both the regional (hemispheric) and multilateral fronts, Latin American countries have adopted increasingly active—though not always unified—positions. Mexico, not a member of the General Agreement on Tariffs and Trade (GATT) until 1986, has become an active participant in the WTO, leading important councils in Geneva, for example, and hosting the 2003 ministerial meeting. At the same time, Mexico is one of the leaders in the Americas in terms of bilateral trade agreements (Ortiz Mena, 2004) and hemispheric integration. In contrast, Brazil, a long-time member of the GATT/WTO, has joined forces with China, India, and South Africa to promote the Group of Twenty (G-20), an informal coalition of developing countries that has been active in demanding liberalization of the agricultural sector in developed countries and in opposing further deregulation in trade-related areas. And Brazil has been the most reluctant participant in hemispheric negotiations for the FTAA (Bahadian and Carvalho Lyrio, this volume). As table 10.3 in Tussie's chapter demonstrates, many other Latin American countries have also been active in the G-20 and other informal coalitions within the WTO.

Conclusion

Latin American economic performance since the 1980s has been disappointing. Debt crises generated prolonged periods of stagnation and economic restructuring, and the enthusiastic embrace of the Washington Consensus delivered little results in terms of economic expansion, reduction of inequality and creation of new comparative advantages. Mexico, which has become a major exporter of manufactured goods to the United States, has been one of the few successful countries in terms of moving away from specialization in primary product exports. Yet, Mexico's difficulties to compete with China and to expand manufacturing production for the domestic market reveal the limitations of its own model (Dussel Peters, this volume; Gallagher and Zarsky, 2007; UNCTAD, 2003).

Given the poor record of the NAFTA and the poor record of the export-oriented model more generally in Latin America, the current spread of RBTAs with the United States is particularly worrisome. These types of agreements appear to be based on an underlying logic that expanding exports and attracting FDI will result in sustained economic growth. The RBTAs disregard the lessons from the East Asian miracle (and the more recent transformation of China), and thus leave little room for an active participation in industrial upgrading and promotion of domestic capabilities.

The criticisms of North-South regional integration developed in this volume should not be seen as a denunciation of globalization. There is little doubt that the fragmentation of production and the expansion of TNCs create *potential* opportunities for technological upgrading and economic growth in developing countries. The Chinese experience, with all its limitations (including inequality and environmental degradation), clearly shows that this is the case. Yet, the realization of these potential opportunities and the reduction of current risks (e.g., dependence, economic duality, and inequality) require a more active state and a broader menu of policy choices than the ones currently available (Evans, 1998). By placing the rights of foreign investors at the top of the development agenda, and by seriously circumscribing governments' opportunities for policy innovation, however, the U.S.–led project of regional integration may make exploiting the opportunities of globalization more difficult and unlikely.

What should be done then? How could Latin American countries respond to the current regional environment? For countries that have yet to sign agreements with the United States, the answer may appear to be relatively simple: they should refuse to negotiate on the current terms. Yet, given the increasing competition between developing countries (in Latin America and outside Latin America), this strategy may require further coordination within regional blocks. The strengthening of Mercosur, for example, may be indispensable if Brazil and other countries in the Southern Cone are to maintain a strong bargaining position vis-à-vis the United States. Advances in multilateral negotiations would also help to reduce the pressure for regional integration at the regional level by opening up other markets and reducing the gains from preferential market access.

Countries that have already signed a free trade agreement with the United States have fewer options. Their challenge may be how to maximize the policy space still available to promote domestic capabilities. Learning how to manage current rules will be particularly important. In the case of investment protection, for example, countries should always assess the risk of investor's claims. More important, as Van Harten (this volume) recommends, countries should also pay more attention to the appointment of arbitrators and should collaborate with other neighbors in mounting effective defenses when international arbitration has already started. In the case of government procurements, countries should discriminate in favor of small and medium firms, something allowed in many agreements.

Adopting all these measures in Latin America (both in the countries that have already signed and in the ones that have not) will ultimately depend on domestic social relations. As Abugattas and Paus (this volume) write, "a key question will be whether governments have the political will to retain and use the available policy space left and the political will and wherewithal to regain spaces that were given up earlier." This may not happen unless new political coalitions emerge as countervailing forces against the growing influence of exporters and TNCs.

Notes

1. The list of countries includes the following: Chile; five countries of Central America (Costa Rica, El Salvador, Guatemala, Honduras, Nicaragua) and the Dominican Republic; Panama; Colombia, Ecuador, and Peru; Uruguay; and the Caribbean countries in the Caribbean Community and Common Market (CARICOM). Outside of the Western hemisphere, the United States has signed trade agreements (or has begun negotiations) with a wide range of developing countries in Asia (Korea, Malaysia, Thailand, Singapore), North Africa and Middle East (Bahrain, Jordan, Morocco, Oman), and sub-Saharan Africa (Southern African Customs Union). We omit Israel from this list because the agreement with the United States only addresses duties on merchandise trade. Details of all U.S. agreements are available on the Web site of the U.S. Trade Representative (www.ustr.gov/Trade_Agreements/Section_Index.html, last accessed February 11, 2008).
2. Parallel to these changes in the productive sphere, the global economy has witnessed a growing prominence of the financial sphere (Glyn, 2006).

Innovations in communication technologies, together with the emergence of new financial actors (mutual and pension funds) and the liberalization of financial flows, have contributed to a rapid expansion of international financial transactions—and its increasing independence from "real" economic operations. This volume, however, will pay relatively little attention to these processes in the discussion of hemispheric regional integration.

3. Latin America has also maintained a relatively traditional insertion in the global economy, particularly when compared to other emerging economies. More than two-thirds of Latin American exports (excluding Mexico) were primary goods or resource-based manufactures in 2004. In Chile, one of the most successful Latin American exporters, 91% of exports were primary based, thus facing severe limits to their future expansion.

4. Here we refer to the Agreement on Trade-Related Investment Measures (TRIMs), the Agreement on Trade-Related Aspects of Intellectual Property Rights (TRIPs), and the General Agreement on Trade in Services (GATS).

5. The only recent RBTA signed by the United States that does not include compulsory investor-state arbitration is the U.S.-Australia agreement.

6. The emergence of both the new system for investment protection and more extensive obligations for granting and protecting private rights over knowledge speaks to the dramatic shift in the distribution of power in the era of globalization. For many decades, developing countries refused to accept international agreements that would reduce their ability to regulate foreign investment, and they sought to relax international regulations on IP management. Indeed, Latin American countries played a leading role in these struggles to preserve national autonomy in the area of investment regulation (Van Harten, this volume) and IP management (Sell, 1998: Chapter 3). Yet, the growing importance of and competition for FDI and the sea change in economic ideology since the early 1980s has led many developing countries in Latin America (and beyond) to reconsider their positions regarding investment protection and IP management. Subsequently, many have come to accept investor-state arbitration and more rigid frameworks for granting and protecting IP.

7. It should be noted, however, that the effect of such agreements on agricultural subsidies in the United States is minor, because U.S. trade officials regard agricultural subsidies as an issue to be addressed at the multilateral level (where European countries are involved as well).

8. In thinking about integration as embodying trade-offs between how much policy autonomy countries sacrifice in exchange for much market access they acquire, it is worth keeping in mind a third option: by remaining outside of both the WTO and RBTAs, countries can retain extensive policymaking autonomy but they also sacrifice MFN access.

What is not available, however, is MFN or better-than-MFN market access in combination with retaining extensive policymaking autonomy; the Uruguay Round removed that exchange from the menu.

9. See Shadlen (2008: Tables 1–3). The findings are based on export volumes measured at the two-digit Standard International Trade Classification (SITC-2).

10. The three leading export sectors for Brazil account for only 27% of the country's exports to the United States, the lowest level of concentration of any country in the Americas (Shadlen 2008: Table 1).

11. Thus, joining DR-CAFTA became a high priority, a change in priorities reflected by the decision to relocate the country's chief trade negotiator from his position in Geneva to Washington, DC (Shadlen 2008).

References

Berry, A. (2005) "The Distributional Impacts of Economic Integration on Latin American Society, and the Institutional Response", Paper prepared for the ESRC Seminar Series Social Policy, Stability and Exclusion in Latin America, London, June 2–3.

Destler, I. M. (1995) *American Trade Politics*, Washington, DC: Institute for International Economics.

ECLAC (2002) *Globalization and Development*, Santiago, Chile: Economic Commission for Latin America and the Caribbean.

Estevadeordal, A., D. Rodrik, A. Taylor, and A. Velasco, eds. (2004) *Integrating the Americas: FTAA and Beyond*, Cambridge, MA: David Rockefeller Center Series on Latin American Studies.

Evans, P. (1998) "Transnational Corporations and Third World States: From the Old Internationalization to the New," in R. Kozul-Wright and R. Rowthorn (eds.) *Transnational Corporations and the Global Economy*, New York: Macmillan Press.

Ffrench-Davis, R. (2005) *Reformas para América Latina. Después del Fundamentalismo Neoliberal*, Buenos Aires, Argentina: Siglo XXI Editores.

Gallagher, K. and L. Zarsky (2007) *The Enclave Economy: Foreign Investment and Sustainable Development in Mexico's Silicon Valley*. Cambridge, MA: MIT Press.

Gereffi, G. (2005) *The New Offshoring of Jobs and Global Development*, Geneva, Switzerland: International Institute for Labour Studies.

Gereffi, G. and D. Wyman (1990) *Manufacturing Miracles*, Princeton, NJ: Princeton University Press.

Glyn, A. (2006) *Capitalism Unleashed: Finance, Globalization and Welfare*, Oxford: Oxford University Press.

Haggard, S. (1995) *Developing Nations and the Politics of Global Integration*, Washington, DC: Brookings Institution.

Lengyel, M. and V. Ventura-Dias, eds. (2004) *Trade Policy Reforms in Latin America: Multilateral Rules and Domestic Institutions.* Basingstoke: Palgrave Macmillan.

Maxfield, S. and J. Nolt (1990) "Protectionism and the Internationalization of Capital: U.S. Sponsorship of Import Substitution Industrialization in the Philippines, Turkey, and Argentina," *International Studies Quarterly,* 34 (1): 49–81.

Narlikar, A. (2005) *The World Trade Organization: A Very Short Introduction.* Oxford: Oxford University Press.

Portes, A. and K. Hoffman (2003) "Latin American Class Structures: Their Composition and Change during the Neoliberal Era," *Latin American Research Review,* 38 (1): 41–83.

Salazar-Xirinachs, J. M. (2004) "The Proliferation of Regional Trade Agreements in the Americas: An Assessment of Key Issues," in V. K. Aggarwal, R. Espach, and J. Tulchin (eds.) *The Strategic Dynamics of Latin American Trade,* Palo Alto, CA: Stanford University Press.

Sell, S. (1998) *Power and Ideas: North-South Politics of Intellectual Property and Antitrust.* Albany, NY: State University of New York Press.

Shadlen, K. (2004) *Democratization Without Representation: The Politics of Small Industry in Mexico.* University Park, PA: Pennsylvania State University Press.

——— (2005) "Exchanging Development for Market Access? Deep Integration and Industrial Policy under Multilateral and Regional-Bilateral Trade Agreements," *Review of International Political Economy,* 12 (5): 750–775.

——— (2006) "Latin American Trade and Development in the New International Economy," *Latin American Research Review,* 41 (3): 210–221.

——— (2008) "Globalization, Power, and Integration: The Political Economy of Regional and Bilateral Trade Agreements in the Americas," *Journal of Development Studies,* 44 (1): 1–20.

Taylor, L. and R. Vos (2003) "Balance of Payments Liberalization in Latin America: Effects on Growth, Distribution and Poverty," in Vos, R., L. Taylor, and R. Paes de Barros (eds.) *Economic Liberalization, Distribution and Poverty: Latin America in the 1990s,* Cheltenham, UK: Edward Elgar.

Thacker, S. (2000) *Big Business, the State, and Free Trade: Constructing Coalitions in Mexico.* New York: Cambridge University Press.

UNCTAD (2000) *World Investment Report, 2000,* Geneva, Switzerland: UNCTAD.

——— (2003) *Trade and Development Report, 2003,* Geneva, Switzerland: UNCTAD.

——— (2005) *World Investment Report, 2005,* Geneva, Switzerland: UNCTAD.

——— (2006) *World Investment Report, 2006,* Geneva, Switzerland: UNCTAD.

Wise, C. (2004) "The FTAA: Trade Preferences and the Art of the Possible," in V.K. Aggarwal, R. Espach, and J. Tulchin (eds.) *The Strategic Dynamics of Latin American Trade,* Palo Alto, CA: Stanford University Press.

World Bank (2004) *Inequality in Latin America. Breaking with History?* Washington, DC: Oficina de América Latina y el Caribe del Banco Mundial.

——— (2006) *DR-CAFTA: Challenges and Opportunities for Central America*, Washington, DC: Central American Department and Office of the Chief Economist, Latin America and Caribbean Regions.

Part I

The Global Environment

Chapter 2

The Transnationalization of Developing America: Trends, Challenges, and (Missed) Opportunities

Michael Mortimore

This chapter examines the transnationalization of developing America.[1] I present data on the extent of transnational corporations' (TNCs) presence in the region, and examine the effects of transnationalization on national economic development. To be sure, a considerable amount of research has taken place on the transnationalization of developing America, especially since the 1990s.[2] I advance the debate by disaggregating among types of direct foreign investment and discussing the opportunities and challenges, potential and real, that distinct types of FDI present to the countries of developing America. The conclusion considers policy responses to best take advantage of the opportunities presented by transnationalization.

Trends

Two data sets can be used for the initial analysis of the transnationalization of developing America. One examines company-level information on sales and exports operations, while the other focuses on the balance of payments information on foreign direct investment (FDI) inflows. The combination of this statistical information allows us to gain a more comprehensive understanding of the presence of TNCs in the region.

The evolution of TNCs in developing America is reflected in their position in the sales of the 500 largest enterprises and the exports of the 200 principal exporters. For the 1990s, these data demonstrate a deepening transnationalization process: the proportion of the sales of the 500 largest companies in the region accounted for by TNCs rose from 26 to 43 percent between 1990–1999 (figure 2.1). In terms of exports, the share of the 200 exporters corresponding to TNCs rose from 19 to 47 percent during 1990–2000. Thus, throughout the nineties the position of TNC operations was strengthening within the context of the largest firms in developing America. That situation began to change in the 2000s, as the TNC sales within that group of companies fell to 29 percent in 2004 and the share of TNC exports within the 200 top exporters of developing America also declined to 36 percent in 2004.

It would be wrong, however, to conclude that the transnationalization of developing America has ended, or that TNCs are no longer playing important roles in the regions' economies. Both local private and state-owned enterprises have certainly gained ground relative to foreign firms within the top 500 (figure 2.1), but this is in large part because they enjoy high international prices for the commodities that they export, which will not be a permanent condition. And in any case, the absolute presence of the TNC operations remains very strong in absolute terms, above the level at the beginning of the nineties. Indeed, consolidated sales of the principal subsidiaries of the fifty largest TNCs operating in the region amounted to U.S.$ 258.6 billion in 2004, ratifying that they have become—and remain—a significant component of the economic and corporate landscapes in developing America.

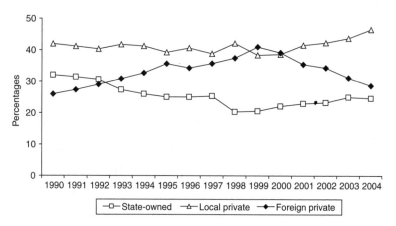

Figure 2.1   Total Sales of the Top 500 Firms in Developing America, by Ownership, 1990–2004

Source: Based on information provided by the Special Studies and Project Department of América Economía, Santiago, Chile, 2005.

According to company-level information, even though the position of the top TNCs has slipped somewhat over the last few years in comparison to local companies, TNCs still possess a hugely significant presence in developing America. Table 2.1 presents data on the fifty largest nonfinancial TNCs in the region. U.S. companies lead the list with twenty-two firms although European companies, taken together, possessed twenty-four affiliates. Three Asian and one Australian firm accounted for the balance. Thirty-one of the companies are manufacturers, eleven are service providers and seven specialize in natural resources. One

Table 2.1 The Fifty Largest Nonfinancial TNCs Operating in Developing America, by Consolidated Sales (Billions of Dollars), 2004

	TNC	Country of Origin	Sector	Sales	% in Developing America	Location of Principal Affiliates
1	General Motors Corp.	United States	Automotive	18.8	10.0	M, B, C, A
2	Telefónica of Spain SA	Spain	Telecom	17.1	45.0	B, Ch, P, M, A
3	Wal-Mart Stores	United States	Retail Trade	14.4	5.0	M, B, A, G
4	Daimler Chrysler AG	Germany	Automotive	14.0	8.0	M, B, A
5	Volkswagen AG	Germany	Automotive	11.9	11.0	M, B, A
6	Bunge	United States	Agro-industry	10.7	42.0	B, A
7	Endesa	Spain	Electricity	9.7	44.0	Ch, B, A, P
8	Ford Motor Co.	United States	Automotive	8.7	5.0	M, B, A
9	Telecom Italy SpA	Italy	Telecom	8.5	22.0	B, A, Ch, Bo
10	Delphi Automotive Systems	United States	Auto Parts	7.0	24.0	M, B
11	AES	United States	Electricity	6.9	72.0	B, V, Ch, A
12	Repsol YPF	Spain	Petroleum	6.7	15.0	A, Ch, P, E, Bo, C
13	Carrefour Group	France	Retail Trade	6.6	7.0	B, A, M, C
14	Royal Dutch Shell Group	Holland/ United Kingdom	Petroleum	6.4	2.0	B, Ch, A, M
15	Unilever	Holland/ United Kingdom	Hygiene/Food products	5.1	10.0	B, M, A, Ch
16	Exxon Mobil Corporation	United States	Petroleum	4.9	2.0	B, C, A, Ch
17	Cargill, Inc.	United States	Agro-industry	4.9	7.0	A, B

Continued

Table 2.1 Continued

	TNC	Country of Origin	Sector	Sales	% in Developing America	Location of Principal Affiliates
18	Hewlett Packard (HP)	United States	Computation	4.9	6.0	M, B, A
19	Nissan Motor	Japan	Automotive	4.8	6.0	M, B
20	Nestlé	Switzerland	Agro-industry	4.7	7.0	M, B, C, Ch
21	BHP Billiton Plc	Australia/ United Kingdom	Mining/metals	4.7	21.0	Ch, P, B, C
22	General Electric	United States	Diverse	4.6	3.0	M, B
23	Lear Corporation	United States	Auto Parts	4.6	27.0	M, B
24	Arcelor	Luxembourg	Steel	4.4	12.0	B, M, A
25	Chevron Texaco	United States	Petroleum	4.2	3.0	B, C, A, V
26	Siemens AG	Germany	Electronics	3.6	4.0	M, B
27	Sony	Japan	Electronics	3.2	5.0	M, B
28	Bayer	Germany	Chemicals	3.1	8.0	B, M, A
29	Iberdrola SA	Spain	Electricity	3.0	24.0	B, M, B
30	Fiat Auto	Italy	Automotive	3.0	5.0	B, A
31	Anglo American Plc	United Kingdom	Mining	3.0	12.0	Ch, B, A, V
32	British American Tobacco	United Kingdom	Tobacco	2.9	12.0	B, M, V, Ch
33	Phelps Dodge Corporation	United States	Mining	2.9	43.0	P, Ch, B, V
34	Portugal Telecom	Portugal	Telecom	2.9	35.0	B
35	The Coca Cola Company	United States	Beverages	2.8	13.0	M, B, A, Ch
36	Whirlpool	United States	Electronics	2.8	21.0	B, M
37	PepsiCo	United States	Beverages	2.7	9.0	M, A, B
38	Philips Electronics N.V.	Holland	Electronics	2.6	6.0	M, B, A, Ch
39	Visteon Corporation	United States	Auto Parts	2.1	11.0	M, B, A
40	Verizon Communications	United States	Telecom	2.0	3.0	V, DR
41	Dow Chemical	United States	Chemicals	2.0	5.0	B, A, M, C
42	E.I. Du Pont de Nemours	United States	Chemicals	1.8	7.0	M, B, A
43	LG Electronics Inc.	South Korea	Electronics	1.8	5.0	M, B
44	Kimberly Clark Corporation	United States	Paper products	1.8	12.0	M, B
45	Nokia	Finland	Electronics	1.7	5.0	B, M

Continued

Table 2.1 Continued

	TNC	Country of Origin	Sector	Sales	% in Developing America	Location of Principal Affiliates
46	BASF AG	Germany	Chemicals	1.7	4.0	B, M, A
47	Sonae SGPS	Portugal	Retail Trade	1.6	18.0	B
48	Électricité de France	France	Electricity	1.6	3.0	B, A
49	Procter & Gamble	United States	Hygiene/Cleaning	1.5	3.0	M, A, B
50	BP Amoco Plc	United Kingdom	Petroleum	1.5	1.0	A, C, V
	Total			263.7		

Notes: M = Mexico, B = Brazil, A = Argentina, Ch = Chile, C = Colombia, V = Venezuela, P = Peru, Bo = Bolivia, DR = Dominican Republic, G = Guatemala, E = Ecuador.
Source: ECLAC (2006).

is a diversified conglomerate. The manufacturers are concentrated in the automotive industry (nine), food products and beverages (seven) and electronics (six). The service providers deal mainly in telecommunications (four), electricity (three) and retail trade (three). Five of the seven natural resource companies are petroleum/gas producers, while the other two are mining companies. Five of the top ten companies are American (General Motors, Delphi, and Ford) and German (Volkswagen and DaimlerChrysler) firms operating in the automotive industry. Three of the top ten companies are Spanish or Italian companies operating in the telecommunications (Telefonica, Telecom Italia), and electricity (Endesa) sectors. Most of the affiliates of the top fifty TNCs by consolidated sales operate in the three largest markets, Mexico, Brazil, and Argentina. With the exception of some Spanish and Italian companies, the TNCs operating in developing America are among the global leaders of their industry. In sum, the major foreign firms in developing America are subsidiaries of leading global firms from the most important source-regions of TNCs, they produce and export some of the principal manufactures of the region, and they provide some of the main services.

In addition to the significant presence of TNCs in the region, balance of payments data on FDI inflows suggest that their presence will be strengthened. Table 2.2 indicates FDI inflows to developing America (excluding financial centers) during 1991–2005. Total inflows rose from an annual average of U.S.$ 20.2 billion during 1991–1995 to U.S.$ 70.7 billion in 1996–2000, before falling thereafter until recuperation began, surpassing the U.S.$ 61 billion level in 2004 to reach U.S.$ 68 billion in 2005. Evidently, developing America had recovered from the sharp decline in FDI

Table 2.2 Net FDI Inflows to Developing America (Billions of Dollars), by Subregions, 1991–2005[a]

	1991–1995[b]	1996–2000[b]	2001–2005[b]	2004	2005
Mexico and the Caribbean Basin	8.4	17.5	23.9	23.8	23.5
Mexico	6.8	12.6	18.8	18.2	17.8
Central America	0.7	2.3	2.3	2.7	2.7
Caribbean	0.9	2.5	2.9	2.9	3.0
South America	11.8	53.2	33.7	37.7	44.5
Mercosur	6.4	36.8	19.9	22.8	20.4
Andean Community	3.7	10.7	9.7	7.7	16.9
Chile	1.7	5.7	5.1	7.2	7.2
Total	20.2	70.7	58.6	61.5	68.0

Notes:
[a] Excludes financial centers. Net FDI inflows are defined as FDI inflows to the reporting economy minus capital outflows generated by the same foreign companies.
[b] Annual average.
Source: Based on statistics from the International Monetary Fund, Balance of Payments Statistics (CD-ROM), March 2006.

inflows at the beginning of the 2000s and the new revitalized inflows no longer depended primarily on privatizations, which suggested that they might be more permanent.[3]

In sum, the operations of TNCs in developing America as a proportion of the total sales and exports of the largest firms in developing America swelled during the FDI boom years and fell off somewhat during the 2000s. FDI inflows enjoyed a strong recuperation during 2004–2005. Thus, available information on the operations of TNCs and FDI inflows suggest that this aspect of the transnationalization of developing America is well advanced and set to deepen further. The next section analyzes the implications of these trends.

Challenges and Opportunities: The Worlds of TNC Operations in Developing America

The approach adopted in this chapter is to focus on the production effects of FDI inflows and TNC operations in order to attain a better comprehension of corporate strategies for investing in developing America (Mortimore, 2000; 2001b) and, thereby, to achieve a more penetrating interpretation of the transnationalization of developing America. From this perspective, it is possible to define four focal points of TNC operations from the perspective of the corporate FDI strategies (table 2.3).[4]

Table 2.3 FDI Focal Points in Developing America, According to the Principal Corporate Strategies

Corporate Strategy/ Sector	Natural Resource-Seeking	Market-Seeking (National or Regional)	Efficiency-Seeking	Strategic Asset-Seeking
Goods	*Petroleum/Gas*: Andean Community, Argentina, Trinidad & Tobago *Mining*: Chile, Argentina, Andean Community	*Automotive*: (Mercosur) *Chemical*: Brazil *Food products*: Argentina, Brazil, Mexico *Beverages*: Argentina, Brazil, Mexico *Tobacco*: Argentina, Brazil, Mexico	*Automotive*: Mexico *Electronics*: Mexico & Caribbean Basin *Apparel*: Caribbean Basin & Mexico	
Services	*Tourism*: Mexico & Caribbean Basin	*Finance*: Mexico, Chile, Argentina, Venezuela, Colombia, Peru, Brazil *Telecommunications*: Brazil, Argentina, Chile, Peru, Venezuela *Retail Trade*: Brazil, Argentina, Mexico & Chile *Electrical Energy*: Colombia, Brazil, Chile, Argentina & Central America *Gas Distribution*: Argentina, Chile, Colombia, Bolivia	*Business Services*: Costa Rica	

The *natural resource-seeking* strategy focuses on the petroleum and gas sector of the Andean Community, Argentina, and Trinidad and Tobago, and the mining sector of Chile, Argentina, and the Andean Community. The *market seeking* strategy is centered on the larger countries of the region. With regard to goods, the best examples are the automobile industry of Mercosur, and food, beverages and tobacco in Brazil, Argentina, and Mexico. In services, the financial, telecommunications, electricity, gas distribution and retail trade industries stand out, especially in South America. The *efficiency-seeking* strategy is concentrated in Mexico (automotive, electronics and apparel) and the Caribbean Basin (apparel). The *strategic asset–seeking* strategy, which is based on TNCs that associate for the purpose of innovation and technology, is not at all evident in developing America.

The data in table 2.3 allow us to conclude that developing America is characterized by the existence of two different "worlds" of TNC operations. The first world is that of Mexico and the Caribbean Basin, where the most significant FDI comes from *efficiency-seeking* TNCs that establish export platforms in this subregion that form part of their regional or international systems of integrated production (Mortimore, 1998c; Mortimore and Vergara, 2003). These local assembly operations of mainly U.S. TNCs are primarily "cost centers" for higher technology activities, such as automotive and electronics (Mortimore, Calderón, and Peres, 1996; 1994), or low-technology activities, such as apparel (Mortimore, 2003a). Global competition in these industries obliges TNCs to search for lower cost, large-scale production sites near major markets for the labor-intensive aspects of their production processes (Mortimore, 2000; UNCTAD, 2002). Mexico offers privileged access to the North American market by way of the North American Free Trade Agreement (NAFTA), whereas six Caribbean Basin countries have achieved special access to the U.S. market by way of the United States—Caribbean Basin Trade Partnership Act (CBTPA)—and have since negotiated a separate trade agreement with the United States (DR-CAFTA).[5] As a result and until recently, Mexico and the Caribbean Basin have witnessed a dramatic improvement in their *international competitiveness*, that is, increased import market shares, in this case for automotive, electronics and apparel in the U.S. market (ECLAC, 2004: Chapter 2; Mortimore, Buitelaar, and Bonifaz, 2000; Mortimore and Peres, 2002; Mortimore, Vergara, and Katz, 2001).

A second world of TNC operations is that of South America, where FDI is primarily from TNCs following *market-seeking* and *natural resource-seeking* strategies. The market-seeking strategy is most evident by European TNCs in telecommunications (ECLAC, 2001: Chapter 4), energy infrastructure (ECLAC, 2005: Chapter 3) and finance (ECLAC, 2003: Chapter 3) especially in the MERCOSUR countries and Chile.

The deregulation and liberalization of these activities, coupled with wide privatization programs and an active internationalization strategy of new (mainly Spanish) TNCs were key factors driving FDI here. One clear result of this FDI was the improvement in the *systemic competitiveness* of these countries, that is, improved services and infrastructure that make exporting easier but do not provide the exports themselves. In contrast to Mexico and the Caribbean Basin, the international competitiveness of these countries did not improve significantly as a result of market-seeking FDI in manufacturing. The FDI following a natural resource-seeking strategy was centered on the Andean Community (ECLAC, 2003: Chapter 2), Chile (ECLAC, 2001: Chapter 2) and Argentina (ECLAC, 2002: Chapter 2); countries that possessed both high quality natural resources, such as petroleum, gas, copper and gold, and facilitating regulatory frameworks. One effect was an improvement in the international competitiveness of these countries' natural resource exports.

The transnationalization of developing America, as presented above, reintroduces in this debates over the benefits for host countries in the region (Mortimore, 1999a; 2001c; 2003b; 2004a). On the one hand, FDI inflows into new activities have played a very significant and undeniable role in transforming the region by modernizing industry and improving services and infrastructure, which is evident, for example, in the upgraded telecommunications network in Brazil, financial services in Argentina, road and airport services in Chile and the export platforms in Mexico and Costa Rica that assemble competitive motor vehicles and microprocessors, among others. On the other hand, certain quite serious and undeniable problems have arisen in different parts of the region with regard to the impacts of FDI and TNC operations (Mortimore, 2004b).

Natural resource-seeking FDI is often criticized for creating enclave activities with few processing activities to integrate it into the national economy, for generating low fiscal revenues from non-renewable resources, and for environmental degradation. Market-seeking FDI is typically considered to create higher cost industrial activities that, in addition to not being internationally competitive, crowd out local firms. And market-seeking FDI in services is prone to regulatory problems that sometimes result in formal investment disputes. Efficiency-seeking FDI is often criticized for perpetuating low-value-added traps based on static rather than dynamic comparative advantages, having weak production linkages with the local economy, crowding out local firms, and leading to a race to the bottom in terms of production costs (wages, social benefits) and a race to the top with regards to incentives (taxes and infrastructure). Finally, the strategic asset-seeking FDI—almost nonexistent in the region—can be very low as a result of unfocused national policies, can stagnate at a low level of scientific and technological development, and can come into tension with national scientific and technology policy goals.

In the remainder of this chapter, I assess, empirically, the opportunities and challenges presented by the transnationalization of developing America. I do so by examining some of the most prominent TNC operations in developing America.[6] The analysis covers efficiency-seeking FDI in the Mexican automotive industry and the apparel sector in the Caribbean Basin, and market-seeking FDI in the electricity and gas industries of the Southern Cone, as well as the absence of strategic asset-seeking FDI in research and development (R&D) in the region.[7]

Efficiency-Seeking FDI in the Automotive Industry of Mexico

The Mexican automotive industry is usually considered one of the great FDI success stories of developing America, as it represented the transformation of a "sitting duck" into a kind of "flying goose" (Mortimore, 1995) and was one of the principal sectors that motivated the negotiation of NAFTA on the part of U.S. TNCs. Investment in new plants converted an uncompetitive industry focused on the national market, which produced antiquated, overpriced and poor quality vehicles, into a highly competitive export platform aimed at the North American market. It was mainly U.S. automobile TNCs (General Motors, Ford, Chrysler,[8] and Volkswagen[9]) that took advantage of the geographical proximity of Mexico, its lower salaries, and its preferential access to the U.S. market via NAFTA to establish modern and competitive export operations to supply the U.S. market with lower cost vehicles and compete better with Japanese and Korean vehicles available there (Mortimore, 1997; 1998a; 1998b; Mortimore, Romijn, and van Assouw, 2000). Between 1985 and 2002, the production capacity of the Mexican automotive industry rose from 400,000 to almost 2,000,000 units and exports rocketed from almost zero to about 1,400,000 units. Mexican plants came to account for 14 percent of vehicle imports to North America. The success of this export platform is impressive, especially in comparison to the less competitive Brazilian automotive industry (ECLAC, 2004: Chapter 3).

The difficulties arise when TNCs' corporate strategies and national policy-makers' development goals become incongruent. In the early 2000s, national authorities in Mexico established a goal of doubling the capacity of the automotive industry and converting the export platforms into manufacturing centers. The initiative has not been successful (Mortimore and Barron, 2005), and the main reason that it failed was that the policy goals of the national government did not coincide with the corporate strategies of the principal TNCs operating in the Mexican automotive industry. The vehicle assemblers were willing to contemplate increased levels of national content in order to meet the rules of origin of the different trade agreements, so long as the parts and components met their global price and quality standards. Yet few auto part companies— TNCs or Mexican—were able to meet those conditions. The principal U.S. auto part companies, especially those spun-off from General Motors (Delphi) and Ford (Visteon), were themselves under intense competitive pressure and facing severe difficulties simply surviving. As a result, they were unwilling and unable to recreate large parts of their U.S. production bases in Mexico, although their assets there are substantial. Non-U.S. auto parts TNCs often lacked the scale necessary to move efficiently from the assembly of imported components to local production. Mexican auto parts producers, with some notable exceptions (i.e., San Luis Rassini, Desc, Nemak, Bocar) often lacked the quality required, as evidenced by certification. Thus, passenger-vehicle exports stalled in the early 2000s and the Mexican automotive industry did not take any major step toward its transformation from an export platform to a manufacturing center.

The Mexican automotive industry represents a forceful example of the problems that can arise with regards to efficiency-seeking FDI (Mortimore, 2004b). Indeed, the case reflects many of the principal shortcomings of efficiency-seeking FDI by principally U.S. TNCs in medium technology industries and exemplifies the kind of weak ripple effects that result. TNC operations in this sector focus on static (low salaries, geographic proximity, and preferential market access) rather than dynamic host country advantages (such as skilled human resources and local technology capabilities). As a result, the local productive linkages are weak owing to the dependence of assembly operations on imported components. This, in turn, results in very limited cluster formation. Severe limits are thereby placed on the industrial and technological upgrading of the industry in Mexico. The Mexican government has not done enough to close the gap between national industrial goals and corporate strategies by designing a strategic vision for the industry that is in keeping with both, by attracting auto TNCs (both vehicle assemblers and auto part manufacturers) that are not yet present in the country, and by implementing measures to integrate the supply base and deepen the value chain in Mexico (Mortimore and Barron, 2005).

Efficiency-Seeking FDI in the Apparel Industry in the Caribbean Basin[10]

In the wake of the debt crisis of the 1980s and in desperate search for foreign exchange, many Caribbean Basin countries established export processing zones (EPZs), which would specialize in producing apparel for the U.S. market. At the time, the global apparel market was organized primarily by the Multifibre Arrangement which allowed major markets to establish import quotas on supplier countries (Mortimore, Lall, and Romjin, 2000). The resultant distortions permitted a number of Caribbean Basin countries to enjoy a major success with regards to their apparel exports to the U.S. market by way of the special market access mechanisms, such as the Caribbean Basin Initiative, the Caribbean Basin Economic Recovery Act of the 1980s, and the United States–Caribbean Basin Trade Partnership Act of 2000.[11] Caribbean Basin countries saw their import market share in the United States rocket from 8.5 percent in 1990 to 16.3 percent in 2000. For many of these countries, the export of apparel was the focus of their access to the U.S. market, which was usually their main export market: El Salvador (90% of exports to United States in 2001), Honduras (81% in 1999), Nicaragua (64% in 2002), Guatemala (63% in 2001), and Dominican Republic (55% in 1999) (Hernandez, Romero, and Cordero, 2006); and the proportion of their apparel exports entering the U.S. market via production sharing was very high in 2001: Dominican Republic (91.8%), El Salvador (85.9%), Honduras (85%) (ECLAC, 2004). The specialization of these countries was mainly simple straight-line stitched articles (T-shirts, sweat suits, underwear) although some more sophisticated operations existed (e.g. women's brassieres). In other words, the use of EPZs to assemble apparel for the U.S. market appeared to be a solution to the difficult economic situation faced by several Caribbean Basin countries: their exports exploded and their international competitiveness, as measured by U.S. import market shares, climbed sharply.

The situation for Caribbean and Central American apparel exporters changed dramatically with the implementation in 2005 of the final tranche of the Agreement on Clothing and Textiles of the World Trade Organization (WTO), which ended the quota system and gradually opened the larger markets to international competition. Many of the principal apparel exports of the Caribbean Basin have fizzled since 2000: the U.S. import market share of Caribbean Basin apparel assemblers plummeted to 10.5 percent (Hernandez, Romero, and Cordero, 2006). It is unlikely that DR-CAFTA will compensate for the competitive disadvantages of the Caribbean Basin countries vis-à-vis lower cost Asian producers.[12]

A brief comparison of the East Asian model with the Caribbean Basin model helps us understand the vulnerability of the latter region's apparel sector. The East Asian model was originally based on the experiences of highly successful textile and apparel exporters in Hong Kong, Taiwan, and South Korea. Many of the firms there evolved from assembly plants to original equipment manufacturers then to original brand manufacturers by establishing themselves as intermediaries between U.S. buyers (especially retailers) and manufacturers. They often established their own global sourcing networks, taking advantage of lower wages and the availability of quotas in different host country assembly sites, as their own domestic competitiveness waned. They moved beyond Original Equipment Manufacture (OEM) to higher value-added upstream products (textiles and yarns) and moved downstream into apparel based on their global assembly networks (ECLAC, 2004: Chapter 2; Gereffi and Memedovic, 2003). Thus, the East Asian model produced an industrial and technological upgrading that results in a continual renovation of the international competitiveness of these integrated companies.[13]

In contrast, the Caribbean Basin model was bound by the production sharing mechanism which locked these countries into solely assembly operations based on lower wages than in the United States (but higher than in Asia). This model had several unfortunate effects. First, it produced what can be called "illusory competitiveness," that is, an improved international competitiveness evident in increased export values and rising import market shares but whose impact consisted of only minor ripple effects in the host economy (Mortimore, 2003a). Second, the focus on static (wage levels, social benefit costs, preferential market access, exchange rate) rather than dynamic (skilled human resources and local technological capacity) host country advantages truncated productive linkages and limited cluster formation because of the dependence on imported inputs (Mortimore, 2002; 1999b). Third, it inhibited the expansion of domestic companies that attempted to combine local apparel manufacture with subcontracting for the foreign companies because they were tied inextricably to their domestic competitive situation (Mortimore, Duthoo, and Guerrero, 1995; Mortimore, Vincens, and Martínez, 1998; Mortimore and Zamora, 1998). Fourth, the fiscal benefit from the operation of the EPZs is minimized due to the ability of the larger apparel TNCs with operations in several Caribbean Basin countries to play one off against another in order to demand continued tax incentives (Mortimore and Peres, 1998). Finally, the Caribbean Basin model lost relative advantages to Mexico when the latter entered NAFTA in 1994,[14] a situation which DR-CAFTA does not significantly improve.[15] In sum, then, this case reflects many of the shortcomings of efficiency-seeking FDI in low-technology industries. Here too, we see a vulnerable export structure that generates weak ripple effects.

Market-Seeking FDI in Electricity/Gas in the Southern Cone

Developing America received a huge amount of FDI in the electricity and gas sector during the FDI boom period, mainly in the Southern Cone. Much of this FDI was driven by a combination of the new internationalization strategies of electricity and gas TNCs and opportunities for investment in the region associated with forceful changes to existing economic models and public policy in the subregion, especially in the form of privatization and deregulation. Structural changes in energy markets that encouraged the internationalization of TNCs began in the United States and the United Kingdom later appeared in the European Union (EU). After that they were transposed to developing America, where the European regulatory framework became the more prevalent one. At the same time, technological change that involved using natural gas to drive the new combined cycle turbines to generate electricity became a new factor affecting the efficiency of the electricity sector as of the 1980s. European energy TNCs tended to take the initiative in developing America as a result of the fact that intra-European mergers and acquisitions had not provided them with the critical mass to compete effectively in more competitive global markets.

The electricity sector of developing America offered many possibilities to energy TNCs in order to achieve their mainly market-seeking objectives. As Mexico continued to maintain significant restrictions on FDI in the energy sector, including electricity, these TNCs focused their investment in the Southern Cone, especially Brazil and Argentina, where the extensive deregulation that included the electricity generation and distribution infrastructure offered the best opportunities. Thus, a new and more intimate interrelationship of the electricity and gas sectors in the Southern Cone emerged at a time when the direct role of the State in the electricity sector was declining and privatization processes produced a strong new role for energy TNCs, especially in electricity. During the 1990s, a huge amount of investment (U.S.$ 77.4 billion) was registered in the electricity and gas sectors of the principal markets of the Southern Cone by TNCs (table 2.4).

The principal aims of host governments were to expand output, make it more efficient, improve quality and modernize the sector. One might have expected such high levels of FDI to have such effects, but, as it

Table 2.4 Private Investment in the Electricity and Gas Sectors of the Principal Southern Cone Countries, 1990–2002 (Billions of Dollars, includes Privatizations)

Country	Sector		
	Electricity	Gas	Total
Argentina	16.0	3.2	19.2
Brazil	43.0	4.9	47.9
Chile	8.0	2.3	10.3
Total	67.0	10.4	77.4

Source: Estimates of Gas Atacama, based on information from the National Electricity Commission of Chile, the Energy Secretariat of Argentina, Ecopetrol, the World Bank, and others.

happened, three quarters of that investment went for the acquisition of existing assets, and only one-quarter for upgrading and/or new green-field investments. As a result, the expansion and modernization of output was not adequate for local needs—in spite of the large amount of FDI that entered the sector—leading to a situation of chronic under-supply. This outcome is quite ironic, considering that since the mid-1990s Southern Cone governments subjected the electricity sector to strong policies of privatization and deregulation precisely so that TNCs would provide the investment necessary to modernize the sector and thereby resolve existing problems of under-investment.

On top of the problem of relatively little *new* investment associated with the privatization of the state assets, numerous problems of a regulatory nature appeared. Difficulties in establishing realistic tariff rates during periods of macroeconomic dislocation led to low long-term profitability for the service providers. In some cases, governments did not respect established contractual commitments (i.e., the currency and the inflation adjustment mechanisms to be used to define tariff rates). In Argentina, the economic chaos associated with the major devaluation of January 2001 led many electricity and gas providers to implement the investor-State dispute settlement options available to them by way of bilateral investment treaties in order to seek international arbitration in the International Center for the Settlement of Investment Disputes (ICSID)[16] (Mortimore and Stanley, 2006; Van Harten, this volume). In the case of Brazil, the National Development Bank avoided similar chaos by acquiring a major shareholding in the AES operation and offering loans to other operators to keep the devaluation from provoking serious losses. These countries reacted in different manners within the constraints that they faced.[17] Thus, the presumed automatic expansion of the electricity infrastructure (both generation and distribution) with the entry of the electricity TNCs did not pan out in practice due to the weak financial situation of the major TNC operators and the changing host country situations they were faced with.

TNCs responded in distinct manners to the growing crisis in the electricity sector of the Southern Cone. The European electricity TNCs were obliged to redefine their strategies in the face of the crisis and some, such as Endesa and Tractebel, took a more aggressive strategy to extend their activities in the Southern Cone into the gas sector to secure more efficient and integrated operations (table 2.5). The few non-European TNCs that had established a significant position in the Southern Cone, such as the U.S. TNCs Enron and AES, were both very much caught up in the financial scandals affecting their firms in their home country to play a very positive role in the evolution of the sector. Enron sold most of its operations in the region. AES opted to redefine its presence there. Both initiated international arbitration against Argentina in ICSID. In other

Table 2.5 Integration of Electricity and Gas Operations in the Southern Cone (by Principal Company), 2004

	Argentina				Bolivia				Brazil				Chile			
	Elec.		Gas		Elec.		Gas		Elec.		Gas		Elec.		Gas	
	G	D	P	T	G	D	P	T	G	D	P	T	G	D	P	T
1. Electricity companies																
AES Co. (US)	X								X	X			X			
Endesa (Spain)	X	X		X					X	X			X	X		X
EDP (Portugal)									X	X						
Suez-Tractebel (France)				X		X			X	X			X	X		
Iberdrola (Spain)									X	X			X			
EDF (France)	X	X							X							
2. Natural gas providers																
Repsol-YPF (Spain)			X	X			X	X	X		X	X				
Total (France)			X	X			X	X				X				X
Petrobras (Brazil)	X		X	X			X	X	X		X	X				X

Notes: Elec. = Electricity, G = Generation, D = Distribution, P = Production, T = Transportation.
Source: ECLAC.

words, the European electricity TNCs ended up as the principal major players remaining in the sector; however, they were not in a financial position to undertake the new investment required to increase and modernize capacity.

Somewhat in desperation, Southern Cone governments looked to petroleum/gas TNCs to pick up the slack. Certain European companies (Repsol and Total) demonstrated a new interest in extending their gas activities toward the electricity sector. The sustained high international price of petroleum provided these corporations with a superior financial position, permitting them to consider a greater presence in the sector. In this case, their aim was to ensure access to the principal gas deposits (in Argentina, Bolivia, and, to a lesser extent, Brazil) and construct transportation facilities to the importing markets (Brazil and Chile). The idea of generating (Argentina and Brazil) and distributing (Argentina) electricity became a distinct possibility. The Brazilian petroleum company, Petrobras, also became a central player in this initiative. Nonetheless, while these companies possess the resources needed to resolve the chronic underinvestment that has plagued the sector, they have been hesitant to commit concrete investments, given the poor regulatory record, in spite of the proposal of a Southern Cone strategy for the integrated electricity and gas sectors.

In turn, some countries are looking for solutions outside the realm of FDI and TNC operations. Bolivia decided to nationalize the petroleum and gas industry, sending its military to occupy the foreign-owned operations in May 2006. Both Bolivia and Argentina are recreating their State petroleum companies in an attempt to face up to existing problems of the energy sector, those that the burst of market-seeking FDI did not resolve. To put it simply, some countries have returned to square one, insofar as the significant inflows of FDI and increased presence of TNCs did not resolve the fundamental problem of insufficient electricity generating capacity.

Strategic Asset-Seeking FDI in R&D

As indicated, globally significant strategic asset-seeking FDI in R&D practically does not exist in developing America. This subsection considers the importance of FDI-driven R&D in local development, considers why developing America lags behind in this area, and the extent to which the situation can be changed.

In the globalizing world economy, the activities of TNCs and their interaction with domestic actors are increasingly important for a country's economic development. TNCs are a central aspect of the international economy, accounting for two-thirds of world trade and more than three quarters of FDI and, even more important, their principal competitive advantages stem from the technology that they develop. TNCs dominate the global spending on business R&D (69%) which drives new technologies and innovation. Recently, TNCs began to internationalize their R&D operations in order to reduce costs.

The internationalization of R&D can bring significant benefits to developing countries. R&D by foreign companies can serve as a training ground and provide challenging, high-skill jobs to scientists and engineers in a host country. R&D may create new research skills and thereby help enhance human resources in a host country. The establishment of R&D activities may bring in new knowledge and research expertise, generate knowledge spillovers to domestic enterprises and non-firm organizations, thus stimulating an R&D culture in a host economy. All of these effects, in turn, can led to the emergence of greater R&D competence, which is necessary for host countries to move up the value chain and into new areas of dynamic comparative advantage. Thus, FDI, R&D, technology, and development can be intimately entwined. Although the trend among TNCs to conduct more R&D in developing countries is accelerating, the trend has for the most part bypassed developing America. Between 1994 and 2002 the share of developing countries in U.S. TNCs' overseas R&D activities rose from 7.6 percent to 13.5 percent, but during the same period developing America's share adropped from 4.0 percent to 3.2 percent. Similarly, future plans among global TNCs indicate further plans to expand R&D activities in Asia, while very few reveal similar intentions for developing America (UNCTAD, 2005).

Developing America would obviously benefit from access to business R&D networks in the form of a strengthened domestic absorptive capacity through technology transfer, human resource training, and local enterprise development, as well as an improved science and technology infrastructure. It is necessary to fully understand why developing America does not succeed in benefiting from this aspect of transnationalization and to implement the necessary policy measures to correct that situation. An UNCTAD questionnaire administrated to investment promotion agencies from different regions found an important part of the explanation as to why developing America underperforms in terms of attracting FDI-based R&D. Contrary to what takes place in the rest of the world, in developing America only two of eighteen investment promotion agencies have policies to actively attract FDI in R&D compared to fifteen of sixteen that do so in developing Asia (UNCTAD, 2005). In order to attract R&D facilities, developing America countries must improve their FDI policy instruments (ECLAC, 2006: Chapter 2). In particular, they need to use targeted investment promotion and incentives in order to operate with the same repertoire of instruments as their competitors. To that end, it would be useful to obtain a higher profile for FDI (and science and technology) affairs within the national economic team. Investment promotion agencies might also play a more important role in the area of policy advocacy related to promoting a stronger national innovation system.

In sum, developing America is seriously underperforming with regards to the amount of business R&D that it attracts, the degree of government support for R&D, and the contribution of universities and public sector research institutions to business innovation in comparison to other developing countries. The principal means of catching up seems to entail first of all the strengthening of national innovation systems. This involves placing greater emphasis on tertiary education, increasing interaction between public and private R&D efforts, and creating the incentives needed to promote innovation in the enterprise sector. Another key area relates to the establishment of better relationships with the TNCs that undertake R&D and capturing a higher proportion of the internationalization of that function. At the same time, to attract FDI in R&D the national innovation system must be relevant to business R&D in any country in which TNCs site R&D facilities, and given the fierce competition for FDI linked to business R&D that exists, national FDI policies have to be competitive in the sense that they be modern, coherent and targeted.

Conclusion

There are different interpretations of what transnationalization means. If we consider simply the increase in FDI and the presence of TNCs, it is clear that developing Americas has undergone a strong transnationalization process which has demonstrated a cyclical upward trend over time. This interpretation, however accurate, in itself does not allow for a firm determination of what these changes mean for economic development.

In order to make that determination, it is necessary to evaluate the impact of FDI and TNC operations on the region. This is a question that is too-often addressed in ideological terms, with believers in the benefits of FDI and TNC operations highlighting the more or less automatic "spillovers" from inward FDI and skeptics citing the danger of globalization, transnationalization and, even, imperialism (Mortimore, 2004b; Mortimore and Sunkel, 2001). This chapter has taken the debate further by presenting findings that are based on a large amount of detailed research in developing America.

The analytical framework employed here entailed examining the FDI inflows and TNC operations in terms of the corporate strategies driving them and the concrete impacts of such on the host economy, especially from the perspective of the international competitiveness of the host country's productive apparatus. It is recognized that during the past fifteen years efficiency-seeking FDI inflows have produced impressive changes in the international competitiveness of the TNC export platforms for manufactures in Mexico and the Caribbean Basin, that natural resource-seeking FDI inflows have done the same for TNC primary product operations of the Andean Community and Chile, and that market-seeking FDI inflows have made a contribution to improving the systemic competitiveness of several services in the Southern Cone. The principal finding of this research is that the overall impact of this trans-nationalization process has been much less profound than expected in terms of the ripple effects on the host economy and companies and numerous and that significant problems have emerged. Table 2.6 summarizes major aspects of the expected benefits and possible problems associated with each of these FDI strategies.

An evaluation of the impact of FDI inflows and TNC presence must incorporate both the benefits and problems that have resulted from the perspective of the corporate strategies driving those investments. For this purpose, several of the most significant examples of focal points of inward FDI and TNC operations were analyzed, as were different aspects of the domestic absorptive capacity of companies of the host countries.

With regards to the TNC export platforms for manufactures in Mexico and the Caribbean Basin, which displayed explosive export growth and impressive increases in market shares in the U.S. market, the central problem was that the mechanisms which permitted the privileged access of those products to the U.S. market (production sharing, NAFTA, and DR-CAFTA) were designed for the purpose of helping U.S. auto and apparel TNCs compete better against Asian competitors in the U.S. market, not for the purpose of helping Mexico and the Caribbean Basin countries upgrade industrially or technologically. As a result, the explosive export growth and impressive increases in market shares in the U.S. market for Mexican-assembled autos and Caribbean Basin-assembled apparel produced relatively little in terms of production linkages, transfer of technology, human resource training or local enterprise development. Thus serious problems of competitiveness arose: Mexican autos could not meet the rules of origin for the trade agreements with Europe and Japan because of its overdependence on U.S.-based suppliers, and the Caribbean Basin apparel exports possessed (illusory) competitiveness solely in the assembly function and these exports eventually collapsed because they could not compete in a U.S. market that opened up to Asian and other competitors.

The electricity and gas industry in the Southern Cone countries was the focus of considerable inflows of market-seeking FDI in the context of new economic models that privatized State service providers and deregulated the industry. The national goals of expanding output, making it more efficient, improving quality and modernizing the infrastructure were only partially met because most of the FDI inflows went into existing assets, not new ones, and very difficult regulatory problems associated

Table 2.6 Impacts of TNC Foreign Investment Strategies on Host Countries

FDI Strategy	Expected Benefits for Host Countries	Principal Problems That Have Appeared
Natural resource-seeking	Increased natural resource exports Improved international competitiveness of natural resources High local content of exports Employment in nonurban areas Tax and royalty income	Enclave-type activities not linked to host economy Low levels of local processing of resources Cyclical international prices Low tax income from non-renewable resources Environmental pollution
Market-seeking (national or regional)	New local economic activities Increased local content New/deepened production linkages Local enterprise development Improved services (quality, coverage, and price) and improved systemic competitiveness	Production of goods and services not internationally competitive (not world class) Weak gains in international competitiveness Regulatory and competition problems Disputes related to international investment obligations Crowding out of local companies
Efficiency-seeking for export platforms	Increased exports of manufactures Improved international competitiveness of manufactures Transfer/assimilation of technology Training of local human resources New/deepened production linkages Local enterprise development Evolution from export platform to manufacturing center	Becoming stuck in the low value-added trap Focus on static rather than dynamic host country advantages Truncated productive linkages: dependence of assembly operations on imported components Crowding out of local companies "Race to bottom" in production costs (salaries, social benefits, exchange rate) "Race to top" in incentives (tax, infrastructure) Limited cluster creation

Continued

Table 2.6 Continued

FDI Strategy	Expected Benefits for Host Countries	Principal Problems That Have Appeared
Strategic asset-seeking	Strengthened domestic absorptive capacity through technology transfer, human resource training and local enterprise development Improved science and technology infrastructure	Unfocused national policy Low propensity to invest in science and technology Stagnation at certain level Tension between corporate objectives and national S&T policy goals

with fixing rates emerged as the principal host countries (Argentina and Brazil) experienced serious macroeconomic dislocation in the early 2000s. The Southern Cone governments became desperate to resolve the problem of electricity generation and distribution capacity that they thought the FDI had remedied. Some tried to interest petroleum/gas TNCs to enter the industry in the context of a Southern Cone strategy. Others attempted to reinvent State petroleum companies to play a role in the industry. Nonetheless, the problem remains.

Across the board, a key factor limiting the developmental impact of FDI inflows and TNC operations is the weak domestic absorptive capacity of the host economies. As we have seen, developing America attracts very little FDI in R&D, a factor that severely limits many of the positive impacts that FDI in R&D can bring, such as introducing new knowledge and research know-how, training scientists and engineers, and creating new research skills. Indeed, developing America underperforms in comparison to other developing regions and transition economies with regards to government support for R&D, the contribution of universities and public sector research institutions to business innovation and, above all else, targeted FDI attraction policies for this purpose.

The experience of developing America suggests that while FDI by TNCs can lead to increased productivity and exports, it does not necessarily increase the competitiveness of the domestic sector, which ultimately determines long-term economic growth. Economic liberalization allows TNCs to exploit existing capabilities more freely but in itself does not provide growth opportunities unless a domestic industrial sector exists which has the necessary absorptive capacity to profit from externalities from TNC activity. As a consequence, over time FDI inflows from TNCs rise in countries where local capabilities are strengthened and new capabilities are created; they stagnate or fall where they are not.

For this reason, it is essential to connect the competitive advantages of TNCs to the improvement of the domestic absorptive capacity of host countries (Lall and Narula, 2006). A common element of all these examples of lost opportunities or meager benefits from inward FDI and the presence TNC operations is weak national policies. The dominant policy framework for attracting FDI during the boom of the 1990s was a package of passive, horizontal policies that relied on opening up the economy, liberalizing, deregulating and privatizing state assets. That framework served to attract huge inflows of FDI; however, it also brought serious problems associated with that FDI and the increased presence of TNCs that the framework was not capable of dealing with.

The single most important element that can help to make the transnationalization of developing America serve the purpose to integrate it into the international market in a competitive manner is the implementation of national policies *designed for that purpose*. The starting point is to define the national development strategy and the role of FDI and TNC operations within that strategy. There exists a global tendency to move from passive to active FDI policies. The former are based on confidence in the business environment (comparative advantages, macroeconomics, institutions, rules of the game) to attract FDI and, by definition, these policies do not distinguish between different types of corporate FDI strategies. The latter entail that countries actively seek FDI through horizontal and vertical measures, including the targeting of specific companies. In the shift from passive to active FDI policies, investment promotion agencies can play a critical role, acting as catalysts for FDI if they work in coordination with other public agencies and in the context of the national development strategy. Developing America, with the exception of Costa Rica and to a lesser degree, Chile, has been left behind and that fact is reflected in the lost opportunities and meagre benefits it receives from transnationalization.

An important upshot of this analysis is that policy toward TNCs matters greatly. Currently, in developing America, the options for active FDI policies are becoming increasingly polarized. On the one hand, the initiative associated with the US-backed Free Trade Area of the Americas (FTAA) implies a significant restriction on the policy space available to host governments (Chang, 2002; IISD/WWF, 2001; UNCTAD, 2006; Abugattas and Paus, this volume; Bahadian and Carvalho Lyrio, this volume) and, in itself, will not drastically alter the existing nature of FDI inflows and TNC operations. Mexico, Chile, Dominican Republic, five Central American countries (Guatemala, El Salvador, Honduras, Nicaragua, and Costa Rica), and three Andean ones (Colombia, Ecuador, and Peru) already are party to trade agreements with the United States. On the other hand, the new populist initiatives in Venezuela, Bolivia, and Argentina are not compatible with more active FDI policies because they attempt to extract higher levels of benefits from *existing* TNC operations, especially in natural resources, and therefore tend to frighten away *new* FDI. Neither the FTAA-equivalent initiative nor the populist initiatives are particularly appropriate for the kind of policies suggested here. A middle way must be sought out if developing America is to take advantage of the opportunities of transnationalization.

Notes

1. In this chapter, the term "developing America" is used to refer to Latin America and the Caribbean, or the Americas minus Canada and the United States.
2. As well as what is indicated in the Bibliography, the annual reports on *Foreign Investment in Latin America and the Caribbean* of the Unit on Investment and Corporate Strategies of the United Nations Economic Commission for Latin America and the Caribbean (ENLAC) have provided a significant amount of research in this regard.
3. It might be mentioned that FDI inflows to developing America during the peak of the 1990s' boom reached the equivalent of almost 6% of GDP, about twice that of developing Asia. More recent inflows have approximated those of other developing regions and economies in transition at about 3% of GDP.
4. We use a modified version of Dunning (1993).
5. See Mortimore (2002 and 1999b). See also the chapters by Philips and Sánchez-Ancochea in this volume.
6. Direct interviews of the companies involved in the TNC operations have proved an invaluable tool for the present analysis.
7. The situation of natural resource-seeking FDI in the region is not dealt with as it is the simplest and most obvious aspect and requires no further analysis.
8. Before its purchase by the German auto TNC, DaimlerBenz.
9. The German auto TNC, Volkswagen, moved its U.S. plant to Mexico to supply the U.S. market from that base.
10. The Caribbean Basin consists of Central America (including Panama), all independent Caribbean Islands, Guyana, and Surinam.
11. The principal mechanism utilized was what was called "production sharing" under which products assembled outside the United States using U.S. inputs were subject to tax only on the value added (mostly wages). This mechanism allowed large U.S. apparel TNCs, such as Sara Lee (Hanes, Bali, Playtex, L'eggs), Fruit of the Loom (BVD, Gitano, Munsinger), and Warnaco (Warner's, Olga, Lejaby) to establish assembly plants in a number of Caribbean economies simultaneously to take advantage of the significantly lower wage levels there.

A group of smaller U.S. apparel manufacturers, which had been forced offshore by competitive pressure, also set up plants to operate as subcontractors.

12. For further discussion of the effects of Asian (particularly Chinese) exports, see the chapter by Dussel Peters in this volume.

13. The textile and apparel industries of China and India are currently evolving in this direction.

14. NAFTA eliminated the trade restrictions and rules of origin that locked Mexico into exclusively an assembler role. It allowed for the incorporation of other operations (textile production, cutting, washing, etc.) into the value chain such that Mexico now possesses the potential to become more of a "full-package" producer (ECLAC, 2004: Chapter 2).

15. DR-CAFTA does provide two *potential* improvements. One, locally produced fabrics can be incorporated into many apparel products for the U.S. market and, if the subregion can produce cheaper fabrics than the U.S. ones, that could improve their competitiveness. Two, Nicaragua (and to a lesser extent, Costa Rica) negotiated a special "tariff preference level" that allows them, within certain stringent limits, to import fabrics from third countries for their apparel exports to the U.S. market.

16. About half of the thirty-eight known arbitration proceedings, with estimated claims in the order of US$ 20 billion stem from the situation in the energy sector of Argentina.

17. Brazil was able to resolve the most serious problems of the electricity/gas sector because it could count on the national development bank, a national petroleum company, and the fact that it never ratified the fourteen bilateral investment treaties that it negotiated. Argentina, on the other hand, could not satisfactorily resolve the biggest problems of the sector because it possessed no national development bank, had privatized its national petroleum company and had ratified about fifty bilateral investment treaties that permitted the electricity and gas TNCs operating there to initiate international arbitration proceedings (Stanley, 2004; Mortimore and Stanley, 2006).

References

Chang, H. (2002) *Kicking Away the Ladder: Development Strategy in Historical Perspective*, London: Anthem Press.

Dunning, J. (1993) *Multinational Enterprises and the Global Economy*, Harrow, UK: Addison-Wesley.

Economic Commission for Latin America and the Caribbean (ECLAC) (1999) *Foreign Investment in Latin America and the Caribbean, 1998*, Santiago, Chile: United Nations.

Economic Commission for Latin America and the Caribbean (ECLAC) (2000) *Foreign Investment in Latin America and the Caribbean, 1999*, Santiago, Chile: United Nations.

—— (2001) *Foreign Investment in Latin America and the Caribbean, 2000*, Santiago, Chile: United Nations.

—— (2002) *Foreign Investment in Latin America and the Caribbean, 2001*, Santiago, Chile: United Nations.

—— (2003) *Foreign Investment in Latin America and the Caribbean, 2002*, Santiago, Chile: United Nations.

—— (2004) *Foreign Investment in Latin America and the Caribbean, 2003*, Santiago, Chile: United Nations.

—— (2005) *Foreign Investment in Latin America and the Caribbean, 2004*, Santiago, Chile: United Nations.

—— (2006) *Foreign Investment in Latin America and the Caribbean, 2005*, Santiago, Chile: United Nations.

Gereffi, G. and O. Memedovic (2003) *The Global Apparel Value Chain: What Prospects for Upgrading by Developing Countries*, Vienna, Austria: UNIDO (*Sectoral Studies* series).

Hernandez, Rene, Romulo Romero, and Martha Cordero (2006) *¿Se erosiona la competitividad de los paísesdel DR-CAFTA con el fin del acuerdo de textiles y vestuario?* Mexico City: CEPAL (LC/MEX/L.691/Rev.2).

International Institute for Sustainable Development/World Wildlife Fund (IISD/WWF) (2001) *Private Rights, Public Problems: A Guide to NAFTA's Controversial Chapter on Investor Rights*, Winnpeg, Canada: IISD/WWF.

Lall, S. and R. Narula (2006) "FDI and Its Role in Economic Development: Do We Need a New Agenda?" in R. Narula, R. and S. Lall (eds.) *Understanding FDI-Assisted Economic Development*, London and New York: Routledge.

Mortimore, M. (1995) "Transforming Sitting Ducks into Flying Geese: The Mexican Automobile Industry," *Desarrollo Productivo*, 26: 9–74.

—— (1997) "The Asian Challenge to the World Automotive Industry," *Economia Contemporánea*, 2: 67–91.

—— (1998a) "Corporate Strategies and Regional Integration Schemes Involving Developing Countries: The NAFTA and MERCOSUR Automobile Industries," *Science, Technology and Development*, 16 (2): 1–31.

—— (1998b) "GETTING A LIFT: Modernizing Industry by Way of Latin American Integration Schemes. The Example of Automobiles," *Transnational Corporations*, 7 (2): 97–136.

—— (1998c) "Mexico's TNC-centric Industrialization Process," in R. Kozul-Wright and R. Rowthorn (eds.) *Transnational Corporations and the Global Economy*, London: Macmillan.

—— (1999a) *Does Foreign Direct Investment Contribute to Economic Growth?* Santiago, Chile: ECLAC (Notes, No. 5).

——— (1999b) "Threadbare: Apparel-Based Industrialization in the Caribbean Basin," *CEPAL Review*, 67: 119–156.

——— (2000) "Corporate Strategies for FDI in the Context of the New Economic Model," *World Development*, 28 (9): 1611–1625.

——— (2001a) "Corporate Competitiveness in Latin America and the Caribbean," *CEPAL Review*, 74: 37–59.

——— (2001b) "Nuevas estrategias de las empresas transnacionales en el proceso de globalización: la oportunidad que representan las SIPIs para algunos países en desarrollo," in F. Javier Beltran de Heredia and Marcos R. Sarasola (eds.) *Innovación tecnológica: desafíos de formación para el empleo y el proceso reciente de inversiones extranjeras en América Latina*, Cátedra. Bilbao, España: UNESCO/Universidad de Deusto.

——— (2001c) *The Region's Precarious International Competitiveness*, Santiago: ECLAC (Notes, No. 16).

——— (2002) "When Does Apparel Become a Peril? On the Nature of Industrialization in the Caribbean Basin," in G. Gereffi, D. Spener, and J. Bair (eds.) *Free Trade and Uneven Development: The North America Apparel Industry after NAFTA*, Philadelphia, PA: Temple University Press.

——— (2003a) *Illusory Competitiveness: The Apparel Assembly Model of the Caribbean Basin*, Maastricht, The Netherlands: United Nations University Institute for New Technologies (INTECH) (Discussion Paper #2003–11).

——— (2003b) *New Options for Attracting FDI*, Santiago, Chile: ECLAC (Notes, No. 28).

——— (2004a) *Attracting FDI and Benefiting from It*, Santiago, Chile: ECLAC (Notes, No. 34).

——— (2004b) "The Impact of TNC Strategies on Development in Latin America and the Caribbean," in D. W. te Velde (ed.) *Foreign Direct Investment, Income Inequality and Poverty: Experiences and Policy Implications*, London: Overseas Development Institute Publication.

Mortimore, M. and F. Barron (2005) "Informe sobre la industria automotriz mexicana," *Desarrollo Productivo*, 162: 7–50.

Mortimore, M. and L. Stanley (2006) "The Obsolescence of Foreign Investment Protection after the Argentine Crisis," *CEPAL Review*, 88: 15–31.

Mortimore, M. and O. Sunkel (2001) "Transnational Integration and National Disintegration Revisited," in B. Hettne, A. Inotai, and O. Sunkel (eds.) *Comparing Regionalisms: Implications for Global Development*, London: Palgrave.

Mortimore, M. and R. Zamora (1998) "La competitividad internacional de la industria de prendas de vestir en Costa Rica," *Desarrollo Productivo*, 46: 13–130.

Mortimore, M. and S. Lall (2000) "Chapter 1—Competitiveness, Restructuring and FDI: An Analytical Framework," in United Nations Conference on Trade and Development (UNCTAD) *The Competitiveness Challenge: Transnational Corporations and Industrial Restructuring in*

Developing Countries, Geneva, Switzerland: UNCTAD/ITE/IIT/ Misc.20.

Mortimore, M. and S. Vergara (2003) "Nuevas estrategias de empresas transnacionales, México en el contexto global," in E. Dussel (ed.) *Perspectivas y retos de la competitividad en México,* Mexico City: Economics Faculty of the National Autonomous University of Mexico (UNAM) and the Entrepreneurial Development Center UNAM-National Chamber of Industry (CANCINTRA).

—— (2006) "Targeting Winners: Can FDI Policy Help Developing Countries Industrialise?" in R. Narula, R. and S. Lall (eds.) *Understanding FDI-Assisted Economic Development,* London and New York: Routledge.

Mortimore, M. and W. Peres (1998) "Policy Competition for Foreign Direct Investment in the Caribbean Basin: Costa Rica, the Dominican Republic and Jamaica," *Desarrollo Productivo,* 49: 9–67.

—— (2002) "La competitividad internacional de América Latina y el Caribe: las dimensiones empresarial y sectorial," in Leticia Campos Aragon (ed.) *La realidad económica actual y las corrientes teóricas de su interpretación: un debate inicial,* Mexico City: Colección Libros de la Revista Problemas de Desarrollo/Nueva Epoca, UNAM.

Mortimore, M., A. Calderón, and W. Peres (1994) "Mexico's Integration into the North American Economy: The Role of Foreign Direct Investment," in IRELA/IDB (ed.) *Foreign Direct Investment in Developing Countries: The Case of Latin America,* Madrid: IRELA/IDB.

—— (1996) "Mexico: Foreign Investment as a Source of International Competitiveness," in J. Dunning and R. Narula (eds.) *Foreign Direct Investment and Governments: Catalysts for Economic Restructuring,* London: Routledge.

Mortimore, M., H. Duthoo, and J. A. Guerrero (1995) "Informe sobre la competitividad internacional de las zonas francas en la República Dominicana," *Desarrollo Productivo,* 22: 9–76.

Mortimore, M., H. Romijn, and R. van Assouw (2000) "CTNCs, Industrial Restructuring and Competitiveness in the Automotive Industry in NAFTA, MERCOSUR and ASEAN," in UNCTAD, *The Competitiveness Challenge: Transnational Corporations and Industrial Restructuring in Developing Countries,* Geneva, Switzerland: UNCTAD/ITE/IIT/Misc.20.

Mortimore, M., L. Vicens, and E. Martínez (1998) "La competitividad internacional de la industria de prendas de vestir de la República Dominicana," *Desarrollo Productivo,* 45: 11–129.

Mortimore, M., R. Buitelaar, and J. L. Bonifaz (2000) "México: un CANálisis de su competividad internacional," *Desarrollo Productivo,* 62, 9–70.

Mortimore, M., S. Lall, and H. Romijn (2000) "Chapter 4—The Garments Industry," in UNCTAD (ed.) *The Competitiveness Challenge: Transnational Corporations and Industrial Restructuring in Developing Countries,* Geneva, Switzerland: UNCTAD/ITE/IIT/Misc.20.

Mortimore, M., S. Vergara, and J. Katz (2001) "La competitividad interna-cional y la política nacional: implicancias para la política de de IED en América Latina," *Desarrollo Productivo*, 107: 9–68.

Narula, R. and S. Lall, eds. (2006) *Understanding FDI-Assisted Economic Development*, London and New York: Routledge.

Stanley, L. (2004) "Acuerdos bilaterales de inversión y demandas ante Tribunales Internacionales: la experiencia argentina reciente," *Desarrollo Productivo*, October(158), LC/L.2181-P: 7–69.

UNCTAD (2002) *World Investment Report 2002: Transnational Corporations and Export Competitiveness*, New York and Geneva: United Nations.

—— (2005) *World Investment Report 2005: Transnational Corporations and the Internationalization of R&D*, New York and Geneva: United Nations.

—— (2006) "Systemic Issues in International Investment Agreements (IIAs)," *IIA Monitor*, 1.

Chapter 3

What Does China's Integration to the Global Economy Mean for Latin America? The Mexican Experience

Enrique Dussel Peters

In the Latin American press, China's increasing presence in the region's energy and raw material sectors, the displacement of Latin America's production and exports in some domestic- and export-oriented sectors, and the diplomatic and "strategic" issues that accompany Chinese investment in sectors such as oil and steel, among other issues, all receive significant attention. However, in contrast to China's presence in the media, the socioeconomic and trade experience of Latin America with China has received much less attention from national and regional institutions. Only recently, for example, have the Economic Commission for Latin America and the Caribbean (ECLAC) and the Inter-American Development Bank (IADB) started analysis of this sort. Nationally, particularly in the cases of Central America and Mexico, systematic and detailed discussions of the changing socioeconomic conditions in China and the ensuing bilateral economic relationships have been even scarcer. At the policy level, there is little analysis and thus little knowledge of the short, medium, and long-term strategy of China's socio-economy, and, more-over, the profound challenges (and opportunities) that China's rapid development bring for Latin America.

This chapter attempts to fill this intellectual and analytical gap. The first section contrasts Mexico's and China's strategies for integration into the global economy since the 1980s. The section presents the basic logic of export-oriented industrialization (EOI) that has become dominant in both countries and highlights not only similarities between the countries in terms of specialization patterns and employment challenges but also points to substantial differences in how EOI is conceived and implemented.

These differences, it is argued, mean that competition in the global economy presents the two countries with different challenges for long-term economic development strategies. The second section examines Chinese development in historical perspective, arguing that the country's rapid integration and extraordinary economic dynamism are unique. The third section examines the effects of China on Latin America, pointing to the differences among Latin American countries, but cautioning against making strong distinctions regarding the effects of China on "northern" versus "southern" Latin America. The fourth section considers the specific trade relationship between China and Mexico.

Mexico and China: Different Strategies for Integration into the Global Economy since the 1980s

Over the course of the 1980s, the new orthodoxy of EOI was widely adopted by policy-makers in Latin America. The lessons of the East Asian miracle, famously summarized by the World Bank in its 1993 report, combined with influential analyses of the "rent-seeking" pathologies associated with earlier import-substituting industrialization (ISI) regimes in Latin America (Krueger, 1978; 1997), led to a categorical rejection of statistic development strategies throughout much of the region and an embrace of export-oriented policies as the key to growth and development. Convinced that creating a market-friendly environment was the best way to generate foreign direct investment (FDI), policy-makers eschewed targeted industrial policy in favor of a neutral or "horizontal" approach, and macroeconomic stabilization became the highest priority of governments that attached great importance to the task of getting the "macroeconomic fundamentals" right.

The argument in favor of EOI builds on the positive association between exports and economic growth or development. Contrary to ISI, EOI stresses that the global economy, through exports, is the "point of reference" for any economic unit (firm, region, nation, group of nations, etc.). Exports, in general, reflect efficiency; that is nonexporting economic units are not efficient from this perspective. It emphasizes neutral or export-oriented production of manufactures to maximize the efficient allocation of factors of production and a specialization among nations according to their respective comparative cost advantages (Balassa, 1981). Moreover, it underlines the central role of manufacturing in economies of the periphery, even though the theoretical justification for doing so has not been sufficiently developed to date. Contrary to structural restrictions or "bottlenecks" imposed by industrialization—as stressed by some ISI-authors—this "intuitive Darwinian rationale for free trade" (Bhagwati, 1991: 17) argues that the degree and the structure of protection in the periphery under ISI had a significant negative impact on the allocation of resources, and subsequently on exports and overall economic structure.

Probably the strongest argument of EOI supporters against ISI's "infant industry" protection and overall policy of state interventions is the "rent-seeking behavior" it generates. As a result of market intervention under ISI—such as import licenses, tariffs, but in general any form of market intervention—economic units in general, including firms and countries, generate perverse (or nonmarket conforming) results in this environment: excess capacity to obtain rents provided by the state, over utilization of promotional instruments, and, in general, an economic structure aimed to "reap" the incentives provided by the state. At the same time, these mechanisms generate perverse social incentives and structures, as, in most of the cases, incentives are not taken by the initially expected groups (potential "modern/industrial" groups), but rather by "rent-seeking" and corrupt groups, which do not have an incentive to modernize/industrialize. The ubiquitousness of rent-seeking from this perspective is one of the most significant obstacles for development (Krueger, 1983; 1992; 1997).

The proposed alternative to interventionist economic management, from this perspective, is for the government to place the creation of the appropriate macroeconomic conditions for development—or the generation of a "market-friendly environment"—at the center of economic policy. Opening the economy by abolishing tariff and nontariff barriers to trade and investment, and combating inflation by means of restrictive monetary and fiscal policies, are the main macroeconomic goals of EOI. The state is minimalist, in this approach, while the private sector is conceived as the motor for future development and industrialization.

The economic development of the East Asian newly industrialized countries (NICs) is put forward as an example of recent EOI successes, and the active role of the General Agreement of Tariffs and Trade (GATT) and its successor the World Trade Organization (WTO), along with multilateral agencies, has increased the ideological dominance of the EOI strategy (Bhagwati, 1988).[1]

Mexico's EOI Strategy since the 1980s

It is in the national and international economic contexts described above that the major pillars and guidelines of trade strategy have developed in Mexico since the 1980s (Aspe Armella, 1993; Dussel Peters, 2000; Salinas de Gortari, 2000; Sojo Garza-Aldape, 2005).[2] Unlike ISI, Mexico's new, liberal EOI strategy has, as a main objective, the achievement of macroeconomic stability, which would "induce" a process of microeconomic adjustment and sectorally nondiscriminatory growth.

Since 1988, the government has viewed as its primary goal controlling inflation rates and the fiscal deficit, as well as attracting foreign investments—as the main financing source of the new strategy, since oil revenues and massive foreign credits were not available and/or sufficient.[3] (or relative prices). The concentration on the stabilization of the macro economy had a number of indirect effects on trade policy. First, the prioritization of macroeconomic stability meant that the Mexican central bank (Banco de México) consistently followed restrictive monetary and credit policies. Second, using the nominal exchange rate as the anti-inflationary anchor created a bias toward strong (and perhaps overvalued) currency, as the government feared that depreciation would have an unwanted inflationary effect by raising the prices of imported inputs. Supported by the massive privatization of state-owned industries in the 1980s and, in the early 1990s, reprivatization of the banking system, the Mexican private sector was to lead Mexico's economy out of the "lost decade" of the 1980s. The massive import liberalization process, initiated at the end of 1985, was supposed to support the private manufacturing sector in order to orient it toward exports, as a result of cheaper international imports. And, as part of the strategy of liberalization and pursuit of nondiscriminatory growth, all sectoral subsidies and sector-specific policies were to be abolished and replaced by neutral policies.

Finally, government policies toward labor unions were of utmost significance. As reflected in the various *Pactos Económicos* (or economic pacts between the public and private sectors, as well as with trade unions) since 1987, only a few (government-friendly) labor unions have been deemed acceptable to negotiate inside firms and with the government, while the rest were declared illegal. This process, which has included violent disruptions of independent labor unions, has made national wage negotiations possible in Mexico within the framework of the respective economic pacts and with the objective to control real wage growth.

Up to 2005, the Mexican government continued, with few exceptions, with a consistent liberalization strategy (Sojo Garza-Aldape, 2005). NAFTA's implementation in 1994 was of fundamental relevance for the liberalization strategy. In a best case scenario, and allowing for a significant structural change towards exports in the Mexican economy, the Mexican economy required an outlet and welcoming market for the commodities/products resulting from Mexico's structural change. This outlet was to be Mexico's main trading partner, the United States, and it is difficult to imagine a successful export orientation without such a market to sell these commodities.[4]

China's Socioeconomic Strategy since the 1980s

The historical, political and ideological context of China's recent development stands in extreme contrast with the case of Mexico and most of

Latin America (Chow, 2002; Dussel Peters, 2005a; Nolan, 2004; OECD, 2002 and 2005; Yifu Lin et al., 2003). In China, the agricultural sector has always been a politically and economically strategic sector. Contrary to most of Latin America—where modernization has been synonymous with industrialization and the agricultural sector has been understood as un-developmental per se—the agricultural sector has remained of substantial political and economic weight: more than 60 percent of China's population lives in rural areas and—as a result of historical experience of food shortages and massive famines during the twentieth century— agriculture continues to be a top priority sector in the country's economic policy. The sector also has a substantial political weight, and the success of the agricultural policy allows for deepening of reforms in other areas.

Since the end of the 1970s, economic policies diminished the weight of state-owned enterprises (SOEs) and collectively owned enterprises by allowing for new forms of property, particularly private and foreign property, as well as property owned by local and regional governments. Yet the central government retains significant influence—and direct ownership—over large companies and industrial groups in China. Contrary to "horizontal policies" in Latin America and Mexico, China's central government granted massive preferential credits, limited capital flows, controlled foreign exchange policies tightly, established tariff and nontariff benefits, in many cases under monopolistic conditions, and provided access to international financial and secondary markets (OECD, 2002; Perkins, 2001). The influence of the central government and its active policies has been massive, particularly through the state-owned banking system, agricultural and technological policies, the control of labor as well as through focused sector and territorial policies (Dussel Peters, 2005a; Perkins, 2001).[5] Thus, either by direct control and ownership—as in the case of the SOEs[6]—or through incentives and policies, the public sector and the Chinese Communist Party exercises substantial weight and control over the Chinese economy (Anguiano, 2004).[7]

Chinese economic policy is also marked by a pragmatic and long-term vision of socioeconomic development, accompanied by instruments, mechanisms, resources, and the coordination of institutions on a local, provincial and central government level. Contrary to most Latin American countries, which have been subjected to structural adjustment programs by the World Bank and the International Monetary Fund (IMF) since the 1980s, China has implemented reforms through "transitional institutions" (Qian, 2003) to allow for a reform process with incentives to generate domestic markets.[8]

Derived from this pragmatic perspective, and in the context of a discussion about "planned market economy" or "market socialism," Chinese economic strategy has passed through different phases since the 1980s.

During the 1980s, sectors such as iron and steel, textiles, transportation of equipment, and, in general, heavy industry and the chemical sector, in which the SOEs had a dominant presence, became the pillars of economic reforms and growth. Since the 1990s, however, the central government has created massive incentives (Dussel Peters, 2005a) in new technologically intensive sectors such as electronics and automobiles in which foreign firms and FDIs have played an increasing role. The central government has allowed for massive incentives for export orientation through a complex tax system, instruments for developing Special Economic Zones (SEZs) and particular products and processes.

In addition to specific territorial and sector instruments, as well as policies focused towards high-tech processes and higher education, among others, macroeconomic policy has played a substantial role in economic development in China. In contrast to the experience of Latin American countries, at least two macroeconomic policies have been significant, namely the exchange rate and financing. Since the 1990s, China's fixed exchange rate has kept its currency systematically undervalued (especially toward the US$) to levels up to over 30 percent since 2000, although the policy was mildly relaxed in 2005.[9] Parallel to these policies, and until 2005, the Chinese central government continued to control capital flows against the pressure of multilateral agencies such as the IMF. Domestic financing for the private sector in China (as a percentage of GDP) has reached levels close to 150 percent in 2003, while it accounted for only 26 percent in Latin America and a mere 19 percent in Mexico (WDI, 2006), Firms in China have thus benefited massively from the (public) banking system as one of the most important central government policies in the last decades.

China's entry into the WTO in 2002 had, rather surprisingly, a qualitative weight similar to entering NAFTA for Mexico: as part of its strategy since the 1990s, it will allow for exports in the manufacturing sector (and the restructuring of its agricultural and service sectors as well as imports in agriculture and services). The issue is of substantial importance in its long-term strategy: manufacturing and urban areas are expected to be the main employment generators, while SOEs and the agriculture and service sectors are expected to shed jobs (Mengkui et al., 2003; OECD, 2005).

Thus, in both nations, exports currently play a strategic role for development, but they are a result of differently conceived and designed strategies of EOI. While Mexico's overall economic policies have relied on horizontal and neutral macroeconomic policies and NAFTA, China has pursued an active and aggressive integration into the global economy through the utilization of a full rage of instruments and policies at the macroeconomic, sector and regional level through tax incentives and massive and focused financing. While Mexico has been substantially integrated into the U.S.-economy since the 1990s, the Chinese economy has integrated increasingly—and its trade and FDI flows are directed—to Asian economies. Before proceeding, it is worth noting that China's remarkable economic performance has rekindled debates over EOI. While institutions such as the OECD (2005)—and particularly the IMF under Anne O. Krueger—stress that China should liberalize its economy and institutions to make its growth trajectory sustainable, other authors such as Rodrik (2006) attribute China's performance precisely to the generation and maintenance of such "transitional institutions."

The remainder of this chapter focuses on three sets of issues and debates: the similarities and differences between China's current economic trajectory and that of fast-growing, export-oriented East Asian economies since the 1960s and 1970s; the experience of China's trade with several specific Latin American countries, particularly distinguishing between South America and Central America and Mexico; and the particular experience of Mexico with China.

China: Another Asian Tiger?

China's export performance has been remarkable in its own right, and particularly remarkable in comparison with large Latin American countries that have also sought to increase exports in the 1980s and 1990s. Indeed, the growth rate of exports of China has been significantly higher than in Latin America and the Caribbean (LACs) countries such as Argentina, Brazil, and Mexico (see table 3.1).

But this is not new; in the 1970s, East Asian countries such as Korea and Taiwan also out-performed their Latin American counterparts in terms of exports. Thus, China's production and export performance could be understood as similar to the performance of other Asian countries, which in the 1960s and 1970s integrated rapidly in the world economy through exports and import-substitution (Gereffi and Wyman, 1990). This is a position taken by several authors (BID, 2005; Mesquita Moreira, 2005), who acknowledge that China's integration to the world economy has been impressive, "but not without precedents—so far—among other recent export-booms" (Mesquita Moreira, 2005: 35). Other authors highlight that China's main challenge for Latin America comes "not from competition with China, but from an eventual bump of its huge financial system that could have serious repercussions in the international capital markets for emerging countries" (Lora, 2005: 35). From this perspective, then, the argument would be that China's integration to the global economy is comparable to other NICs in different periods.[10]

Yet such perspective understates the importance of the Chinese case, failing to recognize the size of China's economy in terms of trade, GDP, economically active population, and other variables. Table 3.2 reflects

Table 3.1 Selected Countries: Export Growth (Average Annual Growth Rate), US$ of 2000, 1970–2004

	1970–1980	1980–1990	1990–2000	2000–2004	1990–2004	1980–2004
Argentina	4.8	5.1	6.6	5.0	6.1	5.7
Brazil	9.9	7.1	6.8	12.8	8.5	7.9
China	—	*5.7*	*14.1*	*23.3*	*16.7*	*11.9*
Hong Kong	*9.4*	*13.6*	*9.0*	*8.7*	*8.9*	*10.8*
China + Hong Kong	—	*9.4*	*11.4*	*17.2*	*13.0*	*11.5*
Japan	9.4	4.7	4.4	3.2	4.1	4.3
Latin America and Caribbean	4.5	5.0	8.2	4.8	7.2	6.3
Mexico	11.6	7.8	13.4	2.9	10.3	9.2
South Korea	20.5	10.8	15.5	11.1	14.3	12.8
World	5.9	5.1	6.8	5.1	6.3	5.8

Source: WDI (2006).

Table 3.2 China and Hong Kong: Selected Variables, World Shares, 1990–2020[a]

	1990	2000	2004	2006	2008	2010	2011	2020
CHINA								
Exports (current $US)	1.56	3.52	5.73	7.31	*9.32*	11.89	13.44	40.20
Imports (current $US)	1.26	3.15	5.56	7.32	9.69	*12.83*	14.77	52.33
GDP[b]	1.63	3.78	4.68	5.21	5.80	6.45	6.81	11.03
CHINA AND HONG KONG								
Exports	3.85	6.55	8.47	*9.63*	10.96	12.46	13.29	23.70
Imports	3.38	6.09	8.09	9.32	10.75	12.38	*13.29*	25.16
GDP[c]	1.98	4.30	5.07	5.51	5.99	6.51	6.79	9.86

Notes:
[a] Assuming the same growth rate of the respective variable than for 2000–2004.
[b] Numbers in italics mean the year China will become the main exporter, importer or producer in terms of GDP.
[c] China's and Hong Kong economy would be the biggest economy in terms of GDP between 2032 and 2038 according to the same estimates.
Source: WDI (2006).

the significant weight of China's economy in terms of trade and GDP. As a result of very high growth rates in trade during 2000–2004, China's economy—together with Hong Kong—will become the biggest in terms of exports and imports beginning 2006 and 2011, respectively. According to the same estimations, China's and Hong Kong's economy together will become the biggest economy during 2032–2038.

These estimations reflect that China's massive integration to the global economy cannot be compared casually with other experiences of East Asian nations. Even the most successful cases of Taiwan and Korea have an economic weight that cannot be compared to China's. China's emergence as a trading power generates important new sources of demand, and it also massively displaces production globally—particularly in manufactured goods—as its exporters compete in world markets.

Similarities and Differences in the Trade Relationship of China with Latin American Countries

Most of the existing analyses of the trade relationship between China and Latin America stress the profound differences between Central America, Mexico, and South America, particularly the Mercosur (BID, 2005; CEPAL, 2005; 2006). While the Northern part of Latin America has substantial problems and a trade structure that competes with China—and is seen as a "loser" reflected in an increasing trade deficit, particularly in the case of Mexico—the Southern part of Latin America has been able to export raw materials and has been thus "successful" also in achieving a trade surplus.

This conclusion should be reconsidered. In reflecting on China's relationship with Latin America, it is particularly important to take a longer-term perspective and take into account China's changing trade structure. Several issues are relevant in this context:

- China's international trade shows a profound integration process with Asia. As reflected in table 3.3—and based on Chinese sources[11]—Latin America and the Caribbean only plays a secondary role for China: even after a rapid growth since 1995 exports and imports to and from Latin America only accounted for 3.1 percent and 4.1 percent in 2005, respectively.
- China's exports to Latin America, with an average annual growth rate (AAGR) of 22.4 percent during 1995–2005, should be divided in two different periods: (1) 1995–2000 with an AAGR of 17.9 percent and (2) 2000–2005 with an AAGR of 27.0 percent. For the latter period—and with the exception of Argentina—all Latin American countries increased their AAGR compared to the first period (see also figure 3.1). Mexico accounts for 23.4 percent of China's exports to Latin America, while the share of Brazil, Chile, and Argentina was of 20.4 percent, 9.1 percent, and 5.61 percent in 2005. Very significant is also the impressive AAGR of China's exports during 2000–2005 to Mexico and Brazil, of 35.5 percent and 31.6 percent, respectively; that

is China's exports to Brazil more than tripled in growth terms between 1995–2000 and 2000–2005.

- China's imports from Latin America have also played so far a minor role in China, with an increasing share during 1995–2005—from 2.1 percent to 3.1 percent for 1995 and 2005—but with an AAGR of 22.4 percent and much higher then total Chinese exports. Contrary to Chinese exports, the imports from Latin America have concentrated heavily in Brazil, Chile, and Argentina, accounting in 2005 for 37.4 percent, 18.5 percent and 14.2 percent of China's imports from LAC, while Mexico's represented only 8.3 percent of the region. As with Chinese exports to LAC, imports have also been much more dynamic for the period 2000–2005, without exceptions, with an AAGR above 30 percent.

- The former trade performance resulted in an overall trade deficit of China with Latin America that has increased substantially since 2002, while prior to 2002 China still achieved a surplus with the region. This change is a result of the increasing exports from Argentina, but particularly from Chile and Brazil to China (see table 3.3), while Mexico is one of the few countries with a deficit since 1995.

Table 3.3   China: Trade Structure for Selected Countries, 1995–2005

	1995	2000	2005	1995	2000	2005	Average annual growth rate (1995–2005)
			Exports				
	($ millions)			(share over total)			
United States (1)	24,713	52,142	162,939	16.61	20.81	21.37	20.8
Hong Kong (2)	35,988	44,969	124,505	24.19	17.95	16.33	13.2
Japan (3)	28,462	41,685	84,097	19.13	16.64	11.03	11.4
Korea (4)	6,689	11,341	35,117	4.50	4.53	4.61	18.0
Germany (5)	5,672	9,308	32,537	3.81	3.71	4.27	19.1
Taiwan (8)	3,099	5,053	16,559	2.08	2.02	2.17	18.2
Free Zones	0	0	0	0.00	0.00	0.00	—
Latin America and Caribbean	3,139	7,153	23,632	2.11	2.85	3.10	22.4
Mexico (22)	195	1,335	5,537	0.13	0.53	0.73	39.7
Argentina (56)	274	611	1,325	0.18	0.24	0.17	17.1
Brazil (25)	759	1,224	4,829	0.51	0.49	0.63	20.3
Chile (41)	411	784	2,151	0.28	0.31	0.28	18.0
Central America	142	372	1,144	0.10	0.15	0.15	23.2
Costa Rica (103)	22	65	229	0.01	0.03	0.03	26.4
El Salvador (93)	36	63	194	0.02	0.03	0.03	18.2
Guatemala (75)	47	139	473	0.03	0.06	0.06	26.1
Honduras (111)	31	62	134	0.02	0.02	0.02	15.6
Nicaragua (120)	5	43	114	0.00	0.02	0.01	35.8
Subtotal	107,763	171,650	479,386	72.43	68.51	62.88	16.1
Rest	41,014	78,911	282,941	27.57	31.49	37.12	21.3
Total	148,777	250,561	762,327	100.00	100.00	100.00	17.7

Continued

Table 3.3 Continued

	1995	2000	2005	1995	2000	2005	Average annual growth rate (1995–2005)
		($ millions)			(share over total)		
				Imports			
United States (4)	16,124	22,365	48,735	12.20	9.93	7.38	11.7
Hong Kong (10)	8,599	9,461	12,232	6.51	4.20	1.85	3.6
Japan (1)	29,008	41,537	100,468	21.95	18.44	15.22	13.2
Korea (3)	10,295	23,269	76,874	7.79	10.33	11.64	22.3
Germany (6)	8,039	10,417	30,668	6.08	4.62	4.65	14.3
Taiwan (2)	14,786	25,516	74,655	11.19	11.33	11.31	17.6
Free Zones (5)	2,255	7,180	55,178	1.71	3.19	8.36	37.7
Latin America and the Caribbean	2,964	5,415	26,707	2.24	2.40	4.05	24.6
Mexico (35)	195	488	2,227	0.15	0.22	0.34	27.6
Argentina (29)	370	930	3,800	0.28	0.41	0.58	26.2
Brazil (14)	1,228	1,621	9,982	0.93	0.72	1.51	23.3
Chile (25)	230	1,339	4,943	0.17	0.59	0.75	35.9
Central America	69	16	1,052	0.05	0.01	0.16	31.2
Costa Rica (52)	29	10	919	0.02	0.00	0.14	41.2
El Salvador (150)	5	0	11	0.00	0.00	0.00	7.5
Guatemala (110)	35	5	95	0.03	0.00	0.01	10.5
Honduras (139)	0	0	14	0.00	0.00	0.00	65.9
Nicaragua (152)	0	0	14	0.00	0.00	0.00	93.7
Subtotal	92,070	145,159	425,517	69.68	64.44	64.45	16.5
Rest	40,057	80,096	234,705	30.32	35.56	35.55	19.3
Total	132,127	225,255	660,222	100.00	100.00	100.00	17.5
				Trade balance			
United States	8,589	29,777	114,204	—	—	—	—
Hong Kong	27,389	35,508	112,273	—	—	—	—
Japan	−545	148	−16,370	—	—	—	—
Korea	−3,605	−11,928	−41,757	—	—	—	—
Germany	−2,367	−1,109	1,869	—	—	—	—
Taiwan	−11,687	−20,464	−58,096	—	—	—	—
Free Zones	−2,255	−7,180	−55,178	—	—	—	—
Latin America and the Caribbean	175	1,738	−3,074	—	—	—	—
Mexico	0	847	3,310	—	—	—	—
Argentina	−97	−319	−2,474	—	—	—	—
Brazil	−469	−398	−5,153	—	—	—	—
Chile	180	−555	−2,792	—	—	—	—
Central America	72	356	92	—	—	—	—
Costa Rica	-7	55	−690	—	—	—	—
El Salvador	31	62	183	—	—	—	—
Guatemala	12	134	379	—	—	—	—
Honduras	31	62	120	—	—	—	—
Nicaragua	5	43	100	—	—	—	—
Subtotal	15,693	26,491	53,869	—	—	—	—
Rest	957	−1,185	48,236	—	—	—	—
Total	16,650	25,306	102,105	—	—	—	—

Source: Own elloboration based on CCS (2006).

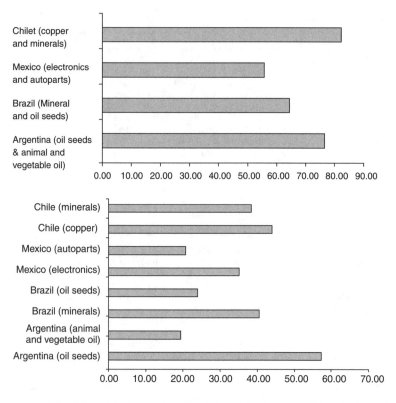

Figure 3.1 Selected Latin American Countries: Main Exports to China, Percentage of the Main One and Two Exports in the Total, 2005

Source: Author's elaboration based on CCS (2006).

The previous discussion would seem to confirm the argument regarding the differences in China's trade within types of Latin America countries, where the Northern region imports from China and runs deficits while the Southern region exports raw materials and generate trade surpluses. Yet a closer look at the data calls into question this simplistic account. First, China's impressive export growth in the last decades, and particularly since the 1990s, has concentrated on industrial and manufactured goods: from garments and textiles to increasingly telecommunications, autoparts, electronics and optical instruments. These are the most significant growth sectors of Chinese exports to most countries and will also be in Latin America. Mexico and Chile are two good examples of this trade structure: in the case of Mexico, 48.1 percent of Chinese exports concentrate only in three chapters of the Harmonized Tariff System (HTS)—electronics, autoparts, and optical instruments—while

Table 3.4 China: Exports and Imports to and from Selected Countries by Main Chapters of the Harmonized Tariff Schedule, 1995–2005

		Million US$						Share			AAGR 1995–2005
		1995	2000	2001	2002	2004	2005	1995	2000	2005	
	TOTAL EXPORTS	148,777	250,561	266,661	325,642	593,647	762,327	100.00	100.00	100.00	17.7
85	Electronics	18,997	46,067	51,322	65,152	129,740	172,406	12.77	18.39	22.62	24.7
84	Autoparts	8,669	27,729	33,626	50,851	118,283	149,835	5.83	11.07	19.65	33.0
62	Articles of apparel, not knitted or crocheted	14,346	18,867	18,967	20,591	28,983	35,038	9.64	7.53	4.60	9.3
61	Articles of apparel, knitted or crocheted	6,938	13,426	13,465	15,988	25,805	30,876	4.66	5.36	4.05	16.1
90	Optical and photographic instruments	2,429	6,348	6,458	7,370	16,266	25,435	1.63	2.53	3.34	26.5
	EXPORTS TO LATIN AMERICA	3,139	7,153	8,219	9,447	18,202	23,632	100.00	100.00	100.00	22.4
85	Electronics	454	1,102	1,313	1,561	3,328	4,729	14.46	15.40	20.01	26.4
84	Autoparts	223	744	963	930	2,134	3,127	7.10	10.41	13.23	30.2
62	Articles of apparel, not knitted or crocheted	346	784	735	914	1,231	1,362	11.02	10.95	5.76	14.7
87	Automobiles	121	206	259	277	641	1,093	3.86	2.88	4.62	24.6
61	Articles of apparel, knitted or crocheted	141	447	489	695	942	959	4.48	6.25	4.06	21.2
	EXPORTS TO ARGENTINA	274	611	574	185	852	1,325	100.00	100.00	100.00	17.1
84	Autoparts	25	97	109	14	146	272	9.15	15.95	20.49	26.9
85	Electronics	46	99	88	17	165	269	16.86	16.25	20.31	19.3
29	Organic chemicals	13	22	28	62	142	171	4.92	3.64	12.86	28.9
87	Automobiles	8	40	41	3	37	96	2.99	6.47	7.26	28.0
72	Iron and steel	0	3	6	8	28	53	0.11	0.57	4.01	67.5

Continued

Table 3.4 Continued

		Million US$						Share			AAGR 1995–2005
		1995	2000	2001	2002	2004	2005	1995	2000	2005	
EXPORTS TO BRAZIL		759	1,224	1,363	1,466	3,675	4,829	100.00	100.00	100.00	20.3
85	Electronics	154	275	365	362	1,020	1,564	20.28	22.44	32.39	26.1
84	Autoparts	64	209	191	163	395	673	8.50	17.07	13.93	26.4
29	Organic chemicals	29	79	100	139	261	320	3.80	6.42	6.63	27.2
27	Mineral fuels	51	67	149	223	533	285	6.70	5.46	5.90	18.8
54	Man-made filaments	2	7	12	41	218	214	0.25	0.53	4.42	60.7
EXPORTS TO CHILE		411	784	816	998	1,690	2,151	100.00	100.00	100.00	18.0
85	Electronics	48	85	89	112	211	279	11.64	10.81	12.97	19.3
62	Articles of apparel, not knitted or crocheted	62	110	126	133	244	267	15.15	14.01	12.41	15.7
61	Articles of apparel, knitted or crocheted	33	86	95	128	237	248	8.02	10.94	11.52	22.4
84	Autoparts	19	49	52	74	126	214	4.64	6.24	9.94	27.4
64	Footwear	44	69	84	113	147	174	10.62	8.82	8.10	14.8
EXPORTS TO MEXICO		195	1,335	1,802	2,864	4,978	5,537	100.00	100.00	100.00	39.7
85	Electronics	79	349	405	662	1,162	1,407	40.66	26.11	25.41	33.3
84	Autoparts	8	208	319	432	846	1,075	3.92	15.57	19.41	64.0
37	Photographic or cinematographic goods	—	0	1	0	173	233	—	0.01	4.21	—
87	Automobiles	0	31	46	74	158	197	0.24	2.30	3.56	83.1
62	Articles of apparel, not knitted or crocheted	19	127	158	343	323	190	9.66	9.48	3.43	26.0

	TOTAL IMPORTS	132,127	225,255	243,567	303,320	560,811	660,222	100.00	100.00	100.00	17.5
85	Electronics	19,418	50,749	55,909	75,218	142,102	174,913	14.70	22.53	26.49	24.6
84	Autoparts	27,578	34,560	40,559	53,469	91,480	96,418	20.87	15.34	14.60	13.3
27	Mineral fuels	5,133	20,652	17,549	20,017	48,027	64,239	3.89	9.17	9.73	28.7
90	Optical and photographic instruments	3,294	7,287	9,778	13,912	40,125	49,958	2.49	3.24	7.57	31.2
39	Plastics	8,018	14,458	15,263	17,633	28,064	33,339	6.07	6.42	5.05	15.3
	IMPORTS FROM LATIN AMERICA	2,964	5,415	6,702	8,902	21,742	26,707	100.00	100.00	100.00	24.6
26	Ores	13	878	1,300	1,387	5,175	7,724	0.42	16.21	28.92	90.1
12	Oil seeds	0	1,078	1,612	1,842	3,615	4,626	0.00	19.90	17.32	216.5
74	Copper	0	792	624	1,056	2,268	2,456	0.00	14.62	9.20	—
85	Electronics	5	146	261	623	1,367	1,765	0.18	2.69	6.61	78.3
27	Mineral fuels	12	120	129	59	1,026	1,625	0.40	2.21	6.08	63.4
	IMPORTS FROM ARGENTINA	370	930	1,281	1,423	3,256	3,800	100.00	100.00	100.00	26.2
12	Oil seeds	24	608	987	785	1,549	2,179	6.54	65.38	57.35	56.8
15	Animal or vegetable oils or fats	75	58	22	246	1,021	733	20.32	6.29	19.30	25.6
27	Mineral fuels	0	0	30	4	205	351	0.00	0.00	9.24	184.9
41	Raw hides and skins	26	62	72	100	106	130	6.95	6.72	3.42	17.6
26	Ores	0	0	0	1	10	91	0.00	0.00	2.39	—
	IMPORTS FROM BRAZIL	1,228	1,621	2,347	3,233	8,656	9,982	100.00	100.00	100.00	23.3
26	Ores	236	448	762	860	2,932	4,048	19.25	27.64	40.55	32.8
12	Oil seeds	2	466	620	1,052	2,055	2,381	0.18	28.73	23.85	100.8
72	Iron and steel	80	57	64	168	657	533	6.55	3.49	5.34	20.8
27	Mineral fuels	1	44	0	0	425	486	0.07	2.70	4.87	88.9
41	Raw hides and skins	25	50	77	110	304	378	2.02	3.06	3.78	31.3

Table 3.4 Continued

		Million US$					Share			AAGR 1995–2005
		1995	2000	2001	2002	2004	2005	1995	2000	2005	
IMPORTS FROM CHILE		230	1,339	1,303	1,580	3,672	4,943	100.00	100.00	100.00	35.9
74	Copper	48	758	564	923	1,994	2,174	20.61	56.63	43.97	46.6
26	Ores	95	312	326	216	979	1,893	41.40	23.31	38.30	34.8
47	Pulp of wood	62	160	243	209	341	383	26.88	11.92	7.76	20.0
23	Residues and wastes from the food industry	6	29	57	110	104	200	2.72	2.17	4.04	41.4
29	Organic chemicals	1	0	1	0	28	63	0.31	0.00	1.27	56.4
IMPORTS FROM MEXICO		195	488	761	1,135	2,132	2,227	100.00	100.00	100.00	27.6
85	Electronics	4	128	187	355	667	783	1.82	26.27	35.14	71.6
84	Autoparts	17	231	348	436	479	459	8.99	47.29	20.63	38.7
26	Ores	0	8	35	33	196	191	—	1.55	8.59	88.5
29	Organic chemicals	3	7	11	71	141	159	1.61	1.34	7.13	48.1
72	Iron and steel	12	7	8	23	174	109	5.92	1.39	4.87	25.1

Source: Own ellaboration based on CSS (2006).

also accounting for 23.9 percent of Chile's imports from China in 2005. Note also that in the case of Chile, 34.3 percent of imports from China were concentrated in the yarn-textile-garment value-added chain.

Table 3.4 provides more detail on the specific trade structure of the main trading partners of China in the region. With the exception of Chile—to which Chinese exports in autoparts still only play a minor role—all Latin American countries are beginning to import electronic and autoparts from China. Yet Latin America's share in total Chinese exports in these two chapters was still below 3 percent in 2005, which means that China still has a huge export-potential to Latin America and particularly to those countries with light and medium manufacturing sectors such as Argentina, Brazil, Mexico, and Venezuela.[12] Unless new trade barriers are imposed, we should thus expect a substantial growth of industrialized exports from China to Latin American in the next decades, particularly in sectors such as autoparts, electronics, garments, textiles, toys, and shoes.

Rather surprisingly, China's total imports are also concentrated in the same three chapters: electronics, autoparts, and optical instruments, as well as mineral fuels, plastics and other raw materials. Contrary to what many would believe, imports in optical and photographic instruments and other manufacturing goods were even more dynamic than imports in mineral fuels during the period 1995–2005. Yet with the important exception of electronics, most of Latin America's exports to China are raw materials and ores, oil seeds, copper, and mineral fuels—they in total accounted for more than 60 percent of Latin American exports to China in 2005. With the important exception of Mexico, which exports electronics and autoparts to China, the rest of the selected countries—Argentina, Brazil and Mexico—only export a few raw materials. In 2005, for example, 44 percent of Chile's exports to China was concentrated in copper; 57.4 percent of Argentina's exports in oil seeds and almost two-thirds of Brazil's exports in ores and oil seeds.

At least three issues stand out from this (albeit preliminary) analysis. First, Mexico's high and increasing trade deficit with China—based exclusively on China's data sources—is the result of Mexico's imports of electronics and autoparts, as well as automobiles and photographic goods. Second, the surplus achieved by countries such as Argentina, Brazil and Chile with China is mainly the result of exports of a few raw materials—which have benefited from high prices. Third, it can be expected that China's manufacturing exports to Latin America will continue to be very dynamic. The trade surplus of the region—and particularly of Brazil—will thus depend on continuous growth in both price and quantities of a small number of exported goods. Otherwise, the trade balance sign can change rapidly.

The Economic and Trade Relationship
between China and Mexico

Having discussed the broad significance of China's emergence as a trading power, and what this event means for Latin America, we now turn to
a specific analysis of the bilateral economic relationship between China
and Mexico. Detailed research on the economic relationship between
China and Mexico is still relatively recent. On the basis of literature since
2004, the following issues are relevant for the proposed discussion:

• Mexican official sources have began to pay more attention to
  China's FDI (see, for example, SE, 2005), stressing that in 2005 339
  Chinese business were established in Mexico, with an estimated
  accumulated FDI of $74 million. Trade and FDI data is, however,
  extremely weak.[13]
• With few exceptions (CANAINTEX, 2006; CNIV, 2006) the Mexican
  private sector has not generated comprehensive information and
  analysis on China and the Chinese-Mexican economic and trade
  relationship.
• There is currently no single public sector publication in Mexico on the
  topic.[14]
• More recently, several studies (Cornejo, 2005; Dussel Peters, 2005a;
  2005b; Oropeza García, 2006; Pescador Castañeda, 2004; Rueda
  Peiro et al., 2004) have undertaken a detailed analysis of specific value-
  added chains such as in the yarn-textile-garment and electronics case;
  in the latter Mexico lost more than 45,000 jobs, 3,200 million $U.S.
  and 500 million $U.S. during 2001–2003 because of Asian and par-
  ticularly Chinese competition (Dussel Peters, 2005a). With different
  methods of analysis most of the results reflect substantial processes of
  displacement of Mexican production and exports both in the domestic
  and export-markets, particularly in the United States.[15] At the same
  time, they also provide some preliminary information of business
  opportunities in China, given the huge growth of its economy.
• Since August 2004, Mexico and China created a Bilateral Commission,
  and since January 2005, a High Level Group to work and solve very
  particular issues—from statistics to bilateral cooperation on industrial
  policy, among many other topics (Gómez Cavazos, 2005). Despite its
  formal establishment, these institutions have not been used to address
  any of the massive and substantial problems between both countries.
• Based on Mexican statistics, China has become Mexico's second trading partner—and only after the United States—since 2003. In 2005
  China accounted for 0.5 percent of Mexican exports and 8.0 percent of
  its imports, with an AAGR of 30.9 percent and 37.5 percent during
  1993–2005, respectively. As a result, and as reflected in figure 3.1,

Mexico has a very "unequal" trade relationship with its second main trading partner: in 2004 the import/export relationship with China was of 31:1 and fell to 16:1 in 2005.

In considering the bilateral relationship, it is worth noting other worrying trends. First, in general terms, China's and Mexico's exports are similar. In both cases manufacturing accounts for more than 90 percent of total exports and autoparts and electronics play a substantial role. Both China and Mexico are also increasingly specialized in temporary imports to be exported.[16] Second, illegal imports from Asia and particularly from China—either through technicalities (new garments are imported as used garments), imports entering the United States as temporary imports and being then imported through NAFTA rules of origin (mainly through Long Beach) and through corruption—could even double registered imports from China: only in the case of garments around 60 percent of domestic consumption is of illegal origin (CANAINTEX, 2006). Lastly, there has been a massive displacement of Mexican exports—particularly in the yarn-textile-garment, furniture, toys, and electronic value-chain—by Chinese exports in the U.S. market (Dussel Peters, 2005a). Considering that Mexico's manufacturing sector has lost 6 percent of GDP during 1988–2005 and more than 14 percent of employment during 2000–2005 (Monitor de la Manufactura Mexicana, 2006), China poses massive challenges for Mexico's productive sector. China and Mexico will compete intensively in the short and medium term in the autoparts-automobile chain.

Conclusions

This chapter seeks to understand—at least preliminary—the implications of China's entry into the world market for Latin America with emphasis on Mexico's experience. The first section concludes that China's and Mexico's strategies currently are highly dependent on their export performance. As discussed, both nations have increasingly supported an export orientation, although as a result of different—even diametrically opposed—development strategies. With a different schedules—in 1994 through NAFTA in the case of Mexico and in 2002 through the accession to the WTO in the case of China—both nations have decided to actively integrate into the world market through exports as one of the main pillars of their development strategy.

Yet China's reforms since the 1980s—with huge challenges, such in Latin America and in Mexico—stands in direct opposition to the EOI followed by Mexico and most of Latin America since the 1980s. One of the main differences among both development strategies to integrate into the global economy is the degree and capability of preparation of each country. While Mexico's integration process—based on EOI's premises—took place rapidly and with little socioeconomic consensus, China allowed for several decades of capacity-building of institutions and productive structures (reflected in the concept of "transitional institutions").

Despite the dominance of the EOI model in Latin America today, the record of market-driven, export-oriented policies in promoting developmental objectives is ambiguous. In addition to disappointing results since the 1980s and 1990s in terms of GDP growth, income distribution, employment generation and balance of payments (Stallings and Péres, 2000), there is also accumulating evidence that Latin America's performance has been poor in comparative terms with Asian countries and particularly with China. While both the Latin American and Chinese models have generated increasing inequality of firms, branches, territories, and workers—between areas that have become integrated into global circuits benefiting from these processes and more backward, less fortunate ones—China has been able to increase overall GDP, GDP per capita and consumption rapidly. In Mexico—and most Latin America—personal consumption and per capita GDP have stagnated, even as inequality continues to rise.

Other differences in economic policy stand out, including the high pragmatism of the Chinese strategy in terms of macroeconomic management—the undervaluation of the exchange rate and massive financing to the productive sector—and the incentives for particular processes and branches with emphasis on high technology. For example, the last Program on Science and Technology in China published in March of 2006 highlights that it has to double—to 2.5 percent of GDP—its expenditure in research and development (R&D) by 2020. In contrast, Mexico and most of Latin America have lacked an upgrading process, particularly in terms of R&D.

Development economics, and particularly multilateral agencies such as the World Bank, IMF, and the Inter-American Development Bank (IADB), are likely to reflect on the performance of Asia, particularly China, and Latin America in the next few years. Are these institutions able to promote a learning process, after implementing "structural adjustment policies" in most of the periphery and particularly in Latin America?

The second section further reflects on the role of China in the global economy, and its relations with Latin America. It concentrates on three specific topics: the historical uniqueness of China's massive integration to the world market, the similarities and differences between different Latin American countries in their bilateral trade relationship with China, and the particular case of Mexico's relationship with China.

On the first issue, the section highlights the uniqueness of China's integration in the world market. As a result of China's size in terms of trade and GDP, China's experience is not comparable to that of other Asian Tigers. Being the main global exporter with an average annual growth rate of 24.9 percent during 2000–2005, China's dynamism results in massive displacement of other international competitors— including those in Latin America. At the same time, China's import performance also allows for significant opportunities, but Latin America—with the exception of raw materials—has failed to use them. In addition, China's size and dynamism profoundly questions the feasibility of Latin America's—and Mexico's—EOI.

When comparing the relations of different Latin American subregions, the analysis concludes that differences between South America (particularly Argentina, Brazil and Chile) and Mexico-Central America are transitory. Thus, it is expected that China will increase its exports in electronics, autoparts, and other light manufacturing products to all Latin American countries, including those in South America. Meanwhile, Chinese exports to China may remain concentrated in just a few raw materials. Is the exporting of raw materials the new Latin America Model (Dussel Peters and Katz, 2006)? Given the lack of significant medium and long-term differences between different Latin American countries in its trade relationship with China, it is of utmost relevance the region as a whole starts a regional bilateral negotiation process with China.

The analysis of Mexico's bilateral trade and economic experience with China shows the rapid deepening of the relations between both countries. China has become the second main trading partner of Mexico since 2003 and has a significant role in specific chapters of the HTS such as electronic and autoparts. In addition, there are massive illegal imports from Asia and China, also as a result of trade barriers such as safeguard quotas and nontariff barriers that make it very profitable to import illegally Asian and Chinese goods. Thus, China's new integration to the world market has not only allowed for massive displacements of Mexico in the U.S. market, but also for domestic production in the Mexican market—questioning Mexico's EOI model and its performance since the 1980s.

Finally, and to conclude, it is worth underscoring that the analysis is preliminary and written with the aim and expectation of generating further debate, research, and discussion on the topic. So far, and as highlighted for the Mexican case, coherent, structured and long-term analysis of the relationship between China and Latin America has been very scarce in the public, private, and academic sectors.

Notes

1. It would take too long in this context, and it is not the objective of the chapter, to develop EOI in depth, and particularly regarding the

association between exports, productivity, economic growth, and overall development. For such a discussion, see Dussel Peters (2000).

2. The hypothesis of this section is that—and as discussed in Dussel Peters and Katz (2006)—Mexico's liberalization strategy has been followed in most of Latin America since the 1980s, either through the export of temporary imports to be reexported or through raw materials.

3. As Aspe Armella (1993) stresses, lowering inflation rate was the crucial targeted variable since high inflation rates, caused in general by domestic demand, but particularly by inertial tendencies of real wages, did not allow for the reduction of the fiscal deficit during the period 1982–1987.

4. At the end of the 1980s, this was not merely a hypothetical possibility. Politicians such as Ross Perot and Patrick J. Buchanan in the United States presented strong criticisms of imports from Mexico. Stepped-up protectionism would have acted against an export orientation in Mexico and EOI in general.

5. For a discussion on the new challenges of unions in China—such as the China Federation of Trade Unions (ACFTU)—see *Businessweek* (2005).

6. In 2003 the SOEs employed more than 66 million persons (staff and workers), while the urban collective-owned employment was of almost 10 million (NBSC, 2005).

7. In 2003 the SOEs employed more than 66 million persons (staff and workers), while the urban collective-owned employment was of almost 10 million (NBSC, 2005).

8. The concept discussed for China by Qian is extremely helpful to understand the country's development strategy since the end of the 1970s: contrary to Latin America, China has massively adopted "transitional institutions"—from property to technology adoption and incentives for different sectors and regions—to integrate into the world market, i.e., in contrast to massive privatization of SOEs, China allowed for the same property status (public property) and incentives for higher efficiency and productivity. As a result after several decades, public property—i.e., from the central government, but also at the state, regional, county, and city level—still plays a substantial role in China's socioeconomy.

9. In July of 2005 the People's Central Bank decided to revalue the Yuan by 2.1%, also as a result of massive foreign exchange reserves (above US$710 billion in 2005) and international pressure for doing so. It is possible that the Yuan will continue with this process, although it is not expected that a substantial change will occur.

10. Implicitly under this argument is also the idea of a "normalization" of the growth curve, i.e., such as in the case of other "Asian Tigers," China's growth rate in terms of exports will fall with increasing income in the future.

11. There are major differences in trade statistics between Latin American—and particularly Mexican—and Chinese sources (Dussel Peters 2005b).

12. As a result, both Argentina and Brazil imposed trade barriers—from tariffs to import licenses—to products from China in 2005, including toys, shoes, and garments.

13. As discussed in Dussel Peters (2005b; 2006), FDI is at least three times higher and while Mexico accounts for US$18.8 billion imports from China in 2005, China registered US$5.5 billion.

14. The lack of a strategy of Mexico's public and private sectors toward China is also reflected in around 1,310 items to which Mexico imposes safeguard quotas as part of the bilateral agreements that Mexico negotiated with China for its entry to the WTO; Mexico was the last country, out of 37 bilateral agreements, that finished negotiations with China. In 2006, again, Mexico is one of the last countries to accept China as a "market economy" in the context of the WTO.

15. The analysis of Garza Limón (2005) is very clear about this topic: "We are bad and late in the Chinese market . . . we cannot continue with a practice . . . defensive or restrictive with China, and continue with accusations of unfair trade and violation of human rights; this is a pretext that justifies inefficiency" (Garza Limón, 2005: 29).

16. The main differences are Mexican oil exports that have increased their share in Mexican exports very recently, accounting for 15 percent of Mexican exports in 2005.

References

Anguiano, E. (2004) Normas sociales para hacer negocios en China. Presented at the International Seminar ";Cómo hacer negocios en China?". Mexico: Bancomext.

Aspe Armella, P. (1993) El Camino Mexicano de la Transformación Económica, Mexico: Fondo de Cultura Económica.

Bair, J. and E. D. Peters (2006) "Global Commodity Chains and Endogenous Growth: Export Dynamism and Development in Mexico and Honduras," World Development, 34 (2): 203–221.

Balassa, B. (1981) The Newly Industrializing Countries in the World Economy, New York: Pergamon Press.

Bhagwati, J. (1988) Protectionism, Cambridge, MA: MIT Press.

——— (1991) "Is Free Trade Passé After All?" in A. Koekkoek and L.B.M. Mennes (eds.) International Trade and Global Development. London: Routledge, 10–42.

BID (Banco Interamericano de Desarrollo) (2005) The Emergence of China: Opportunities and Challenges for Latin America and the Caribbean. Washington, DC: BID.

Businessweek (August 22, 2005) "A New China for Organized Labor."

CANAINTEX (Cámara Nacional de la Industria Textil) (2006) Several documents, Available: http://www.canaintex.org.mx/, last accessed July 2006.

CEPAL (2005) *Panorama de la inserción internacional de América Latina*, Tendencias 2005. Santiago, Chile: CEPAL.

Chow, G. C. (2002) *China's Economic Transformation*. Malden, MA: Blackwell.

CNIV (Cámara Nacional de la Industria del Vestido) (2006) Several documents, Available: http://www.cniv.org.mx/, last accessed July 2006.

Cornejo, R. (2005) "México y la competitividad de China," in Sergio Cesarín and Carlos Moneta (compilers), *China y América Latina*, Buenos Aires, Argentina: REDEALAP/BID-INTAL, 235–268.

Dussel Peters, E. (2000) *Polarizing Mexico. The Impact of Liberalization Strategy*. Boulder, CO/Londres: Lynne Rienner Publishers.

———— (2005a) *Economic Opportunities and Challenges Posed by China for Mexico and Central America*. Bonn: DIE/GDI.

———— (2005b) "El caso de las estadísticas comerciales entre China y México: Para empezar a sobrellevar el desconocimiento bilateral," *Economía Informa*, 335: 50–59.

———— (2006) "La relación económica y comercial entre China y México: propuestas para su profundización en el corto, mediano y largo plazo," Paper presented at the First Forum "La relación económica y comercial entre China y México," Organized by the Economic Commission for Latin America and the Caribbean (ECLAC), Mexico's Foreign Ministry, and the Mexican Senate, Mexico City, March 6–7, 2006.

Dussel Peters, E. and J. Katz (2006) "Dos vías de desarrollo en América Latina: exportaciones temporales y transformación de materias primas," in K. J. Middlebrook and E. Z. Miramontes (eds.) *Producción de exportación, desarrollo económico y el futuro de la industria maquiladora en México*. Mexico: Universidad Autónoma Metropolitana.

Garza Limón, C. (2005) "El ambiente de negocios en la República Popular China," *Economía Informa*, 335: 24–30.

Gómez Cavazos, I. A. (2005) "Condiciones y potencial de las relaciones México-República Popular China." *Economía Informa*, 335: 5–10.

Gereffi, G. and D. L. Wyman (1990) *Manufacturing Miracles. Paths of Industrialization in Latin America and East Asia*. Princeton, NJ: Princeton University Press.

Krueger, A. O. (1978) *Liberalization Attempts and Consequences*. Cambridge, MA: Ballinger Publishing Company.

———— (1983) *Trade and Employment in Developing Countries*. Vol. 3. Chicago, IL: University of Chicago Press.

———— (1992) *Economic Policy Reform in Developing Countries*. Oxford: Blackwell.

———— (1997) "Trade Policy and Economic Development: How We Learn," *The American Economic Review*, 87 (1): 1–22.

Lora, E. (2005) "¿Debe América Latina temerle a la China?" Documento de Trabajo 536 (BID), 1–40.

Mengkui, W., L. Baipu, and L. Zhongyuan (2003) "Cambios estructurales, retos y perspectivas de la economía China," Beijing: DRC. Available: http://www.drc.gov.cn/new_product/drcexpert/showdoc.asp?doc_ id=124853, last accessed July, 2004.
Mesquita Moreira, M. (2005) "El surgimiento de China: oportunidades y desafíos para América Latina y el Caribe," presented at the Conference "La competitividad latinoamericana y el reto asiático," Institute of the Americas, UCSD, August 28.
Monitor de la Manufactura Mexicana (2006) *Monitor de la Manufactura Mexicana*, vol. 2, no. 4, Mexico: Centro de Estudios Empresariales UNAM-Canacintra y Canacintra.
NBSC (National Bureau of Statistics of China) (2004) *China Statistical Yearbook*, Beijing: NBSC.
Nolan, P. (2004) *China at the Crossroads*. Cambridge: Polity Press.
OECD (Organization for Economic Co-operation and Development) (2002) *China in the World Economy. The Domestic Policy Challenges,* Paris: OECD.
────── (2005) *OECD Economic Surveys: China,* Paris: OCDE.
Oropeza García, A. (2006) *China. Entre el reto y la oportunidad,* Mexico: UNAM/Consejo Argentino para las Relaciones Internacionales.
Perkins, D. H. (2001) "Industrial and Financial Policy in China and Vietnam," in J. E. Stiglitz and S. Yusuf (eds.) *Rethinking the East Asian Miracle*, Washington, DC: World Bank, 247–294.
Pescador Castañeda, A. (2004) "China, un nueva reto para la política exterior mexicana del Siglo XXI," in Instituto Matías Romero/SRE (ed.) *Los retos para la política exterior de México en la actual coyuntura*. Mexico: Instituto Matías Romero/SRE.
Qian, Y. (2003) "How Reform Worked in China," in Dani Rodrick (ed.) *In Search of Prosperity. Analytic Narratives on Economic Growth*, Princeton, NJ: Princeton University Press, 297–333.
Rodrik, D. (2006) *What's So Special about China's Exports?* Cambridge, MA: NBER (Working Paper Series 11947).
Rueda Peiro, I., N. S. Domínguez and M. L. González Marín (2004). *La industria de la confección en México y China ante la globalización*. Mexico: UNAM.
Salinas de Gortari, C. (2000) *México. Un paso difícil a la modernidad*. Mexico: Plaza & Janés Editores.
SE (Secretaría de Economía) (2005) *Inversión de China en México,* Mexico: SE.
Sojo Garza-Aldape, E. (2005) *De la alternancia al desarrollo. Políticas públicas del gobierno del cambio,* Mexico: Fondo de Cultura Económica.
Stallings, B. and W. Péres (2000) *Crecimiento, empleo y equidad. El impacto de las reformas económicas en América Latina y el Caribe,* Mexico: FCE/ CEPAL.
WDI (World Development Indicators) (2006) *World Development Indicators*.
Yifu Lin, J., F. Cai, and Z. Li (2003) *The China Miracle. Development Strategy and Economic Reform,* Hong Kong: Chinese University of Hong Kong.

Chapter 4

Investment Treaty Arbitration and Its Policy Implications for Capital-Importing States

Gus Van Harten

The policy impact of any project of economic integration depends, in part, on how the rules of integration are to be interpreted and enforced. In international law, rules governing states are typically subject to various forms of dispute settlement among states. In the case of the World Trade Organization (WTO), states took the step of authorizing the compulsory international adjudication of disputes by tribunals that are supervised by an appellate body. Even so, WTO adjudication remains an intergovernmental regime. It is only rarely that states have gone so far as to give an international tribunal the comprehensive jurisdiction to rule on claims by individuals against states. Under the European Convention on Human Rights (ECHR) and under European Union (EU) law, individuals may bring claims for compensation for an alleged breach of treaty by a state, before the European Court of Human Rights and the European Court of Justice, respectively. But individualized adjudication of this sort is much the exception in international law, all the more so if one includes only those cases where individuals may be awarded money compensation as a remedy for losses caused by the exercise of regulatory authority by the state.

It is thus noteworthy that the newly emerged system of investment treaty arbitration goes well beyond the ECHR and EU law in the degree to which it gives foreign investors, but not other individuals, the right to bring claims against states and receive damages via compulsory international arbitration. The system—based on hundreds of investment treaties concluded from the late 1960s and mainly in the 1990s—existed in relative obscurity until about ten years ago when the present torrent of investor claims under the treaties began. The importance of this system lies in the unique extent to which it establishes international arbitration as a

vehicle to protect international business from prohibited forms of
regulation by states. In this chapter, the aim is to elaborate upon this
system in order to shed light on what its emergence means for capital-
importing states[1]. The discussion begins with an overview of how the
system combines various elements in an unprecedented way. In particular:
(1) the system gives arbitrators comprehensive jurisdiction over investor
claims relating to the regulatory activity of states without requiring investors first to exhaust domestic avenues for redress before bringing an
international claim; (2) it allows investors to receive damages as a remedy
in public law; and (3) it provides for the enforcement of awards in a large
number of countries by incorporating the treaty-based enforcement
structure of international commercial arbitration.

After examining the uniqueness of the system, the discussion turns to
the context for its emergence as a mechanism to regulate sovereign conduct, as evidenced by the recent explosion of investor claims. This is followed by a discussion of why capital-importing states may have decided
to submit to this powerful mechanism of adjudicative control in bilateral
investment treaties (BITs) and in bilateral or regional trade agreements,
after rejecting proposals for a multilateral investment treaty for much of
the twentieth century. A subtheme in this respect is the position of Latin
American countries within the system, three aspects of which are significant. First, in the nineteenth century, they were newly independent
Latin American states that originally elaborated doctrines of international law to defend their adjudicative sovereignty against the assertion
by capital-exporting states of expansive international standards of investor protection. Second, most Latin American countries abandoned this
historical position in short order during the late 1980s and early 1990s
by consenting to numerous investment treaties with major capital-
exporters in Europe and North America. Third, Latin American countries appear to have paid more, both figuratively and literally, for their
consents to the system, given that they have been the targets of more
investor claims than other capital-importing regions. In these respects,
the Latin American experience illuminates how the system may be used
to discipline states while also pointing to tentative explanations for why
capital-importing countries agreed of late to such rigorous control by
international tribunals.

Overview of the System of Investment
Treaty Arbitration

A Hypothetical Case

To illustrate how investment treaty arbitration operates, one may consider
the hypothetical case of a Spanish company that owns a mine in a Latin

American country, via a locally incorporated firm that is 100 percent owned by the Spanish investor. Let us assume that the government of the host country has introduced new environmental regulations that reduce the profitability of the investor's mine. The investor believes the regulations are unfair and an expropriation of its assets, and seeks compensation for the market value of the mine including lost profits over the next twenty years, which amounts to a claim of US$120 million. The host government, on the other hand, sees the regulations as a legitimate exercise of its inherent public authority as the sovereign and refuses to pay compensation.

After a few months, negotiations break down and the Spanish company brings an arbitration claim. However, it does so not under the host country's investment treaty with Spain but under an investment treaty between the host country and the Netherlands. The investor, it appears, anticipated the passage of the regulations and, shortly before they were enacted, transferred ownership of its local mining firm to a Dutch holding company which is in turn owned by the Spanish company. The investor did so based on earlier advice that the Dutch treaty offered more favorable protection than the Spanish treaty because it allowed claims under arbitration rules that provide for the presiding arbitrator of a tribunal to be appointed by the International Chamber of Commerce (ICC) and because it did not require the investor to choose either to bring a treaty claim or to pursue remedies in domestic law. Thus, the investor was more confident in bringing the claim under the Dutch treaty while at the same time its local mining firm attempts to overturn the regulations in the host country's courts.

The arbitration is conducted by a tribunal of three members and the hearings take place in Paris at the Court of International Arbitration of the ICC. However, the tribunal has the authority to select another jurisdiction as the legal "seat" of the arbitration, depending on the tribunal's assessment of that jurisdiction's suitability, and it chooses Sweden as the seat of the arbitration (although the tribunal is physically located in Paris). After hearing the evidence and arguments presented by the parties, the tribunal sustains the investor's claim and awards US$15 million in damages plus US$250,000 in costs and arbitration fees. Notably, in the course of its ruling, the tribunal decides that there is no express provision in the Dutch treaty to prohibit forum-shopping or parallel claims and, therefore, the claim is allowed to proceed in spite of the investor's transfer of ownership to the Dutch holding company and the concurrent pursuit of domestic remedies by its local firm.

In response, the host government declares that the tribunal misinterpreted the treaty and applies to set aside the award in Sweden. The application is unsuccessful after the Swedish court decides that, although the tribunal applied an overly broad definition of expropriation, the court does not have the authority to intervene under Swedish law implementing the 1958 New York Convention on the recognition and enforcement of foreign arbitration awards, which is incorporated into the Dutch investment treaty for the purpose of enforcing awards. Nevertheless, the host government maintains that the award is invalid and obtains a judgment from its own supreme court striking it down. In response, the investor seeks to enforce the award against the host country's assets in other countries. The investor is unable to locate substantial assets of the host country in Europe but, because the award is enforceable under the New York Convention, the investor is able to bring an action in the United States for an order enforcing the award against two ships, docked in a U.S. port, that are owned by the host country.

The story could go on but I shall put it to rest here. The reason for telling it is not to suggest that all claims under investment treaties end in an award against the state; many do not. Rather, it is to highlight the novelty and complexity of the system as well as some of the legal strategies that investors employ within it. The next step is to examine more closely how various features of the system make it uniquely far-reaching as a form of international adjudication.

The Uniqueness of the System

Investment treaty arbitration should be understood as an exceptionally powerful system to control states through the wide-ranging review of their regulatory conduct by untenured adjudicators whose decisions are subject to limited review in foreign courts, typically, rather than in the courts of the host state. The system is novel in that it combines various features in a manner that goes beyond other adjudicative regimes in international law. Each of these features is outlined below. Together, they constitute tribunals established under investment treaties as the closest the world has come to an international adjudicative body endowed with comprehensive jurisdiction over individual claims in the regulatory sphere.

The Individualization of Claims

Customary international law presumes that the resolution of a dispute involving a foreign national is in the first place a matter for the domestic law of the host state. States are not subject to compulsory adjudication of disputes within their territory, whether by international tribunals or foreign courts. A dispute arising from one state's treatment of an investor of another state could conventionally trigger a claim of diplomatic protection by the investor's home state, but the investor could not make an independent claim under international law.[2] Also, a claim of diplomatic protection by the home state could only be made once the investor had exhausted local remedies, in order to give the host state an opportunity to address the complaint before any resort to international law.[3] Even then, the dispute could be referred to international adjudication only with the consent of the host state and, with one minor exception, no international tribunal has been granted comprehensive jurisdiction over disputes between states and foreign investors.[4] Before the recent wave of consents by states to compulsory arbitration under investment treaties, such disputes were typically resolved through diplomatic negotiation.

This conventional method of resolving regulatory disputes in the international sphere rests on the assumption that an investor's entitlement to protection under international law derives from rights of its home state.[5] By authorizing investors directly to advance international claims for damages, investment treaties give them the ability to decide when and how to threaten or initiate claims and, in general, investors can be expected to bring claims and represent their interests more vigorously than would their home state because investors do not have an interest to settle or moderate claims for reasons of the public interest. Investors, unlike states, do not face the prospect of ever having to defend an investment treaty claim. By implication, individualization expands the opportunities for arbitrators to adopt a broad approach to their jurisdiction and to the standards that regulate states (Sands, 2005: 130–138). Investors have advocated a more expansive approach to state liability than that adopted by the states parties, including the home state, in many North American Free Trade Agreement (NAFTA) cases to date, for example. Of course, this is not surprising: private claimants in a one-way system of adjudication will naturally favor a liberal approach to investor protection and state liability. What is important is that by allowing investors to make the claims and present the arguments, the system fosters an environment in which arbitrators can adopt interpretations of the treaty that go beyond the unanimous submissions of the states that negotiated it.[6] This environment does not exist in international custom and under most treaties where access to adjudication is limited to states.

However, individualization in itself is far from a unique development. It is only when individualization is combined with other novel features of investment treaties that the full significance of the present system becomes clear. The first of these features involves the nature of the state's consent to arbitration.

The Prospective Consent to Compulsory Arbitration

Historically, individuals were occasionally authorized to bring claims against states before international tribunals that were created in the aftermath of war or revolution (Collier and Lowe, 1999: Chapters 1 and 3). From the Jay Treaty of 1794 to the Iran-U.S. Claims Tribunal, established in 1981, states have allowed international tribunals to settle regulatory disputes arising from the sovereign treatment of foreign nationals and, in some cases, claims could be brought directly by investors. Yet these historical tribunals did not have *comprehensive* jurisdiction because their authority was retrospective in nature. That is, their authority was granted only after the dispute had arisen and it was limited to a distinct period, series of events, or subject matter.

A retrospective consent is very different from an advance consent to compulsory arbitration. With a retrospective consent, the state is much more able to anticipate the implications of its commitment to arbitrate. By giving a prospective consent in an investment treaty, the state exposes itself in principle to claims by any foreign firm with economic interests subject to regulation by the state. Also, in contemporary investment treaties, jurisdictional concepts (such as "investment" and "investor") and the applicable standards of review (such as the obligation of the states parties to provide "fair and equitable" treatment of investors, or to compensate for any "deprivation" of investor assets) are open to varying interpretations. Thus, unlike historical claims tribunals, the present system encompasses future disputes involving an indeterminate class of claimants in relation to a wide range of governmental activity. In doing so, it allocates a substantial sovereign power to private arbitrators.

The Dynamic of State Liability

In making a claim under an investment treaty, an investor seeks damages for losses caused by the respondent state's alleged violation of the standards of investor protection stipulated in the treaty. Where a tribunal concludes that a state has violated the treaty, it may award damages to the investor. Awards are primarily compensatory but they also have a deterrent effect by imposing what may amount to a catastrophic fiscal sanction on the state for irreversible regulatory choices. This creates a serious potential for a "regulatory chill" on states that deem themselves vulnerable to claims, as indicated by case studies of Canadian policy initiatives that were abandoned in the face of pending or threatened NAFTA claims by U.S. investors, although the actual extent and intensity of this deterrence is difficult to measure (Been and Beauvais, 2003: 132–134). What is clear is that, although damages awards respond to the specific circumstances of each individual claimant, a finding of illegality and retrospective award of compensation against the state has wider implications for the state's regulatory position (Harlow, 2004: 80 and 85–86). Most importantly, investment treaties extend state liability in matters of public law to legislative and judicial acts of the state, with major implications for the domestic constitutional order (Harlow, 2004: 62; Rabkin, 2005: 40–41).

To illustrate, in the *CME* arbitration, the Czech Republic was ordered to pay an amount of compensation to a U.S. investor that was equivalent to the country's national health care budget (Kellner, 2003) after the tribunal decided that Czech regulators had cajoled the investor into divesting itself of a popular TV station. Adjusted for population size and gross national income, the amount awarded was comparable to an award of US$19 billion against the United Kingdom, $26 billion against Germany, or $131 billion against the United States.[7] It was followed by a raft of claims against the Czechs by other investors in cases involving the collapse of a domestic bank, an unsuccessful bid for a mobile phone network, and the seizure of a jet by Czech customs authorities (Peterson, 2003). Although difficult to quantify, it is likely that the *CME* award will deter regulatory measures that are opposed by foreign investors, not only in the Czech Republic but also in other capital-importing states. In this respect, the system's use of damages as a remedy in public law, which is itself exceedingly rare in the international context, significantly alters the bargaining relationship between international business and the state.

The Removal of the Duty to Exhaust Local Remedies

Many investment treaties remove the customary rule that a foreign investor must exhaust local remedies before an international claim can be brought (Been and Beauvais, 2003: 83–86; UNCTAD, 2003: 31–37). The duty to exhaust local remedies is very well established and, outside of investment treaty arbitration, no regime that allows individual claims discards it. Its removal under the present system is aimed, no doubt, at boosting the confidence and security of investors, but it leads to a number of other, less desirable consequences. First, domestic courts are no longer presumed to be capable of delivering justice and investors (unlike other foreign nationals) are no longer assumed to have a responsibility to take into account the domestic means of redress. Second, the host state's legal system may be denied an opportunity to itself correct any wrongs done to foreign investors and, as a result, states may be found liable for acts of their officials without any possibility for review by their courts. In turn, this creates what are at times astonishing opportunities for investors to bring parallel claims against states, under investment treaties as well as domestic law, in relation to a single dispute with the host state. States have responded to investors' attempts to bring parallel claims of this sort by arguing, for instance, that investors should not be able to bring a treaty claim where the claimant (or a domestic company owned by the claimant) is concurrently pursuing local remedies. Most tribunals have rejected these arguments, however, and read the treaties liberally to permit parallel claims.[8] And while this may be defensible as a form of interpretive gap-filling where the treaty is silent or ambiguous on the matter, it creates further uncertainties from a governmental perspective, by remodeling the system into one that is autonomous of the domestic courts and that effectively duplicates their remedial function. Again, no other international adjudicative regime does this.

The Facilitation of Forum-Shopping

Investment treaties concluded by the Netherlands, Switzerland, the United Kingdom, and the United States, in particular, usually facilitate forum-shopping by investors by allowing claims to be brought by foreign companies without imposing minimum thresholds of control by natural persons in the country of incorporation. Thus, the treaties allow investors to assume the nationality of a state party to the treaty simply by establishing a holding company in accordance with that state's laws, enabling multinational firms—though they lack actual business ties to the relevant state to acquire its nationality and the benefits of its treaty network (Muchlinski, 1999: 622–624; UNCTAD, 1999a: 37–38). Some countries, such as the Netherlands, appear to have positioned themselves as platforms for this type of forum-shopping by combining liberal rules of incorporation under their domestic law with a flexible approach to corporate nationality in their investment treaties. In such circumstances, a host government must assume that an investment treaty may open the door to claims by any firm incorporated in the territory of the other state party, regardless of whether the firm's ownership structure winds its way through a series of other companies in other jurisdictions.[9]

With forum-shopping, investors can select the jurisdictional link within their corporate structure from which to bring a claim under the most favorable conditions, or even to bombard a state with multiple claims under different treaties in relation to the same dispute. In the *CME* arbitration, the American billionaire Ralph Lauder used a Dutch holding company to bring parallel claims in a dispute with the Czech Republic, first under the Czech Republic's BIT with the United States and then (several months after the first tribunal was established) under the Czech Republic's BIT with the Netherlands. Mr. Lauder lost the first case but won the second, and was thus able to collect a sizeable award, as discussed above.[10] Likewise, in *Tokios*, a majority of the tribunal permitted a claim against the Ukraine by a Lithuanian company that was 99 percent owned by Ukrainians, who were thus allowed to leverage their ownership of a foreign firm into a treaty claim against their own state, in effect opening the system to claims by domestic investors who shift capital to a foreign platform and then re-invest it in their home country.[11] Most recently, in *Aguas del Tunari v. Bolivia*, the tribunal allowed a claim by the U.S. firm Bechtel that, after it became apparent that there was a great deal of public opposition to its privatized water utility in Bolivia, cleverly "migrated" the business from the Cayman Islands to the Netherlands—again, by shifting its legal ownership to a newly created Dutch company—thus enabling it eventually to bring a claim under the Netherlands-Bolivia BIT.[12]

In each of these cases, flexible rules of nationality in an investment treaty, aided by the tribunal's liberal approach to its jurisdiction, produced a major expansion of the scope of the system. They also revealed that ambiguity in the language of investment treaties may be read by tribunals so as to protect much more than the actual flows of capital between the states parties to a treaty, given that actual flows need not correspond to the legal structure for the international ownership of assets (UNCTAD, 2004: 238, fn. 15). Investors can make themselves Dutch or Lithuanian by a mere transfer of assets among companies without any accompanying commitment of capital to the host economy. Despite the bilateral framework of most of the treaties, in the stark words of the *Tokios* tribunal, "The origin of the capital is not relevant to the existence of an investment."[13]

The International Enforceability of Awards

Lastly, we turn to the question of enforcement. Clearly, the force of an arbitration award rests in large part on the prospect of enforcement against the state, without which investment treaty arbitration would more resemble mediation or conciliation than compulsory adjudication. Now that military force is prohibited, absent authorization by the UN Security Council, as a method of enforcement under international law, capital-exporting states have integrated an alternative which taps into the collective authority of domestic courts across the globe to enforce awards by seizing assets within their territory. This powerful means of enforcement is borrowed from the treaty structure of international commercial arbitration; specifically, investment treaties allow investors to seek enforcement of awards under the New York Convention and the Panama Convention, as well as the International Center for the Settlement of Investment Disputes (ICSID) Convention.[14]

To backtrack a little, there are three main ways in which investment treaty awards can be enforced. First, if a state refuses to abide by an award it may be subjected to diplomatic and economic pressure from the home state of the investor, from other capital-exporting states, from the capital markets, and from international financial institutions. Second, investment treaties typically obligate states to enforce any awards issued under the treaty, which allows investors to seek enforcement in the courts of any state party to the treaty, including their home state. Third, where a treaty provides for enforcement under the New York Convention, the Panama Convention, or the ICSID Convention (and many investment treaties provide for all three), investors can seek enforcement in the courts of any state party to any of these treaties. This option for enforcement is exceptionally powerful because so many states have ratified the relevant treaties: about 165 states are party to the New York Convention or the ICSID Convention, or both, for example. On the basis of this structure, investment treaty awards are supported, at least on paper, by the most wide-ranging and potent system of international enforcement ever devised for the adjudication of individual claims in the regulatory sphere.

Summary

With this combination of elements—the prospective consent, the use of damages as a public law remedy, the invitation to parallel claims and forum-shopping, and international enforceability—investment treaties establish a unique mechanism of international review which constrains the policy choices of states where those choices affect economic interests of international business. It was noted at the outset that investment treaty arbitration is the closest that the world has come to a system of international adjudication that provides for comprehensive jurisdiction over individual claims in the regulatory sphere. Yet it is also a system that is accessible only by one class of individuals: those with enough foreign wealth to contemplate claims. For the most part, this means multinational firms.

The Emergence of the System

The Expansion of Investment Treaties

Let us turn now to the emergence of investment treaty arbitration as a system. It is necessary at the outset to distinguish investment treaty arbitration from other forms of investment arbitration. This is best done by examining the state's consent to arbitrate. States can consent to the arbitration of future disputes with foreign investors in three ways: by contract, by domestic legislation, and by treaty. First, a state can accept an arbitration clause in a contract with a foreign investor, in which case the state is typically regarded as acting in a private (rather than a sovereign) capacity and its consent as limited to a commercial relationship with another private party. Second, a state can consent by enacting a law that authorizes foreign investors to submit any investment dispute with the state to international arbitration. Third, a state can conclude a treaty that likewise provides for the compulsory arbitration of disputes with foreign investors. In the latter two cases, the state consents generally to investment arbitration pursuant to either domestic law or international law (Paulsson, 1995: 233 and 240). The state's consent is general because it authorizes the arbitration, at the instance of the investor, of any future dispute concerning the state's exercise of regulatory authority in relation to foreign investors. Unlike contract-based arbitration, which relies on the specific consents of private parties, both legislation and treaty-based arbitration engage a wide range of disputes within the regulatory sphere. They expose the state to claims by a broad class of potential claimants in relation to any governmental activity affecting foreign investors in the absence of a contract between investor and state (Afilalo, 2001: 4; Wälde, 1996: 434–436).

The first treaties to incorporate general consents by states to investment arbitration were a handful of BITs signed in the late 1960s, typically between a newly independent country and the former colonial power (Dolzer and Stevens, 1995: 126). In the 1970s and 1980s, general consents in BITs became more common, though not universal; further, the scope of such treaties was often limited to a narrower body of disputes involving, for example, the amount of compensation that a state should pay for an expropriation (Parra, 2000; UNCTAD, 1998: 8–10). Only in the 1990s did the inclusion of far-reaching general consents become the norm. Of the 2,400 BITs signed to date, approximately 2,000 were signed during and after the 1990s (UNCTAD, 2000: 1 and 4; UNCTAD, 2005a: 1–2). Also, a number of important regional treaties were concluded in the 1990s, including NAFTA and the Energy Charter Treaty, both of which authorize compulsory investment arbitration. NAFTA in particular was a watershed in that it incorporated an investment chapter as part of a trade agreement, providing for the arbitration of investor claims in relation to investment but not the agreement as a whole.[15] Moreover, given that NAFTA governs more capital flows than other investment treaties—from the United States into Canada and Mexico, and from Canada into the United States—it has led to more claims and a more comprehensive body of jurisprudence than other investment treaties.

Existing investment treaties do not establish a global system of investor protection, especially in the absence of investment treaties between capital-exporting states, but the wide geographic coverage of existing treaties—supported by the infrastructure of the New York Convention and the ICSID Convention—has founded investment treaty arbitration as a general mechanism to regulate states in a very far-reaching way. Of course, variations among treaties create a degree of complexity and uncertainty regarding the scope and content of the obligations assumed by states and, for this reason, it is not possible to draw conclusions about how a dispute will be resolved without examining the language and structure of the relevant treaty. But there remains an international system designed to protect investors and regulate states by the use of international arbitration and, in this respect, the hundreds of investment treaties that constitute the system are unified by three main features. All subject (1) a wide range of regulatory activity by states to (2) broadly framed international standards of review that are (3) enforceable by the compulsory arbitration of investor claims.

The Explosion of Investor Claims

Evidence of the system's emergence is offered by the sudden and rapid growth in investor claims against states over the past decade. From 1996 to 2005, the ICSID in Washington, for example, registered four times as many investor claims as in the previous thirty years, and the increased rate of claims appears to be sustaining. By July 2006 there were 111 ICSID claims pending, more than all the claims registered at ICSID during its entire history until 2002. Dozens of claims were brought against Argentina in the aftermath of its financial crisis, which explains the spike in claims in 2003, but the rate of claims has remained relatively high, averaging twenty to thirty per year.

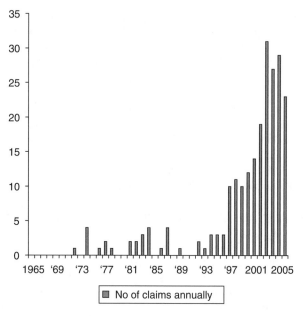

Figure 4.1   ICSID Claims Registered Annually: 1965–2006

Source: Compiled by author from ICSID data.

In tracking the system's expansion, the growth of ICSID arbitration is only part of the story. First, it does not include cases in which an investor and a state settled a dispute before the claim was registered at ICSID. Also, ICSID is the only forum for investment treaty arbitration that is required to publicize claims; others, such as the International Court of Arbitration of the ICC and ad hoc tribunals established under the UNCITRAL Rules, operate under the presumption that claims shall be kept confidential unless both disputing parties agree otherwise. For this reason, it is not possible to assess accurately the extent to which the use of investment treaty arbitration has expanded.[16] At minimum, the ICSID experience indicates rapid and continuing growth.

On the basis of this experience, it can also be said with confidence that the primary targets of investor claims to date are middle-sized capital-importing states, especially in Latin America and the former Soviet Bloc. A fairly reliable picture is obtained by reviewing those claims that have led to a widely available award on jurisdiction.[17] To the end of March 2006, seventy-five claims had reached this stage at ICSID and elsewhere, of which thirty were brought against Latin American countries, sixteen against the former Soviet Bloc, ten against countries in the Middle East and North Africa, eight against Asian countries, and eight against either Canada or the United States. Just two claims were filed against sub-Saharan African countries and only one against a Western European country. Further, of these seventy-five claims, 76 percent were brought against a lower-middle or upper-middle income country, and the average gross domestic product (GDP) per capita of the respondent state was (US) $11,148. Small and low-income countries have generally avoided claims, with no jurisdictional awards to March 2006 against a Central American or Caribbean country, and only two involving sub-Saharan Africa. Likewise, countries with large markets—including Western Europe and the large developing or transition states (China, India, Brazil, and Russia)—have avoided claims.[18] One explanation for this greater exposure of middle-sized states is that smaller countries may not host investments that are sizeable enough to warrant a treaty claim, whereas large countries have more bargaining power to refuse to conclude investment treaties in the first place or to deter claims by investors seeking to maintain favorable relations with the government of a major market or exporter of natural resources.

For those countries that are likely to suffer claims, the system's impact on governmental decision-making is difficult to assess in light of the confidentiality that infuses the system and the challenges of confirming whether and in what sectors policy initiatives have been abandoned or modified by states in order to preclude or settle claims. What is clear, however, is that the system has given arbitrators the authority to review and discipline states, and that many arbitrators are prepared to apply this authority in a far-reaching way. In sixty-six of the seventy-five awards to March 2006, for example, the tribunal decided that it had jurisdiction over the claim. Of these cases, fifty-six proceeded to the merits (with ten claims settled following the jurisdictional award), leading to a finding by the tribunal that the respondent state violated the relevant treaty in

Table 4.1 Damages Awards to Date (July 2007)

Award	Sector	Damages (US$)[a]	Ranking
CMS (Argentina)	Natural gas	149,081,000	5
Azurix (Argentina)	Water	182,400,000	4
Siemens (Argentina)	Data processing	248,700,000	3
Enron (Argentina)	Natural gas	128,800,000	6
Pope & Talbot (Canada)	Softwood lumber	462,000	22
S.D. Myers (Canada)	Waste disposal	6,126,000	14
MTD (Chile)	Construction	7,163,000	12
American Manufacturing (Congo)	Battery manufacturing/ commercial import	9,000,000	11
CME (Czech Republic)	TV broadcasting	350,758,000	2
Occidental Petroleum (Ecuador)	Oil exploration and production	75,075,000	7
Wena Hotels (Egypt)	Hotel management	20,601,000	8
Petrobart (Kyrgyz Republic)	Natural gas	1,414,000	20
Swembalt (Latvia)	Shipping	2,882,000	16
Nykomb (Latvia)	Natural gas	1,600,000	19
Metalclad (Mexico)	Waste disposal	16,685,000	9
Feldman (Mexico)	Tobacco export	1,700,000	18
Tecmed (Mexico)	Waste disposal	7,027,000	13
Sedelmayer (Russia)	Security services	2,761,000	17
CSOB (Slovak Republic)[b]	Banking	1,050,000,000	1
Maffezini (Spain)	Chemicals production	299,000	23
AAPL (Sri Lanka)	Agriculture	598,000	21
PSEG (Turkey)	Electricity	12,100,000	10
Average award		99,086,000	
Average not including CSOB		55,863,000	
Average not including Canada and Spain		113,605,000	

Notes:

[a] Rounded to the nearest thousand and approximated in some cases where interest and foreign exchange rates were not clear from the award.

[b] Note that, in *CSOB* [*Ceskoslovenska Obchodni Banka v Slovak Republic* (Jurisdiction) (May 24, 1999), 14 ICSID Rev 251, 17(3) World Trade and Arb Mat 189] the tribunal based its jurisdiction on the incorporation into a contract of the compulsory arbitration clause in a BIT that the claimant had not shown to be in force. As the origins of the respondent state's consent were connected to a BIT, I have included the case in the data presented here.

Source: Compiled by author from publicly-available awards.

twenty-seven of these cases and that there was no violation in eighteen, with eleven cases pending as of July 2007. Finally, twenty-three claims led to a damages award against the host state in a wide range of sectors, including oil and natural gas, water, electricity, waste disposal, construction, hotel management, shipping, broadcasting, and banking. The average award was for roughly (US) $99 million, although this figure is inflated by a number of large awards against Slovakia, the Czech Republic, Argentina, and Ecuador.

In total, seven awards to date have been for more than $20 million. However, these awards have a disproportionate significance because they signal to all capital-importing states the added fiscal risks and burdens that are now associated with the regulation of foreign-owned assets within their territory, as a factor in the regulatory relationship between governments and multinational firms. Indeed, they highlight the importance of the system's potential to sanction nearly any state measure that imposes significant costs on international business. For example, in the eleven damages awards issued to date against countries in the western hemisphere, the impugned measures included a legislative devaluation of the national currency in the face of a financial crisis (Argentina—various), a legislative ban on hazardous waste exports (Canada—SD Myers), an administrative investigation of a firm's compliance with export quotas (Canada—Pope & Talbot), an approval of an investment project (Chile—MTD), an order refusing refunds of value-added tax (Ecuador—Occidental Petroleum), a refusal to issue a waste disposal permit and an order establishing an ecological park (Mexico—Metalclad), a denial of a tax refund (Mexico—Feldman), and a denial of the authority to operate a landfill (Mexico—Tecmed). The point here is not that all of these measures were well planned and prudent in every respect, but rather that they are varied in purpose and, more fundamentally, that they all arose from regulatory as opposed to commercial acts of the host state. This reflects the character of the system as a uniquely internationalized form of public law adjudication.

The advent of investment treaty arbitration is an important development in international political economy because of its power as a regulatory mechanism that has been applied mainly to developing and transition countries. Barring some innovative forum-shopping strategies by investors, few treaties—namely, NAFTA and the Energy Charter Treaty—realistically expose major capital-exporting countries to claims, and so the great majority of claims will likely continue to be brought by Western firms against governments in Latin America, the Middle East, Northern Africa, Asia, and the former Soviet Bloc. The typical scenario is a claim under a treaty between a capital-importing country and a major capital-exporter for which the former country is not itself a significant source of investment. In this scenario, the capital-importer assumes major liabilities to foreign firms without achieving formal legal benefits for its own nationals. Extended to hundreds of treaties, the effect is to regulate capital-importing states intensively without imposing binding obligations on either home states or investors. This lopsided arrangement reflects the evolution of a treaty system in which the negotiating agenda was always driven by the dominant capital-exporters in Western Europe and North America (Muchlinski, 2000: 1049).

Explanations for the Emergence of the System

Once imperial legal regimes were dismantled in the nineteenth and twentieth centuries, developing states have opposed rigorous international standards of investor protection asserted by capital-exporting states. And, from an early stage, it was Latin American writers who fashioned legal doctrines to support the aspirations of capital-importing states for greater autonomy over their natural resources and economic affairs. According to the Calvo doctrine of jurist and diplomat Carlos Calvo, the use of force to protect the financial interests of foreign investors is prohibited under international law and, upon entering a state's territory, foreign investors must respect local laws and subject themselves to the domestic courts; further, the only protection to which they are entitled under international law is equal treatment to that enjoyed by nationals (Calvo, 1896: 118–164; Shea, 1955: 9–21). According to the Drago doctrine of Argentine foreign minister Luis Drago, the use of force by states to collect debts owed to their nationals is prohibited under international law; as Drago put it, "Pecuniary obligations shall not be converted into chains for South America" (Drago, 1907: 692; Stowell, 1908: 960). Both doctrines found increasing support in the twentieth century among newly independent countries and, as such, they foreshadowed more recent conflicts about the content of standards and the appropriate means of dispute settlement in investment law.

On the other hand, multinational firms and major capital-exporting states pushed for an international regime that would protect foreign investors against the threat of nationalization and expropriation, as well as less direct risks involving the potential closure of markets, loss of access to resources, or competition from state-backed firms in the developing world. From the 1920s, numerous proposals were advanced for a multilateral code that would enshrine investor-friendly standards of protection, such as the 1929 Draft Convention on the Treatment of Foreigners (Kuhn, 1930), the 1959 Abs-Shawcross Draft Convention on Investments Abroad (Abs and Shawcross, 1960), a Uruguay Round proposal for a multilateral investment treaty as part of the WTO agreements (Dillon, 2002: 100), and the draft Multilateral Agreement on Investment prepared by the Organization for Economic Cooperation and Development (OECD, 1998). Typically, these proposals originated in business lobbies and in international organizations dominated by capital-exporting states, and in all cases they were rejected by capital-importing countries (and, more recently, by constituencies within capital-exporting states themselves) (Walter, 2001: 58–60). On the other hand, alternative proposals emphasizing the discretion of states to regulate foreign investors, especially the Havana Charter of 1948, became a nonstarter for the major capital-exporters and for international business organizations (Fatouros, 1961: 80 and 101).

It is remarkable, therefore, that capital-importing states have consented of late to as rigorous a system of investor protection as that established by investment treaties and trade agreements that allow for compulsory arbitration of investor claims. Given the historical background, why did so many capital-importing states—whose governments are the primary targets within the system, but whose nationals do not own sufficient assets abroad ever to contemplate bringing claims—buy into this regime? At a general level, the emergence of the system can be linked to various trends associated with globalization, especially the growth of multinational firms (Hart, 1996: 39–44; Muchlinski, 1999: 25–33) and the liberalization of international finance (Kelsey, 2003: 158; Kozul-Wright and Rowthorn, 1998: 84–85). Added to this is the political emphasis on liberalization and deregulation that was dominant during the 1990s in many countries and international financial institutions. In many cases, a flood of BITs was ratified after the government of a developing or transition country adopted a neoliberal approach based, in part, on the promotion of foreign investment through the signaling of a high level commitment to investor protection.

Even so, international business has heralded the purportedly reciprocal benefits of investor protection since the 1920s and yet it was only in the 1980s and 1990s that these efforts really bore fruit. This indicates the significance of structural factors that coalesced in recent decades to intensify the pressure on developing countries to attract foreign private capital. Those identified in the literature include the 1980s' legacy of tight international credit, capital flight, the Third World crisis, the maturing of the process of obtaining control over natural resources, the decreasing cohesion of the Third World, the loss of bargaining options after the fall of the Soviet Bloc, and reductions in Western official aid (Haggard, 1995: 6–7; Hart, 1996: 79; Sornarajah, 2001: 12 UNCTAD, 1999b: 29–30). Added to this is direct and indirect pressure from financial institutions and capital-exporting states themselves (Peter, 1995: 251). Perhaps most importantly, the increasing mobility of international capital has put multinational firms in a stronger position to demand legal concessions from host states.

These conditions have expanded the clout and prestige of international capital in a world of many states, most of whom compete eagerly to attract investment and to promote "their own" national centers of capital (Vandevelde, 1998: 633–635; Morrissey, 2001: 64–65). This leads to a further explanation for the expansion of the system, lying in the dynamic of inter-state competition. States conclude investment treaties to attract investment but the degree to which any single treaty makes a state more attractive to investors depends on the extent to which the treaty assures more favorable treatment than that provided by competing investment destinations. States with less to offer in terms of their domestic market and resources may attempt to compensate for this by offering more in terms of legal guarantees that are favorable to investors. Cumulatively, the proliferation of treaties intensifies the competitive pressure on states to attract capital by liberalizing standards: as more states agree to investor-friendly rules, the bar rises as to what qualifies as a hospitable climate for investment. The result is a bidding up of state concessions to international capital (Guzman, 1998: 671–672).

The presence of this competitive dynamic and the recent timing of the system's consolidation and emergence indicate that the movement toward investment treaty arbitration reached a tipping point in the early 1990s once several hundred BITs had been ratified. But it offers little explanation for why individual states moved more quickly than others and why some, to this day, have not consented to the system. Each country will no doubt have its own reasons for concluding a one treaty or another. By looking at trends in a particular region, one may identify as market leaders those states that committed to compulsory arbitration at an early stage, thus undermining whatever wider regional solidarity existed to limit concessions to foreign investors. This targets opportunities for further research on which conditions played the most important role in prompting states to adopt reforms that in turn triggered the ratification of treaties with major capital-exporting states and, in particular, to examine the motivations of whichever regime held office at the key period and to analyze its relationship to those capital-exporters with whom BITs were first concluded. In Latin America, the record indicates that the regional leaders were Panama (which conceded to the system during the mid-1980s), followed first by Uruguay and Bolivia (late 1980s) and then by Argentina (early 1990s).[19] On a cursory examination, it seems that each of these countries changed its policy after a new government came to power and implemented a program of rapid liberalization and deregulation,[20] suggesting that the earliest Latin American consents to the system—and the consequent ratcheting up of competitive pressure on other countries—were a core feature of the neoliberal project of the 1980s and 1990s in that region (Gwynne and Kay, 1999: 13–17; Harvey 2005, 98–106). Even so, reliable conclusions about the origins of the

Table 4.2 BITs Ratified by Latin American Countries (June 1, 2005)

Country	# of BITs	First Major Ratifications	Key Period[a]
Belize	2	1982 (UK)	1982
Panama	11	1985 (UK, Switzerland, France)	1982–1985
Uruguay	21	1990 (Germany)	1987–1991
Bolivia	18	1990 (Germany, UK)	1987–1991
Argentina	53	1992 (Spain, Switzerland, Sweden)	1990–1994
Paraguay	19	1992 (UK, Switzerland, Taiwan)	1992–1994
Peru	26	1993 (Switzerland)	1991–1994
Venezuela	21	1993 (Italy, Netherlands)	1990–1994
Chile	36	1994 (France)	1991–1995
Mexico	12	1994 (US, Canada)	1992–1996
Ecuador	21	1995 (UK, Argentina, Venezuela)	1993–1996
Nicaragua	11	1995 (Spain)	1994–1996
El Salvador	20	1997 (Spain, Switzerland)	1994–1996
Costa Rica	13	1998 (Germany, Canada)	1982–1984/ 1997–1999
Guatemala	4	2004 (Spain)	2000–2004
Brazil	None	—	—
Colombia	None	—	—
Suriname	None	—	—
Honduras	NA	—	—

Note:
[a] Reflecting the period of signature and ratification of early BITs with major capital-exporting state.

system would require more careful research into the relevant political history of individual countries and their BIT programs in order to ground a comprehensive account of the expansion. Such an inquiry is beyond the scope of this chapter.

Most importantly, most capital-importing states have by now consented to numerous investment treaties with major capital-exporting states, regardless of the path they took. The most pressing policy questions, therefore, do not relate to why states entered the system but to the implications for governmental decisions in the here and now. Assuming that the development strategies of capital-importing states may conflict with the business priorities of multinational firms operating within their territory, let us consider some of these implications, even if space limitations permit only a brief review in this respect.

Some Policy Considerations

The advent of investment treaty arbitration demonstrates that a project of economic integration can be built on a variety of legal foundations, each of which may regulate policymaking in very different ways from a governmental perspective. Investment treaty arbitration stands out in this respect because of its unprecedented disciplinary power, but also because of the extent to which capital-importing states have consented to a model of investor protection that was beyond their reach for much of the twentieth century. The decision of so many developing and transition states to consent to compulsory arbitration in this way is a major policy decision in its own right because, above all, it transfers a core segment of the state's adjudicative authority in the regulatory sphere to international tribunals and foreign courts.

Perhaps the most troubling aspect of the present system is that the power to determine the legality of sovereign acts has been delegated to private arbitrators who lack, in the objective sense, key hallmarks of judicial independence and accountability in public law. I shall return to this below. More broadly, in assessing their position within the present system, capital-importing states must first adopt the assumption that their regulatory conduct in a wide range of fields—industrial development, taxation, public health and environment, broadcasting, utilities regulation, and so on—now falls within the comprehensive jurisdiction of international arbitrators. Further, the scope of investment treaties has been read and constructed by arbitrators to encompass activities of states that are in turn regulated by other regimes, such as the WTO or the International Monetary Fund (IMF). Thus, investment treaties establish an additional disciplinary mechanism that capital-importing states must consider as part of the policymaking process, one that is less predictable and less manageable because it can be activated directly by private firms, rather than by other states or by an international organization, and because it carries the risk of a fiscally crippling damages award. The Argentine experience has demonstrated quite dramatically that multiple claims may be brought against a state within a short period in response to regulatory decisions that are general in scope and that do not specifically target foreign investors, whether individually or as a group.

For this reason, developing countries should take cognizance of the system (and yet not be unduly intimidated by it) by assessing the extent to which the interaction between regulation and foreign ownership in important sectors introduces a risk of claims. Foreign investors with diversified or long term interests in the host economy are less likely to jeopardize their relationship with the host government by bringing a treaty claim. On the other hand, many firms have shown a willingness to use the treaties creatively to challenge perceived mistreatment or as leverage in the wider political arena. In order to manage this liability, states need to establish systems to track the ownership and nationality of major assets within their territory and, where possible, they should adjust potentially unsafe measures in order to minimize the likelihood that they will be found to violate the applicable treaties. That said, anticipatory planning of this sort is hindered by the propensity of some arbitrators to adopt the presumption that investment treaties should be interpreted liberally in favor of investors, and to award damages even where the state in question did not maliciously or negligently harm the claimant. On this basis, numerous tribunals have adopted an expansive approach to their jurisdiction and to the standards of review,[21] and, as such, they have greatly expanded the incumbent fiscal risks for governments.

Where a government initially faces a claim, a primary concern is the appointment of the members of the tribunal. Arbitrators do not have security of tenure and thus they are not independent in the judicial sense. As such, they are uniquely open to a perception of bias in favor of investors because, in an individualized system of state liability, the market for arbitrators will reflect the attractiveness of the system to potential claimants. It is all the more important, therefore, that governments strive to ensure that those appointed to tribunals have a reputation for fairness and balance, and that they do not display an obvious predisposition in favor of investors. A host state has control over who it appoints to a tripartite tribunal and it must not squander this opportunity by appointing a favored lawyer or academic or diplomat within the local establishment; rather, it should appoint someone who has shown a reasonable degree of sympathy for governmental priorities in the past and who is likely to be respected by the presiding arbitrator of the tribunal. With respect to borderline issues in an adjudication, the state-appointed arbitrator could play a vital role in countering the views of the arbitrator appointed by the claimant, or in at least producing a well-reasoned dissent that improves the prospects for annulling or setting aside the award.

More importantly, capital-importing countries should take an active interest in the appointments process for the presiding arbitrator of a tribunal, given that he or she will be called upon to resolve conflicts between the party-appointed arbitrators and, typically, to draft the award; in other words, the presiding arbitrator is the key figure in the adjudicative process. Investment treaties and the applicable rules of arbitration generally provide for presiding arbitrators to be appointed by a designated authority, in the absence of agreement between the investor and state or between the party-appointed arbitrators. In rare cases, investment treaties designate an independent, state-based, and broadly representative entity such as the International Court of Justice as the appointing authority. But in most cases this crucial power is given to an institution that is dominated by capital-exporting states (e.g., ICSID) or by private business (e.g., the International Court of Arbitration of the International Chamber of Commerce or the Arbitration Institute of the Stockholm Chamber of Commerce). Capital-importing countries should avoid granting such power to the latter private institutions because, where they are designated, individuals who are appointed by business will decide whether private investors are entitled to public compensation; indeed, the investor in question may well be a member of the business organization that makes the appointment. This quite obviously undermines judicial independence to the distinct disadvantage of capital-importing states.

Most investment treaties provide for the chairman of the ICSID Administrative Council (that is, the President of the World Bank) or the ICSID secretary-general to appoint presiding arbitrators. Thus, international officials exercise appointing authority who are themselves chosen, for the most part, by the U.S. administration, with the concurrence of the other major capital-exporters that dominate the World Bank's voting system. Even so, opportunities do exist for capital-importing states to exert influence over the ICSID appointment process by way of their membership in the World Bank and, in particular, to object to the manner in which ICSID exercises its authority in cases where, for example, ICSID fails to appoint arbitrators from the roster of candidates designated by states under the ICSID Convention. Capital-importing states may also wish to identify those arbitrators whose past performance has unduly favored investors, and argue that their re-appointment by ICSID to future tribunals would be unfair to respondent states. Interventions of this sort should be made with caution and, ideally, in conjunction with other states, but they are appropriate in principle given the extent to which the present system, as designed by capital-exporting states, neglects the principle of security of tenure in adjudicative decision-making in the regulatory domain, in favor of a system of case-by-case appointment which is institutionally slanted in favor of claimants.

In the actual arbitration of claims, it is suggested that the respondent state undertake a spirited defense of its interests without being perceived to create needless delay or repetition, following the general practice of the United States, which rigorously litigates nearly every turn in the adjudication of NAFTA investment claims against it. The benefits of this strategy relate more to the deterrence of future claims than to the specific case at hand. In order to mount a cost-effective but spirited defense, host governments should seek to develop in-house expertise in investment arbitration, perhaps in concert with other states that have successfully defended claims (Mexico comes to mind). The least attractive, but not unheard of, scenario would be that of the ill-prepared government which is faced with a claim by a legally sophisticated and well resourced investor, which turns in desperation to a major law firm whose primary client base is multinational firms, and which is later induced to settle or to limit its options in the litigation in order to save costs.

In the face of an award against it, a capital-importing state should consider the option of refusing to pay the award, especially where the tribunal has produced a poorly reasoned or imbalanced decision and awarded substantial compensation to the investor. The avenues for appeal provided within the system are limited in that they allow for the annulment or setting aside of an award only in instances of jurisdictional error or procedural impropriety, and typically not for errors of law. As such, the system places core questions of public law in the hands of untenured adjudicators who are appointed by a process that does not balance the interests of capital-exporting and capital-importing states. The consequent perception of bias weakens the legitimacy of the system and gives respondent states a credible platform in some cases to refuse to pay awards. The Argentine case is the most telling example; that is to say, it may be understandable for that country to offer only partial compensation to investors who are awarded damages in claims arising from the country's financial crisis, in light of the widespread suffering that the crisis caused to domestic investors and to ordinary Argentineans, as well as the fact that the majority of foreign bondholders accepted a discount of roughly 66 percent on the repayment of Argentine loans (Thomson, 2005). Lastly, as a precautionary step and to deter claims, capital-importing states should insulate their assets abroad from seizure and remove their assets from jurisdictions that adopt an aggressive approach to the enforcement of foreign arbitration awards.

A more fundamental issue is the competitive pressure that provokes states to consent to investment treaty arbitration in the first place. This pressure calls for capital-importing states to work toward a strategy in common for the revision of investment treaties, one that addresses the problems of forum-shopping and parallel claims and, above all, that withdraws the power of private arbitrators to rule on such fundamental matters in the regulatory domain. As such, capital-importing states may wish to seek amendment or joint interpretations of the more offensive aspects of their investment treaties with capital-exporting states, while also reviewing their treaties with other capital-importing states in order to ensure, in particular, that they do not designate a private business organization as an appointing authority. More broadly, both capital-importing and capital-exporting countries have good reason to support a plurilateral code that establishes an international investment court that is staffed by tenured judges and that is given jurisdiction over all investor claims under existing investment treaties.[22] Reform in this area has more likelihood of success if it focuses on institutional aspects of the system and if it provides for entry into force of a plurilateral code based on a modest quorum of capital-exporting and capital-importing states. For capital-importers, it is preferable to create an international investment court in which they have some say in the appointment process than to maintain a system of arbitration, institutionally biased against host governments, in which they have little say at all.

Beyond the legal and institutional context, capital-importing countries should examine whether their investment treaties have delivered the anticipated benefits in terms of increased foreign investment or (in the case of trade agreements) greater access to foreign markets. If not, they should in general be abrogated at the earliest opportunity unless the other state party agrees to accept amendments that narrow the treaty's constraints on host governments to those that are required to stimulate actual capital flows between the states parties. Without concrete evidence that treaty-based arbitration provides this benefit to capital-importing countries more effectively than the contractual and legislative alternatives (Egger and Pfaffermayr, 2004; Hallward Driemeier, 2003; Tobin and Rose-Ackerman, 2005), the case for capital-importing states continuing to subject themselves to far-reaching investment treaties is weak. A preferable alternative would be to limit the state's exposure to compulsory arbitration by relying on the tool of contract-based consents that are tied to specific investment projects. The contract-based option enables more informed and careful planning by governments about whether they should submit to compulsory arbitration in exchange for a binding commitment by a known investor to commit capital in a particular sector. This method of consent is more consistent with the judicious use of legal concessions by capital-importing countries as part of a wider development strategy in the context of international integration (Rodrik, 2001: 27–33). Given that investment treaty arbitration is the most intrusive legal regime to which capital-importing states have ever subjected themselves in their effort to improve their attractiveness as an investment destination, it should be resorted to only where less onerous alternatives demonstrably fail to deliver the same advantages. There is no point selling the farm if all one needs is a new tractor.

Notes

1. "Capital-importing" refers here to states whose inward stock of FDI exceeded their outward stock in 2004 by a ratio of at least 2:1. These include, e.g., Angola, Argentina, Brazil, Cameroon, Chile, China, Croatia, Czech Republic, Ecuador, Egypt, India, Indonesia (2000 data), Kenya, Malaysia, Mexico, Morocco, New Zealand, Nigeria, Pakistan, Peru, Philippines, Poland, Romania, Turkey, and Venezuela (UNCTAD 2005b, Annex Table B.2).
2. For e.g., *Nottebohm* (*Liechtenstein v. Guatemala*), [1955] ICJ Rep 4, 23–24; *Barcelona Traction, Light and Power Co* (*Belgium v. Spain*), [1970] ICJ Rep 3, 9 ILM 227 (cited as *Barcelona Traction*), para 35–36.
3. *Ambatielos Claim* (*Greece v. United Kingdom*) (1956), 12 RIAA 83, 103; *Interhandel Case* (*Switzerland v. United States*) [1959] ICJ Rep 6, 26–27.

4. The exception is the Central American Court of Justice of 1907–1918: Hill, 1981: 41–42.

5. *Barcelona Traction* (note 2 above) para 78.

6. For e.g., *Pope & Talbot Inc v. Government of Canada* (Merits, Phase 2) (April 10, 2001), 13(4) World Trade and Arb Mat 61, para 79; *GAMI Investments, Inc v. Government of the United Mexican States* (Merits) (November 15, 2004), 17(2) World Trade and Arb Mat 127 (cited as *GAMI*), para 29–30.

7. *CME Republic BV v. Czech Republic* (Merits) (September 13, 2001), 14(3) World Trade and Arb Mat 109 (cited as *CME* [Merits]), para 80 (separate opinion of I Brownlie).

8. For e.g., *CMS Gas Transmission Company v. The Republic of Argentina* (Jurisdiction) (July 17, 2003), 42 ILM 788, para 78 and 80; *Azurix Corp v. The Argentine Republic* (Jurisdiction) (December 8, 2003), 16(2) World Trade and Arb Mat 111, para 99–100; *Siemens AG v. The Argentine Republic* (Jurisdiction) (August 3, 2004), 44 ILM 138 (cited as *Siemens*), para 151 and 160; *Petrobart Ltd v. Kyrgyz Republic* (Merits) (March 29, 2005), SCC Rules, SCC Arbitration Institute Case No 126/2003 (cited as *Petrobart*), 65–66; *Sempra Energy International v. Argentine Republic* (Jurisdiction) (May 11, 2005), ICSID Case No ARB/02/16 (cited as *Sempra*), para 42.

9. For e.g., *GAMI* (note 6 above) para 29–30 and 38 (permitting a U.S. shareholder of 14% of a Mexican company's shares to make a claim against Mexico under NAFTA Chapter 11 regarding alleged injuries to the domestic company—as opposed to direct injuries to the shareholder itself—despite the domestic company's pursuit of relief in the Mexican courts); *Waste Management Inc v. United Mexican States* (Merits) (April 30, 2004), 43 ILM 967, 16(4) World Trade and Arb Mat 3, para 85 ("The nationality of any intermediate holding companies is irrelevant to the present claim").

10. *CME* (Merits) (note 7 above) para 396; *CME Republic BV v. Czech Republic* (Damages) (March 14, 2003), 15(4) World Trade and Arb Mat 83 and 245, para 432–433.

11. *Tokios Tokelès v. Ukraine* (Jurisdiction) (April 29, 2004), 16(4) World Trade and Arb Mat 75 (cited as *Tokios*), para 21, 38, and 80.

12. *Aguas de Tunari SA v. Republic of Bolivia* (Jurisdiction) (October 21, 2005), 18(2) World Trade and Arb Mat 271 (cited as *Aguas del Tunari*), para 69, 73, and 237, and para 4 and 10 (dissenting opinion).

13. *Tokios* (note 11 above) para 80.

14. United Nations Convention on the Recognition and Enforcement of Foreign Arbitral Awards (the New York Convention) (New York, June 10, 1958; 330 UNTS 3); Inter-American Convention on International Commercial Arbitration (the Panama Convention) (Panama, January 30, 1975; 14 ILM 336); Convention on the Settlement of Investment Disputes Between States and Nationals of Other States (the ICSID Convention) (Washington, March 18, 1965; 4 ILM 524).

15. Other trade agreements concluded by the United States follow the NAFTA model, including the Chile-U.S. Free Trade Agreement, the Singapore-U.S. Free Trade Agreement, the Morocco-U.S. Free Trade Agreement, the Dominican Republic-Central American Free Trade Agreement (DR-CAFTA), and the proposed Peru-U.S. Trade Promotion Agreement.

16. An important exception is NAFTA, under which the states parties have adopted a general practice of publishing materials that relate to Chapter 11 arbitration, regardless of the applicable arbitration rules.

17. Widely available meaning available online at ICSID www.worldbank. org/icsid, last accessed August 1, 2007; Investment Treaty Arbitration http://ita.law.uvic.ca/, last accessed August 1, 2007; or NAFTA Claims http://naftaclaims.com/, last accessed August 1, 2007.

18. There was an award in one claim against Russia, one against Spain, and eight against Canada or the United States (each targeted by the other's investors under NAFTA)

19. Belize is treated as an exceptional case in that it has ratified just two BITs, only one of which is with a major capital-exporting country, the United Kingdom, also the former colonial power; the other is with Cuba (ratified in 1999).

20. Namely, during the administrations of President Carlos Menem in Argentina (1989–1995), President Víctor Paz Estenssoro in Bolivia (1985–1989), and Presidents Julio Sanguinetti and Luis Alberto Lacalle in Uruguay (1985–1990 and 1990–1995), and during the U.S.-friendly period of General Manuel Noriega and President Nicolas Barletta in Panama (1983–1987).

21. For e.g., *Emilio Agustín Maffezini v. Kingdom of Spain* (Jurisdiction) (January 25, 2000), 16 ICSID Rev 212, 124 ILR 9, para 54–56 and 64; *CSOB* (note 20 above) para 57 and 64; *Tokios* (note 11 above) para 31–32 and 52 (majority opinion); *Siemens* (note 8 above) para 85 and 120; *Noble Ventures v. Romania* (Merits) (October 12, 2005), ICSID Case No ARB/01/11, para 52; *Continental Casualty Company v Argentine Republic* (Jurisdiction) (February 22, 2006), ICSID Case No ARB/03/9, para 80; *Petrobart* (note 8 above) 62–63; *Sempra* (note 8 above) para 94; *Aguas de Tunari* (note 12 above) para 244–247.

22. For a more elaborate discussion, see Van Harten (2007: Chapter 7).

References

Abs, H. and H. Shawcross (1960) "The Proposed Convention to Protect Private Foreign Investment," *Journal of Public Law* 9: 115.

Afilalo, A. (2001) "Constitutionalization Through the Back Door: A European Perspective on NAFTA's Investment Chapter," *NYU J Int'l L & Pol* 34: 1.

Been, V.L. and J.C. Beauvais (2003) "The Global Fifth Amendment: NAFTA's Investment Protections and the Misguided Quest for an International 'Regulatory Takings' Doctrine," *NYU L Rev,* 78: 30.

Calvo, C. (1896) *Le Droit International,* 5th ed., Paris: A Rousseau.

Collier, J. and V. Lowe (1999) *The Settlement of Disputes in International Law,* Cambridge: Cambridge University Press.

Dillon, S. (2002) *International Trade and Economic Law in the European Union,* Oxford: Hart.

Dolzer R. and M. Stevens (1995) *Bilateral Investment Treaties,* The Hague: Kluwer Law International.

Drago, L. (1907) "State Loans in Their Relations to International Policy," *American Journal of International Law,* 1: 692.

Egger P. and M. Pfaffermayr (2004) "The Impact of Bilateral Investment Treaties on Foreign Direct Investment," *Journal of Comparative Economics,* 32: 788.

Fatouros, A. (1961) "An International Code to Protect Private Investment— Proposals and Perspectives," *UTLJ,* 14: 77.

Guzman, A.T. (1998) "Why LDCs Sign Treaties That Hurt Them: Explaining the Popularity of Bilateral Investment Treaties," *Va Journal International Law,* 38: 639.

Gwynne, R.N. and C. Kay (1999) "Latin American Transformed: Changing Paradigms, Debates and Alternatives," in R.N. Gwynne and C. Kay (eds.) *Latin American Transformed,* London: Arnold.

Haggard, S. (1995) *Developing Nations and the Politics of Global Integration.* Washington, DC: Brookings Institution.

Hallward-Driemeier, M. (2003) "Do Bilateral Investment Treaties Attract Foreign Direct Investment? Only a Bit...and They Could Bite," World Bank Policy Research Working Paper No 3121, June 2003, 4–5 and 22–23, Washington, DC: World Bank.

Harlow, C. (2004) *State Liability: Tort Law and Beyond,* Oxford: Oxford University Press.

Hart, M. (1996) "A Multilateral Agreement on Foreign Direct Investment— Why Now?" in P. Sauvé and D. Schwanen (eds.) *Investment Rules for the Global Economy,* Toronto: C.D. Howe Institute.

Harvey, D. (2005) *A Brief History of Neoliberalism,* Oxford: Oxford University Press.

Hill, H.M. (1981) "Central American Court of Justice," in R. Dolzer, H.M. Hill, R.E. Hollweg, K.J. Madders, and A. Rustemeye (eds) *Encyclopedia of Public International Law,* 1.

Kellner, T. (2003) "The Informer: Call It the Ronald *Lauder* Tax," *Forbes Magazine,* 171: 9 (April 28, 2003).

Kelsey, J. (2003) "The Denationalization of Money: Embedded Neoliberalism and the Risks of Implosion," *Social and Legal Studies,* 12: 155.

Kozul-Wright, R. and R. Rowthorn (1998) "Spoilt for Choice? Multinational Corporations and the Geography of International Production," *Oxford Review of Economic Policy,* 14: 74.

Kuhn, A.K. (1930) "The International Conference on the Treatment of Foreigners," *AJIL*, 24: 570.

Morrissey, O. (2001) "Investment and Competition Policy in the WTO: Issues for Developing Countries," *Development Policy Review*, 20: 63.

Muchlinski, P.T. (1999) *Multinational Enterprises and the Law*. Oxford: Blackwell.

——— (2000) "The Rise and Fall of the Multilateral Agreement on Investment: Where Now?" *International Law*, 34: 1033.

Organization for Economic Cooperation and Development (OECD) (1998) *The MAI Negotiating Text*. Paris, OECD.

Parra, A.R. (2000) "ICSID and Bilateral Investment," *ICSID News*, 17 (1): 7.

Paulsson, J. (1995) "Arbitration without Privity," *ICSID Rev*, 10: 232.

Peter, W. (1995) *Arbitration and Renegotiation of International Investment Agreements*. The Hague: Kluwer Law International.

Peterson, L.E. (2003) "Investors Emboldened by Arbitral Verdict against Czech Republic," *Investment Law and Policy Weekly News Bulletin* (April 11, 2003).

Rabkin, J.A. (2005) *Law Without Nations?* Princeton, NJ: Princeton University Press.

Rodrik, D. (2001) "The Global Governance of Trade As If Development Really Mattered," New York: UNDP.

Sands, P. (2005) *Lawless World*, London: Penguin.

Shea, D.R. (1955) *The Calvo Clause*. Minneapolis: University of Minnesota Press.

Sornarajah, M. (2001) *The Settlement of Foreign Investment Disputes*. Boston, MA: Kluwer.

Stowell, E.C. (1908) "La Doctrina Drago." *American Journal of International Law*, 2: 959.

Thomson, A. (2005) "Argentina Revels in Power of Peso," *The Financial Times*, June 30, 2005.

Tobin, J. and S. Rose-Ackerman (2005) *Foreign Direct Investment and the Business Environment in Developing Countries: The Impact of Bilateral Investment Treaties* New Haven, CT: Yale University (Working paper).

UNCTAD (1998) *Bilateral Investment Treaties in the Mid-1990s*. Geneva: United Nations.

——— (1999a) *Scope and Definition*, UNCTAD Series on Issues in International Investment Agreements. New York: United Nations.

——— (1999b) *Trends in International Investment Agreements: An Overview*, UNCTAD Series on Issues in International Investment Agreements. New York: United Nations.

——— (2000) *Bilateral Investment Treaties—1959–1999*, New York: United Nations.

——— (2003) *Dispute Settlement: Investor-State*, UNCTAD Series on Issues in International Investment Agreements. New York: United Nations.

——— (2004) *World Investment Report 2004*. New York: United Nations.

——— (2005a) "Occasional Note: Many BITs Have Yet to Enter Into Force," New York, United Nations.

————— (2005b) *World Investment Report 2005.* New York: United Nations.
Van Harten, G. (2007) *Investment Treaty Arbitration and Public Law.* Oxford: Oxford University Press.
Vandevelde, K.J. (1998) "The Political Economy of a Bilateral Investment Treaty," *American Journal of International Law*, 92: 621.
Wälde, T.W. (1996) "Investment Arbitration Under the Energy Charter Treaty—From Dispute Settlement to Treaty Implementation," *Arbitration International*, 12: 429.
Walter, A. (2001) "NGOs, Business, and International Investment: The Multilateral Agreement on Investment, Seattle, and Beyond," *Global Governance*, 7: 51.

Chapter 5

Policy Space for a Capability-Centered Development Strategy for Latin America

Luis Abugattas and Eva Paus

During the last two decades, Latin American countries have pursued an agenda of widespread market liberalization, commonly referred to as the Washington Consensus. These policies have left Latin American economies—with few exceptions—with a new/old comparative advantage in natural resources, a shrinking manufacturing sector, a growing informal sector, low investment ratios, slow economic growth, more unequal income distribution and rising poverty rates.

The aim of our chapter is threefold: (1) to outline key components of a new development agenda—a capability-centered development strategy—with a particular focus on industrial policies and tax policies (subsection 2); (2) to sketch out a conceptual framework for analyzing the policy space available for implementing such an agenda and to assess the frontiers of possibilities (subsection 3); and (3) to identify the potential constraints, external and internal, that could prevent the adequate implementation of the specific measures identified as main components of the new agenda for development (subsection 4).

We argue that the World Trade Organization (WTO) has dramatically restricted the external policy space for Latin America. Bilateral agreements with the United States have further tightened the space with respect to a number of important policy instruments. Low tax ratios impose a severe limitation on the internal space for implementing a capability-centered strategy. But the willingness to use the policy space still available and to push for an expansion of its boundaries may no longer exist in countries, where importers, agro-industrialists, and foreign multinationals constitute the dominant coalition of interests.

A New Development Agenda for Latin America:
The High Road to Development

After twenty years of neoliberal reforms, most South American economies have returned to a comparative advantage based on primary products in agriculture and mining, while the exports of most Central American countries have come to be dominated by assembled labor-intensive products (e.g., Reinhardt and Wilson, 2000). Even Chile, upheld in many contexts as Latin America's development success story, did not succeed in creating a technologically more advanced structure of production during the 1990s (Albala-Bertrand, 2006). After the lost decade of the 1980s, Latin America's GDP grew at a paltry rate of 2.6 percent between 1990 and 2002 (CEPAL, 2005: 15). Such rates of growth are insufficient to address the pressing social problems in the region.

There exists a large literature that analyzes the dismal development results of Washington Consensus policies in Latin America and offers new policies for the future. Some authors blame the poor outcomes on the insufficient and incomplete application of neoliberal reforms, and thus urge a deepening of market liberalization (e.g., Singh et al., 2005; Krueger, 2004; both cited in Rodrik, 2006). But critics of the Washington Consensus refute the proposition that free markets in general, and free trade policies in particular, can provide a solid foundation for development (e.g., Shafaedin, 2006; Gallagher, 2005; Paus, 2004; Rodrik, 2001). They stress that—with rare exceptions—latecomers in the development process have caught up with some form of protectionist measures and active government intervention (e.g., Chang, 2005; Rodrik, 2004; Amsden, 2001). And they highlight the disjuncture between the theoretical underpinnings of the neoliberal model where markets are perfect and complete and the realities in most developing countries where markets are riddled with failures and imperfections (e.g., Lall, 2005; Stiglitz, 1998; Arndt, 1988).

Natural resource exports can make an important contribution to development through generation of foreign exchange and tax revenue. But they cannot form the basis for sustained development, as they generate few technological spillovers, provide little basis for a move up the value chain, and are beset by declining relative prices. These very arguments provided the rationale for import substituting industrialization (ISI) more than fifty years ago. The fact that ISI, as pursued in many Latin American countries, had deficiencies does not invalidate the arguments about the need for structural change and comparative advantage in higher value added production. Rather, a new development agenda has to be cognizant of the policy mistakes of the ISI era, especially the absence of effective reciprocal control mechanisms for industrial policies and the blind belief in the absence of government failures.

At the beginning of the twenty-first century, the global economic environment is dramatically different from what it was in the 1950s and 1960s, the heydays of ISI. Thanks to China's seemingly insatiable demand for primary products, commodity prices have been rising in recent years, leading to higher economic growth in many Latin American countries.[1] The commodity price boom provides a propitious context in which to adopt a new development friendly strategy in the region. But that strategy has to be informed by today's global realities that provide new opportunities and pose new challenges for Latin America.

Global Capitalism in the Twenty-first Century: Development Challenges and Opportunities

The entry of China, India, and Central Europe onto the global capitalist stage is perhaps the most significant change in today's global economy. The resulting doubling of the global labor force alters the range of possibilities for Latin America's new comparative advantages. Wages in Latin America are relatively too high for countries to compete any longer in the production of unskilled-labor-intensive commodities. And productivity is often relatively too low to compete successfully with more technologically advanced countries, including with China and India, in the production of highly skill-intensive goods and services.[2] As a result, Latin American countries face a twofold challenge. On the one hand, China and other Asian developing countries are displacing Latin American exports in the major markets. On the other hand, Latin America's imports from these countries are displacing domestic production, which has given rise to increasing demands for trade remedy actions by domestic producers.

But China and India also offer significant potential opportunities to Latin American countries. The increasing buying power of emerging Asian economies and the resurgence and consolidation of regionalism among developing countries have led to a "new geography of international trade" (UNCTAD, 2004). Currently more than 40 percent of developing country exports are destined for other developing countries, and developing countries' share of global demand is growing steadily. Latin American countries need to generate the skill base, or more broadly the knowledge-based assets, to develop new comparative advantages higher up on the value chain to confront the challenges of the intensified international competition and to reap the benefits from new market opportunities.

The increasing fragmentation of production processes across national borders is the second distinctive characteristic of the current globalization process. It opens up new possibilities for Latin American countries to attract foreign direct investment (FDI) and reap technological spillovers, and for indigenous producers to become part of the global networks of transnational corporations (TNCs). But the growing competition for

FDI in conjunction with the ongoing process of global production shifting have left developing countries less time to reap the potential benefits of FDI, raised the threshold for host country firms' participation in global value chains, and increased the pressure on indigenous companies for constant upgrading (e.g., Paus, 2005; Yusuf, 2003).

The third important feature of today's global capitalism is the high cross-border mobility of financial capital. Access to the global capital market provides valuable opportunities for developing county producers to raise capital for investment purposes. But with international short-term capital transactions of well over $1 trillion a day, the potential for financial volatility has increased considerably. A sudden massive capital outflow can wreak havoc with a country's macroeconomic stability. Developing countries need to find ways to reduce the likelihood of a financial and foreign exchange crisis, whether it is of their own making or the result of contagion effects from other countries.

Latin America at the Crossroads

In general, Latin America is not well prepared to master the challenges of globalization and take advantage of its opportunities. Of course, Latin American countries are not all alike, occupying different places on the spectrum of economic diversification, development, and exposure to short-term financial capital flows. Each country has to find new comparative advantages, and thus a sustainable basis for development, in accordance with its country-specific endowments, path dependency, and institutional characteristics. But for all countries, productivity growth and a move up the value chain provide the only shot at the high road to development. The low road of insufficient productivity growth and declining wages is not a road to development, but it is the de facto default option.

All indications are that Latin America is currently heading down the low road. Under the neoliberal strategy, the productivity record of the region has been dismal (e.g., Paus, 2004; IADB, 2001). Labor productivity in Latin America grew at an average annual rate of 0.7 percent during the 1990s, a third less than in Asia, and only slightly higher than in Africa (IADB, 2001: 12).[3]

An expansion of domestic technological capabilities, macroeconomic stability, the requisite infrastructure improvements as well as institutions conducive to fostering these elements are important ingredients for increased productivity growth and the ongoing creation of new comparative advantages. The global competitiveness index (GCI) of the World Economic Forum presents the most far-reaching attempt to capture this multiplicity of factors into one single index. It is based on an elaborate weighting of quantitative data as well as survey results where dozens of respondents in each country assess a set of claims about their particular country ranging from "1" (low) to "7" (high).[4] The results give us some indication of Latin

America's relative competitiveness at this juncture (and of some of the reasons for its discouraging productivity performance over two decades).[5]

The Global Competitiveness Report for 2005–2006 includes 117 countries. The average GCI score for Latin America (3.5) is right between Africa (3.4) and Transition Economies (3.7), and significantly lower than in Asia (4.1). Some of the sub indices underlying the GCI highlight the key areas where Latin America is not comparing well with competitor regions, namely education, technological capabilities, and a business-enabling environment with access to loans and appropriate infrastructure (see table 5.1).[6]

Table 5.1 Competitiveness Indicators in Comparative Perspective

Region/ Country	Macro Stability Index	Public Institut. Index	Firm Level Technol. Absorption	Infra-Structure Quality	Public School Quality	Access to Loans
Africa (n=23) (GDP* p.c. : $ 3,600)						
Average	4.05	3.91	4.1	3.1	2.8	2.6
Stand. Dev.	0.58	0.63	0.6	0.9	0.8	0.7
Asia (n=24) (GDP* p.c. : $ 11,990)						
Average	4.77	4.45	4.9	4.0	3.7	3.5
Stand. Dev.	0.66	1.06	0.8	1.4	1.1	0.8
Transition Economies (n=24) (GDP* p.c. : $ 8,992)						
Average	4.45	4.10	4.2	3.2	3.9	3.0
Stand. Dev.	0.47	0.65	0.7	0.9	0.9	0.7
Industrialized countries (n=23) (GDP* p.c. : $ 31,324)						
Average	4.81	5.82	5.4	5.7	5.4	4.5
Stand. Dev.	0.45	0.45	0.6	0.8	0.6	0.6
Latin American Countries (n=21) (GDP* p.c. : $ 6,995)						
Average	4.25	3.90	4.0	3.1	2.6	2.7
Stand. Dev.	0.59	0.69	0.6	0.8	0.7	0.6
(GDP* p.c. : $ 3,600)						
Argentina	4.59	3.96	4.0	3.6	3.2	2.1
Bolivia	3.69	3.71	3.1	2.1	2.1	2.0

Continued

Table 5.1 Continued

Region/ Country	Macro Stability Index	Public Institut. Index	Firm Level Technol. Absorption	Infra- Structure Quality	Public School Quality	Access to Loans
Brazil	4.14	4.06	4.8	2.8	2.2	2.8
Chile	5.66	5.58	4.9	4.9	2.8	3.9
Colombia	4.61	4.55	3.9	2.9	3.0	2.5
Costa Rica	3.62	4.32	4.6	2.6	3.7	2.6
Dominican Republic	3.63	3.24	4.3	3.1	1.5	2.5
Ecuador	4.84	2.93	3.3	2.8	2.0	2.2
El Salvador	4.42	4.45	4.3	4.6	2.7	3.5
Guatemala	4.24	3.22	3.8	2.6	1.9	2.4
Guyana	3.13	3.10	3.0	2.2	2.8	2.3
Honduras	4.11	3.61	3.5	3.0	2.3	2.3
Jamaica	3.63	4.14	4.4	3.6	3.0	2.6
Mexico	4.76	4.03	4.2	3.5	2.8	2.6
Nicaragua	3.88	3.74	3.4	2.4	2.2	2.1
Panama	4.03	3.90	4.2	3.6	2.7	3.9
Paraguay	4.16	2.97	3.0	2.0	2.0	2.3
Peru	4.53	4.27	4.1	2.5	1.8	3.2
Trinidad and Tobago	5.23	3.73	4.2	3.3	3.7	3.3
Uruguay	3.85	5.19	3.7	3.8	3.9	2.2
Venezuela	4.46	3.23	4.4	3.2	2.0	2.6

Note:
* PPP. 2004.
Source: Calculated based on Porter et al. (2005).

At a time when education and knowledge acquisition are more important than ever to achieve sustained economic growth, it is particularly grave that Latin America scores the lowest in the world regarding the quality of public education, 2.6 compared with 2.8 for Africa and 3.7 and 3.9 for Asia and Transition Economies, respectively.[7] The poor quality assessment is matched by and partly reflective of poor quantitative indicators. In 2000, the average gross enrolment rate in secondary schools was 72 percent in Latin America, compared to 91 percent in East Asia and 95 percent in Eastern Europe (IADB, 2005b: 6), with completion rates in Latin America much lower than in the other regions. One bright light for the future is that the number of students enrolled in technical subjects at the tertiary level is, comparatively speaking, quite high in several Latin American countries (UNCTAD, 2005: 296).

On average, the technological abilities of Latin American firms are insufficient to confront the global challenges. The average score for "firm level technology absorption" is not much different from that in Africa and Transition Economies, though considerably lower than in Asia.[8] The fact that TNCs in Latin America source only a small percentage of their inputs in the host countries is a powerful reflection of limited domestic technological capabilities. In 2002, TNCs in Costa Rica and Mexico sourced less than 3 percent of their inputs domestically (Paus and Gallagher, 2006: 19, 25). TNCs are also not inclined to move more research and development (R&D) intensive activities to the more advanced Latin American destinations because of the "lack of a growing, highly skilled work force" (Kearny, 2005: 16).[9]

Latin America also lags behind in access to information and communication technology (ICT). In 2004, fixed line access per 100 inhabitants was 17.3 for Latin America and 53.1 for the high-performing Asian economies. For Internet users the respective figures were 14.4 versus 56.5, and for personal computers 8.1 versus 57.5 (IADB, 2005a: 117). The low level of R&D spending in Latin America is another indicator of the region's relative technological deficiencies. All Latin American and Caribbean countries together spend $1 billion less on R&D than South Korea on its own with $12 billion (IADB, 2005a).

The pursuit of Washington Consensus polices with a hands-off government approach to economic development is one important reason why FDI has not provided a major impetus for the expansion of indigenous knowledge-based assets. When indigenous producers have imperfect information and face high financing costs, risk, or barriers to entry, they are not likely to compete successfully with TNCs. National and local governments ignored the importance and pervasiveness of market failures. They did not support the private sector—directly and pro-actively—in competing effectively with foreign investors and developing the national capabilities necessary to benefit from positive spillover effects.

Changing Gears: Policies for the High Road to Development

The new development strategy has to be a capability-centered strategy, where the expansion of domestic knowledge-based assets is at the core of achieving comparative advantages beyond primary products and unskilled labor-intensive goods.[10] Such an expansion will lead to increased investment rates and productivity growth, if the general business framework is favorable in terms of requisite infrastructure, competitive nontraded services, competition in the markets, and pro-competitive input prices (e.g., Abugattas, 2005a).

Since market failures and inadequacies are especially prevalent in the context of the expansion of domestic technological and learning capabilities, a capability-centered strategy requires activist government policies. They have to be strategic and long term, yet dynamic and flexible in response to changing national and global circumstances. Generally speaking, the strategy needs to delineate policies in four critical areas and specify their interactions and complementarities: (1) industrial policies that address market failures and realize positive externalities; (2) public finance policies which identify sources and agency for increased expenditures on infrastructure, education, and technological and technical training; (3) development-friendly macroeconomic policies that aim to increase stability and reduce financial volatility; and (4) pro-poor policies which pay deliberate attention to poverty reduction rather than rely exclusively on trickle-down effects. These policies have to be complemented with an environment-friendly approach that does not opt for short-term economic gains at the expense of long-term environmental degradation. Country-specific considerations will determine the exact nature of such a development plan, and the relative importance and role of each of its constituent elements. Here we offer some general considerations, which are summarized in table 5.2.

Table 5.2 A Capability-Centered Development Strategy

Policy Set	Rationale	Policy Tools

A. *Industrial Policies* Horizontal or sector/ sub-sector-specific	Address market failures, realize positive externalities, infant industry considerations	Protection
		Subsidies (grants and fiscal expenditures)
		Performance requirements
		Government Procurement policies
		Coordination policies (match-making)
		  Cluster formation
		  Linkage formation
		Technology transfer mechanisms and assistance
		Information provision
		Financing mechanisms

B. *Public Finance Policies*	Need for creating "fiscal space" for, inter alia: improvements in education, infrastructure, technological learning complex, support for private sector	Tax policies Tapping natural resource rents Borrowing (foreign and domestic) Management of foreign debt (reduction or rescheduling) Public investment Public-private partnerships

Continued

Table 5.2 Continued

Policy Set	Rationale	Policy Tools
C. *Development-Friendly Macro-policies*	Increase macroeconomic stability, and setting basic prices right for development	Control over short-term capital flows Interest rate policies Exchange rate management
D. *Pro-poor Policies*	Need to supplement market outcomes	Targeted interventions

There are many potential reasons for the need for industrial policies. The fact that knowledge development does not happen overnight based on a blue print, but over time through learning-by-doing means that private firms will not and cannot seek out new opportunities without help that compensates for their currently higher costs. Such support, especially in the critical early learning phase, could come in the form of temporary protection or through subsidies linked to particular performance goals. If such activities are not deemed profitable in the medium-run, private sector companies will simply not invest. When the financial system is biased against affordable loans to small and medium-sized enterprises, when the capital market is underdeveloped thus making it difficult to raise venture capital or funds for long-term projects, then pro-active financial policies are needed. When information is imperfect, when there are barriers to entry in new markets, when agglomeration economies are not realized because of coordination failures in investment, when there are acute human capital and skill deficiencies in particular technological areas, then targeted policies are required to overcome these market failures.

Active public policies are also needed to overcome the time-lag that exists between the launch of basic reforms, for example in education and training or the creation of a national innovation system, and the achievement of the desired outcomes (Abugattas, 2005a). The imperatives of the new realities of globalization deny Latin American countries the luxury to wait until such reforms deliver all their promises. There is the need to address the short-term requirements of the productive sectors in order to develop knowledge-based assets that provide competitive advantages and allow countries to confront the challenges of globalization.

Industrial policies can be horizontal (available for all producers) or specific (restricted to particular firms or subsectors). Targeted intervention is justified when resources are limited (financial as well as institutional) and particular subsectors hold out the promise of particularly high development payoffs, for example, because they are technology intensive with a broad impact on the economy through spillovers and productivity growth, and face a high income elasticity of demand. With the minimization of government intervention under neoliberalism, Latin American countries abolished many of their prior industrial policies, ranging from the drastic decline in tariff protection, to the elimination of subsidies, to a shrinking range of action of development banks, if those persisted at all. While some industrial policies persisted—for example the support of the automobile industry in the Mercosur—it was only in the second half of the 1990s that targeted policies reemerged in some countries. Nearly all of them have been in the form of fiscal incentives and loans to sectors other than manufacturing (Peres, 2006).

A capability-centered development strategy requires increased expenditures in key areas of infrastructure, education and training, and financial incentives or grants in targeted areas. Higher expenditures can be financed either through additional tax revenues, or resources from abroad, or borrowing or debt reduction or rescheduling, or rationalizing current expenditures. The more sustainable way of increasing resources is through increasing tax revenues without compromising the competitiveness of the productive apparatus of the country.

The industrial and tax policies (as well as the policies in the other two areas not discussed here in detail) have to be articulated in the context of a long-term development plan, which guides government policies beyond the duration of any particular government. The national development plan needs to lay out priorities, quantifiable targets, time duration and agency for the achievement of different goals and institutional responsibility for the different policies.

Policy Space for a Capability-Centered Development Strategy: A Conceptual Framework

Policies for a capability-centered development strategy cannot be formulated in the abstract, as a utopian model for development in a political vacuum. They have to be conceptualized within the realm of possibilities, recognizing the degrees of freedom that countries effectively have to implement policies within existing international and domestic constraints.

Based on Hamwey (2005) we distinguish between *external policy space* and *internal policy space*. The former is circumscribed by international agreements and global market expectations, while the latter is constricted by domestic institutional capabilities, resources, and the political economy behind a particular government's agenda. A country's *available policy space* is then confined to the intersecting set of the two policy spaces. The boundaries of the available policy space are not fixed, over time and across countries. They vary with differences in bilateral agreements and in internal constraints like the development-mindedness of a government and its willingness and ability to push the boundaries of the available policy space.

External Constraints on Policy Space

In assessing the external constraints on available policy space we consider two main dimensions: the constraints resulting from countries' adoption of internationally binding and enforceable commitments, and the effects of globalization on national sovereignty and policy options. In the first case, policy space is relinquished as an act, at least in principle, in the exercise of national sovereignty. In the second case, policy space is limited as a result of the new emerging realities of a global capitalist market and the behavior of private actors.

Binding International Commitments

The results of the Uruguay Round reflect a fundamental paradigm shift. Under the General Agreement on Tariffs and Trade (GATT), developing countries had a high degree of flexibility in their choice of development strategies and policies. The special and differential treatment (S&DT) accorded to developing countries was grounded in preferential market access to developed countries' markets, flexibility in the application of disciplines, and more broadly nonreciprocal trade relations between developed and developing countries. Under the WTO, the basic objective of trade disciplines is to oblige all market participants to abide by the same rules. The "single undertaking" nature of multilateral negotiations and the adoption of common obligations for both developing and developed countries achieved such objective. S&DT is limited to transition periods which give developing countries time to comply with obligations, and to best endeavor clauses which call on developed countries to provide technical assistance to help developing countries implement their obligations.

Compared with the GATT, these obligations were expanded to deal with domestic policies beyond the border such as subsidies, technical standards and sanitary rules. And the trade-related agenda was broadened to incorporate intellectual property rights (TRIPS), investment (TRIMS) and services (GATS). WTO rules were understood as embodying "sound economic policies," reinforcing and securing the Washington Consensus and providing "good governance" by constraining the possibilities for special interest groups to lobby for public policies at odds with the supposedly optimal policy mix. The substantive legitimacy of WTO rules was sought in economic welfare considerations with its claims about the welfare-enhancing effects of free trade rules.

An analysis of the constraints emerging from international commitments has to be broadened beyond the WTO agreements to incorporate the effects of the emergence of a multilayered structure of international agreements. Latin American countries, for example, are adopting commitments at different levels of integration: multilateral, regional, interregional, bilateral, and potentially hemispheric, if the Free Trade Area of the Americas (FTAA) process is brought back to life. Multilevel rule making is emerging in virtually every policy area, with the various levels in a state of constant flux. Increasingly, international agreements are covering a wider range of policy areas, many of which used to be considered the exclusive domain of domestic policies. Regional and bilateral agreements, particularly those signed between Latin American countries and the United States and the European Union (EU), have incorporated areas beyond those covered by the WTO agreements, such as government procurement, investment, competition, labor rights, environment, and trade and corruption. In areas already covered by the WTO, bilateral and regional agreements tend to enshrine even deeper commitments.

The extent to which binding commitments adopted in international agreements constrain policy options depends on whether provisions are subject to voluntary acceptance, as in the case of the plurilateral agreement on government procurement in the WTO, or whether they are part of a single undertaking where countries must adopt them, as the case of government procurement provisions in the bilateral agreements. In the first case there is the possibility of retaining policy space by not entering into commitments. Another factor is the extent to which the agreements allow for maintaining some reservations to the general obligations, as is the case of the GATS where reservations can be inscribed in the commitments or in agreements with negative lists where parties can maintain nonconforming measures.

In the context of the Doha Development Round negotiations, the issue of policy space played a prominent role in all the negotiating areas, in which a number of proposals to regain and retain policy space were on the table. The WTO Ministerial Meeting in Hong Kong in December 2005 brought perhaps the clearest admission to date that the WTO agreements might not be—by definition—development friendly. Members decided in favor of a "round for free" for least developed countries (LDCs), where these countries were not expected to make any new commitments in all the negotiating areas. The final outcome of the Round itself and its possible effect on policy space are uncertain, as negotiations were suspended in July 2006.

Regional agreements among Latin American countries have not significantly infringed upon the policy autonomy of participating countries,

since enforcement mechanisms are limited, and flexibility has been provided by the nature of the processes in which political negotiations have
played a dominant role. Regionalism has not yet been effectively integrated into the countries' national development policies. Where governments have tended to comply with their regional commitments, it has
only been to the extent that those did not directly collide with national
economic policies (ECLAC, 2006). Regional agreements, however, can
also increase policy space for Latin American countries. For example,
local content requirements, which are proscribed in some bilateral agreements, could be replaced by regional rules of origin.

Since trade agreements and bilateral investment treaties (BITs) need to
account for a wide range of possible situations, they are generally crafted in
vague, open-ended terms. Thus, the exact specification of implied policy
constraints is often left to dispute settlement proceedings. The Dispute
Settlement Body (DSB) of the WTO has played an important role in
providing definitive interpretations or amending provisions of the agreements; and it is likely that the DSB will come under increasing pressure to
legislate through interpretation and filling in the blanks in WTO disciplines
(Barfield, 2001; Bronckers, 1999). BITs tend to be imprecise in many areas
regarding the substantive legal standards to be applied leaving considerable
discretion to panels to interpret the scope of the obligations emanating
from the agreements (see the discussion of Van Harten, this volume). In
addition, issues arising from non-violation complaints, both in the WTO
and in other agreements, can also have an effect on available policy choices
(Hsu, 2005).[11] In the context of multilayered binding and enforceable
commitments, potential *rule-making by adjudication* adds additional complexity in defining the needed policy space for the implementation of a
capability-centered development policy.[12]

Global Market Constraints

In today's global economy, foreign investors' actual or anticipated
response to domestic development policies has emerged as a significant
constraint on the policy options available to developing countries.
Policy-makers are held accountable by the international markets. If a
policy is not perceived as business-friendly, from the perspective of
international capital and the developed countries governments, it can
evoke strong negative reactions in international markets (e.g., a higher
risk assessment and lower credit rating), with significant domestic
repercussions.

Perceived best practices legitimate some policies and delegitimize
others. Benchmarking with standards for a "business-friendly" environment set by policies in other countries may act as a constraint on policy
options. This is of particular significance in a context in which Latin
American countries are competing for FDI and other financial flows.

Finally, expanding globalization with its growing standardization of production has raised the bar for national producers to become integrated into global value chains. Increasingly, producers need to have adopted quality standards (e.g., ISO standards) before being even considered as a potential input supplier to TNCs. The growing expectation that producers meet product, environmental, and labor standards established by the industry itself has an important impact on policy space in that it may call for government measures to support private producers in achieving such standards.

Internal Constraints on Policy Space

Internal constraints on policy space may make it difficult for many countries to take advantage of the external space still permitted. The internal policy space is defined by the availability of resources that can be deployed to implement a development policy, by the institutional capabilities of the state to manage the instruments of such policy, and by the size of the country. These three factors define to a large extent the capacity of countries to implement development policies. That is particularly true, since the existing external constraints imposed under the international trade agreements tend to leave space mainly for policies that require government resources and institutional capabilities. But government capacity has to be matched by government willingness to implement a capability-centered development strategy, which depends on the economic interests that dominate a government's policy agenda.

The development and upgrading of infrastructure and human capital, and the implementation of different instruments of industrial policies require resources. They entail significant public investment or expenditure, and/or financial transfers or tax revenue made available to private producers. Therefore, the availability of resources to finance a capability-centered development strategy is a key factor shaping the internal policy space. Resources can be derived from taxes on international transactions or on the domestic economy, from the appropriation of a higher share of the rent generated by natural resource–based production activities, or from financial transfers from abroad.

Institutions are a crucial factor for the development and implementation of proactive development policies (e.g., World Bank, 2002; Malik, 2002; Rodrik et al., 2004). Policy instruments that are permitted by international rules cannot be used in the absence of the requisite institutional capacities. The WTO subsidies agreement, for example, allows certain types of subsidies for R&D, the WTO agreement on agriculture allows support for farmers. However, the implementation of such subsidies and support measures requires domestic capacities that many developing countries may not have.

It is often argued that developing countries cannot pursue interven-tionist policies similar to the ones implemented by the high-performing Asian economies because they lack requisite institutional capacities (World Bank, 1993). In other words, the risk of government failure is assumed to be high, since the capacity of the government machinery is low (World Bank, 1994). It is ironic then that many of the analysts, who question the feasibility of industrial policies on the grounds of inexistent institutional state capacities, have high expectations that the same bureaucratic cadres will be able to manage the complex institutions and regulatory frameworks required by the second and third generations of the market-liberalizing reforms they promote.

Institutional development requires government resources, among other things. The state has to be able to compete with the private sector for skilled personnel and to undertake the required investments. The range of policy options that can be implemented to foster economic and social development can be broadened or constrained depending on existing institutional capacities.

Country size also plays a role in determining the internal policy space. Certain policy alternatives, for example for industrial policies and macro-economic management, might be open for countries with large internal markets, such as Brazil and Mexico; but they may be outside the range of possibilities for medium-sized and small countries. The issue of size has been brought onto the agenda of trade negotiations at the multilateral and regional levels, where small economies have insisted on their special needs for retaining policy space to address their particular challenges.

Finally, the political economy behind a government's policy agenda is the key determinant of whether a government has any interest in using the internal policy space or in pushing for the expansion of its bound-aries. Sánchez-Ancochea (this volume) argues that even though all Central American governments enthusiastically supported and signed DR-CAFTA, differences in class dynamics explain the different degree of acceptance and implementation of the agreement across countries.

Effective Policy Space:
Availability versus Utilization

The effective policy space for implementing a capability-based develop-ment strategy is defined by the intersection of the external and internal policy spaces. These policy spaces are not completely independent from each other. International commitments, for example, can have a favorable or a negative impact on the availability of resources. And greater institu-tional capabilities make it easier to retain or regain external policy space in the negotiation and administration of international trade agreements.

The boundaries of the external policy space are not written in stone. The paradigm shift from the GATT to the WTO is an example par excellence. But rules and disciplines can also change on a smaller scale. As the Washington Consensus started to lose legitimacy, the dynamics of multilateral negotiations during the post-Uruguay Round period have been shaped by the struggle of developing countries to retain and regain policy space. The elimination of three of the four "Singapore issues" from the WTO work program decided at the 2003 Cancun Ministerial Meeting (competition, investment, and transparency in government procurement) allowed the retention of policy space in highly sensitive areas. Developing countries have also succeeded in regaining policy space in a number of areas. The most prominent examples include (1) the amendment introduced to the TRIPS agreement allowing access to affordable drugs to developing countries suffering from epidemics; (2) the extension of the transition periods for LDCs under the same agreement; (3) the extension of the timeframe for eliminating export subsidies for a number of developing countries; and (4) the granting of numerous waivers allowing developing countries to depart from obligations.

The potential for redefining the external policy space is quite different at the different layers of integration. At the multilateral level, the possibility of *coalition building* among developing countries, and also among like-minded countries including developed countries, has opened the door for attempts to increase the existing policy space with a certain degree of success. The situation is different in bilateral agreements with developed countries, like those signed between Latin American countries and the United States. Power asymmetries and agreement competition among countries substantially limit the possibilities for a Latin American country to retain policy space during the negotiations or to expand the exogenous policy space once the agreement is signed (Shadlen, 2008).

However, the fact that international commitments and market realities might leave some space for internal policy autonomy does not necessarily imply that countries will make effective use of it, even if the internal conditions allow it. A government's political will and the overall orientation of its development policies determine whether available policy space will be used and whether a government is likely to press for an expansion of that space. Thus, the utilization of the effective policy space for a capability-based development strategy depends on the existence of a development-oriented leading political coalition willing to shift gear and implement policies outside the variants of neoliberal conventional wisdom. In this context, it is important to note that other external constraints on policy space derive from the particular nature of the relationships between a country and the international financial institutions, the International Monetary Fund (IMF) and the World Bank.[13]

In sum, Latin American development policies need both domestic and international legitimacy and thus require a complex balance between the demands and expectations of domestic stakeholders and of international markets. Synchronizing national development policies and objectives with binding and enforceable multiple-dimensional commitments in different layers of integration has become the core of statecraft for Latin American and other developing countries (Abugattas, 2004). In the context of multiple and simultaneous intrusive trade agreements, Latin American countries are challenged to preserve the required policy space for a new capability-based development strategy, while reaping the benefits of effective integration into the international economy.

The Realities of Available Policy Space

Ultimately, an analysis of available policy space has to be undertaken at the country level. For example, among the countries that have signed bilateral agreements with the United States the available policy space varies with the differentiated reservations that countries have inscribed, under the "negative list" approach, in the substantive commitments emanating from those agreements. Here we will use specific examples to illustrate how the WTO and other agreements affect the space for specific policies of a capability-centered agenda (summarized in table 5.3) and how the internal space is constricted.

Table 5.3   External Constraints on Policies for a Capability-Centered Strategy

Policy Tool That Might Be Affected	GATT	WTO Agreements	NAFTA-Type Bilateral and Regional Agreements
Industrial Policies			
• Protection	Bound Tariffs	Bound Tariff	Dismantling of applied tariffs
• Subsidies	Plurilateral Agreement	Agreement on Subsidies y Countervailing Measures	No covered
• Performance requirements	Not Covered	TRIMS Agreement	Investment provisions: prohibition
• Government procurement	Plurilateral Agreement	Plurilateral Agreement	Commitments on market access and national treatment
• Technology transfer	Not covered	TRIPS Agreement	TRIPs plus provisions
Public Finance Policies	No significant impact	No significant impact	• Tariff revenue loss • Potential Constraints in tapping natural resource rents and increasing tax burden on FDI (Investment provisions)

Continued

Table 5.3   Continued

Policy Tool That Might Be Affected	GATT	WTO Agreements	NAFTA-Type Bilateral and Regional Agreements
Development-Friendly Macroeconomic Policies	No impact	GATS provisions on payments and transfers, commitments on financial services liberalization	Commitments on opening capital account Commitments on payments and transfers Financial services wide liberalization
Pro-poor Policies	No effect	No effect	No direct effect

Industrial Policies

The rationale for industrial policies derives from infant industry considerations, coordination and information externalities, strategic trade policy, promotion of productive restructuring and compensation for the time-lag between the point when structural reforms are implemented and when they come to fruition. Many analysts agree that WTO agreements limit the space for industrial policies, through the agreement on subsidies and countervailing measures, the agreement on agriculture, TRIMS, TRIPS, and the GATS (e.g., Gallagher, 2005; Wade, 2003; World Bank, 1993). But they also concur that the agreements still allow some space for active public development policies. However, in many cases, the external policy space left is in areas which demand domestic resources and institutional capabilities that are outside the range of possibilities for many developing countries.

In the past, protective tariff and nontariff barriers and tariff sequencing were the most common industrial policy instruments. Today protection is no longer an option, due to market access commitments under the WTO as well as regional and subregional agreements. The different Regional and Bilateral Trade Agreements (RBTAs) in Latin America have accomplished their liberalization objectives, with few exceptions. And bilateral agreements with the United States incorporate significant liberalization (more than 80 percent of total trade) when entering into force. Currently more than 85 percent of total trade in the Western Hemisphere is tariff free. Negotiations under the WTO, based on bound tariff levels and the current liberalization proposals under consideration, might have a further significant impact on MFN liberalization (Bachetta and Bora, 2003). Protection is now only a policy option for a small number of sensitive agricultural products.

The alternative to protection at the border is support for domestic undertakings through subsidies. The WTO agreement on subsidies and countervailing measures (ASCM) has imposed considerable constraints on industrial policy options (e.g., Ayala and Gallagher, 2005). The existing rules leave a certain margin for subsidies by developing countries, and the Agreement on Agriculture also provides some policy space to support the agricultural sector through, inter alia, its *de minimis* provisions. In the ASCM most Latin American countries are sheltered from action by the requirement that the complainant has to demonstrate injury before taking action. Latin American countries have not used this flexibility to the extent possible, as a result of deliberate self-constraint. Bilateral agreements between the United States and Latin American countries are silent on the question of subsidies for goods, deferring on this issue to WTO rules.

The WTO rules on subsidies apply to trade in goods only. Thus there is ample policy space for Latin American countries to use these instruments in the case of services, which constitute a very dynamic segment of world trade.[14] U.S. bilateral agreements explicitly exclude subsidies from the rules on trade in services. Given the crucial role played by services in economic development and the potential they offer for Latin American countries to alter their pattern of integration into the world economy, a capability-centered development strategy should try to maximize the use of the available policy space to promote these activities.

A central element of a capability-centered development strategy is the realization of positive externalities from FDI. In this area, multilateral agreements impose drastic limitations on policy options. Under the TRIMS, the WTO prohibits the use of local content requirements or trade balancing measures widely used in the past. The specific commitments on market access and national treatment, which countries might voluntarily undertake on commercial presence under the GATS, might also impose limitations on policy space.

The bilateral trade agreements with the United States incorporate even stronger binding constraints on FDI-related policies. They go far beyond those incorporated in traditional BITs that aimed to protect investment once it had been undertaken in a country. The investment commitments in the new agreements extend a country's obligations to the pre-establishment phase assuring market access and national treatment to foreign investors (Peterson, 2004; and UNCTAD, 2000).

The proscription of any type of performance requirement on FDI significantly constrains the possibilities to foster linkages with domestic producers and to promote positive spillovers. In addition, limitations on mandated joint ventures might negatively affect the potential to promote technology transfer. Bilateral agreements with the United States prohibit all performance requirements either implemented through legal mandate or as a condition for particular benefits for FDI. Market-based constraints that reflect the anticipated or actual response of foreign investors to domestic policies are of particular importance in government policies toward FDI, as the latter is increasingly footloose, with the exception of natural resource seeking investment.

Government procurement policies that grant preferences to local production over imports have been actively used to promote domestic sectors. The Government Procurement Agreement in the WTO is a plurilateral agreement to which very few Latin American countries are signatories. The bilateral agreements, on the other hand, incorporate strong rules about government procurement extending national treatment to imports. For example, under the Dominican Republic-Central America Free Trade Agreement (DR-CAFTA) and the U.S.-Peru Agreement, Latin American countries have, for all practical purposes, forgone public procurement as a potential instrument of industrial policy.

The commitments on intellectual property rights (IPRs) in international agreements seriously affect the capacity of the Latin American economies to access and adapt technologies. Besides the increased cost of "knowledge" resulting from enforced IPRs (World Bank, 2002), the agreements limit the capacities of the national state to implement policies facilitating the transfer of foreign technology to domestic firms. Fink and Maskus (2004) argue that developing countries may want to opt for different standards of protection of IPRs than those prevailing in countries with different technological and financial capabilities, and that TRIPS still leave some room to adjust IPR norms to domestic needs. However, that limited policy flexibility has been forgone in the bilateral agreements with the United States, which have significantly deepened the commitments by Latin American countries.

International commitments do not constrain the other potential tools for implementing a capability-centered development strategy, such as, inter alia, coordination policies, technical assistance and information provision. However, those require adequate institutional capacities.

Fiscal Policies

Tax ratios in Latin American countries range from below 9.3 percent in Panama to a high of 17.5 percent in Uruguay. Such ratios do not compare too badly with other latecomers in the development process, though a few countries stand out with substantially higher rates (see table 5.4). Nonetheless, in most cases the tax ratio is still not sufficient to address the requirements of a pro-active development policy. The problem is compounded by the loss of revenues from trade, and by the burden of foreign debt servicing which compromises a significant share of fiscal revenues in many countries of the region. Furthermore, the growth of

Table 5.4 Tax Revenues as a Share of GDP, circa 2003

Country	Tax Revenue/GDP	Year
Latin America		
Argentina	9.4	2002
Bolivia	13.3	2003
Brazil	12.2	1998
Chile	16.2	2003
Colombia	13.9	2003
Costa Rica	13.5	2003
Dominican Rep.	15.7	2002
Guatemala	10.3	2003
Mexico	11.7	2000
Nicaragua	15.3	2003
Panama	9.3	2001
Paraguay	9.5	2003
Peru	12.9	2003
Uruguay	17.5	2001
Venezuela	11.3	2003
Africa		
Algeria	32	2002
Cote d'Ivoire	14.9	2001
South Africa	25.1	2003
Tunisia	20.6	2003
Uganda	11.8	2002
Asia		
India	9.1	2003
Indonesia	13.0	2001
Korea	15.4	2001
Malaysia	17.6	2003
Philippines	12.3	2003
Thailand	15.4	2003
Transition Economies		
Belarus	14.2	2002
Bulgaria	19	2003
Czech Republic	16.4	2003
Estonia	15.5	2001
Hungary	22.2	2003
Poland	17.4	2002
Slovenia	21.6	2003

Source: World Development Indicators, online, accessed April 2006.

the informal sector has been eroding the tax base making it more difficult to overcome the resource constraints on internal policy space.[15]

There are a number of reasons why the need for increased tax ratios is
particularly pressing in Latin America. First, in concordance with the
neoliberal paradigm, public sector investment rates declined considerably
in most Latin American countries, leading to a relative deterioration or
insufficient improvement in key infrastructure areas.

Second, for a number of Latin American countries, trade taxes traditionally generated a significant share of tax revenue, which declined
considerably as tariffs were reduced, shifting the tax effort to other taxes
and contributions that are more difficult to enforce. Taxes on international trade as a percentage of tax revenue declined from 16.5 in 1990 to
7.2 percent in 2003 in Peru, from 23 percent to 4.5 percent in Costa
Rica, and from 19 percent to 11 percent in Guatemala. Over the period
from the early 1980s to the late 1990s, Haiti, El Salvador, Costa Rica,
Chile, Trinidad and Tobago, and Panama recovered less than 70 percent
of lost tariff revenue through other taxes, whereas Argentina, Bolivia,
Guatemala, Ecuador, Uruguay, Barbados, Honduras, Colombia, and
Peru had a recovery rate of more than 70 percent (IMF, 2005: 26–27).

The IADB (2004) estimates that completion of the FTAA would
imply a loss of tax revenue close to 1 percent of GDP for the Andean
Community countries and the Central American countries, and to
between 0.2 and 0.4 of GDP for MERCOSUR countries. Fernandez de
Cordoba and Vanzetti (2005) estimate the loss of revenues from the
Most Favored Nation tariff reductions considered in the current WTO
negotiations at close to $11 billion for the Latin American region. For
most countries of the region the estimated revenue losses exceed the
expected welfare gains from trade liberalization!

Third, the Transition Economies, which have about the same average
GDP per capita as Latin American countries, are seeing a huge increase in
revenues through external transfers, which puts them in a better position
to promote a capability-centered development strategy. European Union
(EU) policies have always reflected the belief that a true common market
can only be achieved and sustained with income convergence among the
member countries. To speed up the convergence process, there has been a
net transfer of development funds (structural funds) from the richer member countries and regions to the poorer ones. In the case of Ireland, for
example, EU structural funds amounted to 2.5–3.5 percent of GDP
during the 1990s.[16] The Cohesion Framework for 2007–2013 allows for
structural funds of up to about 3 percent of GDP for the new member
states, depending on their income gap relative to the EU average (Council
of the European Union, 2005).

One source of increased tax revenue lies in the abolition of the differential tax treatment that many Latin American governments have

accorded to domestic and foreign investors via tax preferences in export processing zones. The "race to the bottom" of competitive tax breaks and subsidies to attract foreign investors makes it difficult for any one Latin American country to break out of this race. But the termination of preferential tax treatment of export activities, as mandated by the WTO, offers a real opportunity for increased tax revenue.

Higher rents on natural resource extraction offer another possibility for increasing government revenues. The case of Chile, which maintains public ownership of a significant share of copper production and recently raised the mining *regalías,* demonstrates that revenues from this source can be increased and utilized for development purposes. Bolivia, Ecuador, and Venezuela are attempting to increase state revenues from the foreign exploitation of oil and gas. But their more drastic measures have generated a negative international market response.[17] The recent experience of Peru shows that even in the case of existing tax stability contracts, revenues from the exploitation of natural resources can be increased. In mid-2006, the government of Alan Garcia was able to negotiate a voluntary contribution from mining companies of around $800 million over five years, to be used for development projects.

Investment provisions in the bilateral trade agreements with the United States may well limit the potential to increase tax revenues from natural resource–based activities and foreign-owned production in other areas. Investment provisions address the issue of "indirect expropriation," by which a foreign investor has recourse to the dispute settlement mechanism if he/she considers that domestic measures are tantamount to indirect expropriation. The new formulation in DR-CAFTA and the U.S.-Peru Agreement does not go as far as the notion of "regulatory taking" incorporated in NAFTA. But coupled with the broad definition of investment, which includes inter alia economic interest, it is likely to lead to future disputes where foreign investors may challenge the capacity of the states to pursue resource-enhancing policies. The recent experience of Argentina, which is facing a large number of investor-state disputes attests to the possible implications of the investment provisions of the agreements (Mortimore and Stanley, 2006).

In the context of the European Structural Funds we saw that financial transfers from abroad can play a significant role in providing necessary resources for implementing a pro-active developmental strategy. Financial transfers are incorporated in most of the trade agreements that the EU negotiates with developing countries, for example the Euro-Mediterranean agreements, and they are on the agenda of the current negotiations with the ACP countries toward Economic Partnership Agreements (EPAs) under the Cotonou Agreement. However, financial transfers are conspicuously absent in agreements signed by the EU with Latin American, such as Mexico and Chile.

The regional integration agreements among Latin American countries have not incorporated mechanisms for transferring resources to less developed member countries to address gaps in the level of development. A rare exception is Mercosur's recent agreement on a very limited amount of structural funds aimed at benefiting Paraguay and Uruguay.

Development-Friendly Macroeconomic Management

Most countries in Latin America have been caught in a "stabilization trap", unable to embark on a route of sustainable growth with equity based on the transformation of the production structures of their economies. An *unfriendly macro environment* has been a crucial factor explaining the observed results in the region (Ffrench-Davis, 2005). Therefore policy discretion is needed to achieve the appropriate macroeconomic balances and basic prices that reflect the particular characteristics of the national economies and promote investments, productive diversification and improve equity (Bradford, 2005) There is growing consensus that policy space should be retained to address, inter alia, the increasing volatility of international financial flows in order to minimize the perverse impacts on the domestic economies.

International commitments adopted in enforceable agreements can seriously undermine the policy discretion needed to assure a development friendly macroeconomic environment. There are at least three sources of constraints with respect to capital controls. The most direct constraint emerges from explicit commitments to maintain unrestricted capital flows, such as the one Chile accepted in the bilateral agreement with the United States. The extent of the commitments with respect to financial services liberalization, in particular cross-border trade in these services, imposes another limitation on policy discretion. This constraint is further aggravated by the fact that Latin American countries which have signed such agreements have committed themselves, a priori, to liberalize fully any new financial service that might emerge in the market, on the only condition that such service has been authorized in the country of origin. Finally, the provisions on investment incorporated in the bilateral agreements, guaranteeing unrestricted transfer of funds to investors and investments also undermine the policy space to control capital flows. By relinquishing policy space to control capital flows, countries are also compromising the possibility to manage exchange rate policies.

Summary and Conclusions

Two decades of neoliberal reforms have left most Latin American countries without a basis for sustained growth and development. Countries are ill-prepared to master the challenges of globalization and take advantages of its opportunities, as limited technological capabilities and productivity growth make it impossible to move up the value chain based on free-market policies. We argue that the high road to development will not be a feasible option unless countries adopt a capability-centered development strategy, where the expansion of domestic knowledge-based assets is at the core of achieving structural change and comparative advantages in higher value-added goods and services.

Such a capability-centered strategy has to encompass proactive policies in four key areas: industrial policies, public finance policies, development-friendly macroeconomic policies, and pro-poor policies. In this chapter we focused on the first two policy sets.

Policies for any development strategy have to be conceptualized within the realm of possibilities, recognizing the degrees of freedom that countries effectively have to implement policies within existing international and domestic constraints. We propose a conceptual framework for understanding the constraints on policy space, arguing that a country's available policy space is confined to the intersecting set of external and internal policy spaces. The external policy space is circumscribed by multilayered international agreements as well as global market expectations, while the internal policy space is primarily constricted by limited domestic institutional capabilities and fiscal resources.

We argue that the fundamental change in understanding of special and differential treatment for developing countries from the GATT to the Uruguay Round has dramatically restricted the external policy space for Latin America. But bilateral agreements with the United States have tightened the space even further, with respect to a number of important policy instruments. Low tax ratios and the difficulties of raising taxes on foreign investors are imposing severe limitations on the internal space for implementing key policies of a capability-centered strategy.

However, it is critical to note that a country's available policy space is a contested space. Differences in development-mindedness of governments and in governments' willingness and ability to push the boundaries of the available space can make the policy space for Latin American countries larger or smaller. In the end, a key question will be whether governments have the political will to retain and use the available policy space left and the political will and wherewithal to regain spaces that were given up earlier.

Notes

1. For Latin America as a whole, GDP grew 5.9% in 2004 and 4.3% in 2005 (CEPAL, 2005: 14).
2. Ten years ago, Adrian Wood (1997) was one of the first to call attention to Latin America's dilemma of being caught in the middle between countries with much lower wages on the one hand and countries with much higher productivity on the other.

3. During the 1980s, Latin America was the region with the lowest labor productivity growth rate in the world, negative 1.4% compared to 3.4% in Asia and 0.3% in Africa.
4. For the exact composition of the GCI see Porter, Schwab, and Lopez-Claros (2005: 36–42).
5. Given the inherent difficulty of assessing survey data across countries, the results have to be taken with the necessary grain of salt.
6. We thank Vidya Sampath for the elaboration of table 5.1.
7. The survey respondents were asked to rank the quality of the public free schools in their country on a scale of "1" (poor quality) to "7" (equal to the best in the world).
8. Survey respondents were asked to assess the ability of companies in their country to absorb new technology, ranging from "1" (not able to absorb new technology) to "7" (aggressive in absorbing new technology).
9. See also Mortimore, this volume.
10. This is not a new term. Evans (2005) emphasizes a "capability-centered approach." UNIDO entitled its 2005 Industrial Development Report *Capability Building for Catching Up*. Other authors use a different terminology; e.g., Amsden (2001) and Paus (2005) focus on the development of knowledge-based assets.
11. These complaints do not result from a breach of a country's obligations under the agreement, but from measures impairing other countries' rights.
12. See, e.g., the ruling in the gambling case brought by Antigua and Barbuda against the United States in the WTO (Pauwelyn, 2005; Wunch-Vincent, 2006). Also, investment disputes arising from Chapter 11 of the NAFTA agreement have shown the profound effect that the interpretation of a countries' commitments can have on policy choices (IIDS, 2001).
13. The international community aiming to assure countries' ownership of their development policies has made repeated calls for the enhancement of the coherence and the consistency between the international monetary, financial and trading systems in support of development (UNCTAD, 2004).
14. Though rules on services are currently negotiated under the WTO, the outcome is far from certain (Abugattas, 2005b).
15. According to ILO data, in 2001, the informal sector in Latin America accounted for 46.3% of total nonagricultural employment, compared to 42.8% in 1990. Only in three out of twelve Latin American countries was the percentage below 40% (Chile, Mexico, and Panama). The proportion of informal employment reached 60% in the cases of Honduras and Peru.
16. For a detailed discussion of the development implications of EU structural funds for Ireland, see Paus (2005).

17. Interestingly enough, at the same time, the House Appropriations Committee in the U.S. Congress approved a bill ordering the Interior Department to renegotiate about 1,000 leases for companies drilling in the Gulf of Mexico to reduce the benefit conferred to oil firms who are producing in publicly owned waters without paying royalties to the government (Andrews, 2006).

References

Abugattas, L. (2004) *Swimming in the Spaghetti Bowl: Challenges for Developing Countries Under the "New Regionalism,"* UNCTAD Policy Issues in International Trade and Commodities (Study Series, No 27).

——— (2005a) "Comentarios y Análisis del Séptimo Congreso Nacional de Industriales," in Sociedad Nacional de Industrias del Perú (ed) *Estrategia Industrial para un Desarrollo Nacional Sostenido,* Lima, Peru: Sociedad Nacional de Industrias.

——— (2005b) *State Support Measures for Services: An Exploratory Assessment with Scanty Data,* UNCTAD. Mimeo. Geneva.

Albala-Bertrand, J. M. (2006) "Cambio de la estructura productive en Chile, 1986–1996: producción e interdependencia industrial," *Revista de la CEPAL,* 88: 167–181.

Amsden, A. (2001) *The Rise of the "Rest." Challenges to the West from Late-Industrializing Countries,* Oxford: Oxford University Press.

Andrews. E. L. (May 11, 2006) "House Panel Urges Reworking of Leases for Oil Drilling in US-Owned Waters." *The New York Times.*

Arndt, H. (1988) "Market Failure and Underdevelopment," *World Development,* 16 (2): 219–229.

Ayala, F. and K. Gallagher (2005) "The Subsidies Agreement at the WTO," IISD, Trade Knowledge Network. Winnipeg, Canada: IISD.

Bacchetta, M. and B. Bijit (2003) *Industrial Tariff Liberalization and the Doha Development Agenda.* WTO Discussion Paper, Geneva: World Trade Organization.

Barfield, C. (2001) *Free Trade, Sovereignty, Democracy: The Future of the World Trade Organization,* Washington, DC: AEI Press.

Bradford, C. (2005) *Prioritizing Economic Growth: Enhancing Macroeconomic Policy Choice* (G-24 Discussion Paper Series, no. 37), Geneva and New York: UNCTAD and Intergovernmental Group of Twenty Four.

Bronckers, M. (1999) "Better Rules for a New Millennium: A Warning against Undemocratic Developments in the WTO," *Journal of International Economic Law,* 2, 4, 547–566.

CEPAL (2004) *Statistical Yearbook for Latin America and the Caribbean, 2004.* Santiago, Chile: CEPAL.

——— (2005) *Balance preliminar de las economías de América Latina y el Caribe,* Santiago, Chile: CEPAL.

Chang, H.-J. (2005) *Developing Countries Need Tariffs. How WTO NAMA Negotiations Could Deny Developing Countries' Right to a Future*, Geneva, Switzerland: South Centre, Oxfam International.

Council of the European Union (2005) "Financial Perspective 2007–2013," 15915/05, CADREFIN 268, Brussels Available at www.consilium. europa.eu/ue/Docs/cms_Data/docs/pressdata/en/misc/87677.pdf, last accessed February 23, 2008.

ECLAC (2006) "Regional Integration in the Western Hemisphere," Santiago, Chile: International Trade and Integration Division.

Evans, P. (2005) "Neoliberalism as a Political Opportunity: Constraint and Innovation in Contemporary Development Strategy," in K. Gallagher (ed.) *Putting Development First. The Importance of Policy Space in the WTO and International Financial Institutions.* London and New York: ZED Books, 195–215.

Fernandez de Cordoba, S. and D. Vanzetti (2005) "Coping with Trade Reforms," Geneva: UNCTAD/ITC/TAB.

Ffrench-Davis, R. (2005) *Reformas para América Latina después del Fundamentalismo Neoliberal,* Argentina: CEPAL-Siglo XXI Editores.

Fink, C. and K. Maskus (2004) *Intellectual Property and Development: Lessons from Recent Economic Research*, New York and London: World Bank and Oxford University Press.

Gallagher, K., ed. (2005) *Putting Development First. The Importance of Policy Space in the WTO and International Financial Institutions,* London and New York: ZED Books.

Hamwey, R. M. (2005) *Expanding National Policy Space for Development: Why the Multilateral Trading System Must Change* South Centre (Working Paper no. 25).

Hsu, L. (2005) "Non-violation Complaints—WTO Issues and Recent Free Trade Agreements," *Journal of World Trade* 39(2): 205–238.

IADB (Inter American Development Bank) (2001) *Economic and Social Progress in Latin America. Competitiveness. The Business of Growth,* Baltimore, MD: Johns Hopkins University Press.

——— (2004) "Fiscal Impact of Trade Liberalization in the Americas," (Periodic Note): January.

——— (2005a) *Education, Science and Technology in Latin America and the Caribbean: A Statistical Compendium of Indicators.* Washington, DC: Inter-American Development Bank. Available: http://www.iadb.org/sds/publication/publication_4357_e.htm/, last accessed February 23, 2008.

——— (2005b) *Expanding the Knowledge Capital of Latin America and the Caribbean: An IADB Strategy for Education and Training,* Washington, DC: Inter-American Development Bank. Available: http://idbdocs.iadb. org/wsdocs/getdocument.aspx?docnum=582514.

IIDS (Instituto Internacional para el Desarrollo Sustentable) (2001) "Derechos Privados, Problemas Públicos: Una guía sobre el controvertido capitulo del TLCAN referente a los derechos de los inversionistas," Winnipeg Canada: IISD.

IMF (International Monetary Fund) Fiscal Affairs Department (2005) "Dealing with the Revenue Consequences of Trade Reform," Available: www.imf.org/external/np/pp/eng/2005/021505.htm, last accessed February 23, 2008.

Kearney, A.T. (2005) "FDI Confidence Index," *Global Business Policy Council*, 8. Available: http://www.atkearney.com/main.taf?p=5,3,1,138, last accessed February 23, 2008.

Krueger, A. (2004) "Meant Well, Tried Little, Failed Much: Policy Reforms in Emerging Market Economies," Remarks at the Roundtable Lecture at the Economic Honors Society, New York University, March 23, 2004.

Kumar, N. and K. P. Gallagher (2006) "Preserving Policy Space at the WTO," Geneva, Switzerland: International Center for Trade and Sustainable Development.

Lall, S. (2005) "Rethinking Industrial Strategy. The Role of the State in the Face of Globalization," in K. Gallagher (ed.) *Putting Development First. The Importance of Policy Space in the WTO and International Financial Institutions*, London and New York: ZED Books, 33–68.

Malik K. (2002) "Trade Liberalization and Development: Some Issues." Paper presented at the IDB-INT/ITP NETAmericas Conference on Integrating the Americas, Washington, DC: November 20–21.

Mortimore, M. and L. Stanley (2006) "Obsolescencia de la proteccion a los inversores extranjeros después de la crisis argentina," *Revista de la CEPAL*, 88: 17–34.

Paus, E. (2004) "Productivity Growth in Latin America. The Limits of Neoliberal Reforms," *World Development*, 32 (3): 427–445.

—— (2005) *Foreign Investment, Development, and Globalization. Can Costa Rica Become Ireland?* New York and London: Palgrave Macmillan.

Paus, E. and K. Gallagher (2006) *The Missing Links between Foreign Investment and Develoment. Lessons from Costa Rica and Mexico.* Boston, MA: Global Development and Environment Institute, Tufts University (Working Paper 06-01).

Pauwelyn, J. (2005) "Rien Ne Va Plus? Distinguishing Domestic Regulation from Market Access in GATT and the GATS," *World Trade Review*, 4 (2): 131–170.

Peres, W. (2006) "El lento retorno de las políticas industrials en América Latina y el Caribe," *Revista de la CEPAL*, 88: 71–88.

Peterson, L. (2004) "Bilateral Investment Treaties and Development Policy-Making," IISD, November.

Porter, M., K. Schwab, and A. Lopez-Claros, eds. (2005) *The Global Competitiveness Report 2005–2006*, Basingstoke: Palgrave Macmillan.

Reinhardt, N. and W. Peres (2000) "Latin America's New Economic Model: Micro Responses and Economic Restructuring," *World Development*, 28: 1543–1566.

Rodrik, D. (2001) "The Global Governance of Trade As If Development Really Mattered," New York: UNDP.

——— (2004) "Rethinking Growth Policies in the Developing World," Available: http://ksghome.harvard.edu/~drodrik/Luca_d_Agliano_Lecture_Oct_2004.pdf/, last accessed February 23, 2008.

——— (December 2006) "Goodbye Washington Consensus, Hello Washington Confusion?" *Journal of Economic Literature*, 44 (4): 973–987.

Rodrik, D., A. Subramanian, and T. Franchesco (June 2004) "Institutions Rule: The Primacy of Institutions over Geography and Integration in Economic Development," *Journal of Economic Growth*, 9 (2): 131–165.

Shadlen, K. (2008) "Globalization, Power, and Integration: The Political Economy of Regional and Bilateral Trade Agreements in the Americas," *Journal of Development Studies*, 44 (1): 1–20.

Shafaeddin, M. (2006) "Does Trade Openness Favour or Hinder Industrialization and Development? Paper presented at the Intergovernmental Group of Twenty-Four of International Monetary Affairs," Geneva, Switzerland: March 16–17.

Singh, A., A. Belaish, C. Collins, P. De Masi, R. Krieger, G. Meredith, and R. Rennhack (2005) *Stabilization and Reform in Latin America: A Macroeconomic Perspective on the Experience since the Early 1990s*, IMF Occasional Paper, February 2005.

Stiglitz, J. (1998) "More Instruments and Broader Goals: Moving Towards the Post-Washington Consensus," United Nations University. World Institute for Development Economics Research. Available: http://www.wider.unu.edu/events/annuel1998.htm, last accessed February 23, 2008.

UNCTAD (2000) "International Investment Agreements: Flexibility for Development," UNCTAD/ITE/IIT/18 Series on International Investment Agreements. New York and Geneva.

——— (2004) "New Geography of International Trade," TD/404: June.

——— (2005) *World Investment Report*. New York and Geneva: United Nations.

Wade, R. H. (2003) "What Strategies Are Available for Developing Countries Today? The World Trade Organization and the Shrinking of 'Development Space,'" *Review of International Political Economy*, 104: 621–644.

Wood, A. (January 1997) "Openness and Wage Inequality in Developing Countries: The Latin American Challenge to East Asian Conventional Wisdom," *World Bank Economic Review*, 11: 33–57.

World Bank (1993) *The Asian Miracle*. Washington, DC: World Bank.

——— (1994) *Adjustment in Africa: Reforms, Results and the Road Ahead*. New York: Oxford University Press.

——— (2002) *World Development Report 2002. Building Institutions for Markets*. Washington, DC: World Bank.

Wunsch-Vincent, S. (2006) "The Internet, cross-border trade in services and the GATS: Lessons from US- Gambling," *World Trade Review*, 5: 319–355.

Yusuf, S. (2003) *Innovative East Asia. The Future of Growth*. A World Bank Publication, New York and London: Oxford University Press.

Part II

The Political Economy of Hemispheric Integration

Chapter 6

The Politics of Trade and the Limits to U.S. Power in the Americas

Nicola Phillips

The puzzle that this chapter seeks to address can be stated quite succinctly: if we accept that the United States possesses a preponderant (and, for some, unprecedented) degree of structural power in both the global and the regional political economies, and by extension in the arena of trade, why does it prove consistently to be unable to secure outcomes consistent with its interests and preferences? This puzzle reveals itself across the arenas of the contemporary global and regional engagement of the United States: the profound difficulty with which the United States is able to exercise the raw material and institutional power capabilities it possesses is evident in its negotiations in multilateral and international organizations, its military strategies and attempts to maintain political and social order, the war on drugs in the Americas, recent strategies to address the political inconveniences posed by Hugo Chávez in Venezuela, and an array of other instances associated with strategies relating to energy, China, the construction of global or regional coalitions around various issue areas, and so on. The question acquires considerable pertinence when thinking about the evolution of both multilateral and regional trade, the latter in a context in which most observers and participants have given the Free Trade Area of the Americas (FTAA) project up for dead, and the United States, over the course of more than a decade, was unable effectively to wield either its coercive power or the "soft" power of consensual hegemony to entrench the particular form of commercial and economic governance it envisaged as the foundation for the regional trade project. Given that this is the region of the world that remains most characterized by economic and commercial dependence on the United States (and the levels of vulnerability implied by that level of dependence), and that this is the region in which the United States is usually deemed to possess the greatest overall degree of hegemonic power, this puzzle becomes all the more compelling.

The puzzle is not entirely a new one and not peculiar to the contemporary period. Rather, it is a question that consistently preoccupied scholars in relation to the post-war period, and was formulated primarily as a concern with the domestic constraints on the "external" power of the United States, particularly in the context of a scholarly conjuncture in which the relationship between the domestic and international determinants of foreign policy was at its height in the field of International Relations (Krasner, 1977; Ikenberry, Lake and Mastanduno, 1988). One could also address the puzzle as a matter of policy failure, and set out all manner of explanations for each instance of failure on the part of the United States in achieving stated objectives, whether these focus on strategic miscalculations, policy mismanagement, unforeseen circumstances, political opposition, legal or normative constraints, or whatever. But I contend that there is something more "structural" at stake here, which takes us beyond a focus on isolated instances of policy failure and does not give the extent of theoretical precedence found in many earlier analyses to the constraints imposed by domestic politics and institutions, even while the latter form a crucial part of the explanation for the nature and persistence of the puzzle itself and are central to the arguments that will be developed here. Rather, I see this puzzle in terms of an intrinsic disjuncture between the structural dimensions of U.S. power and what we might call its "agential" dimensions, which issues both theoretical and empirical challenges to dominant understandings of U.S. power in the contemporary period.

The premise from which this chapter starts is that the existence of structural primacy (or hegemony), which reaches across the terrains of "structural power" identified usefully by Susan Strange (1987), is frequently not accompanied by an ability to exercise preponderant control over outcomes and unilateral dominance over the processes in which the United States is engaged. It is important to be clear from the outset that the power of the United States, whether understood as hegemony, primacy or domination, has never and will never approximate "absolute" power, and indeed that these concepts do not imply as much. To argue that there are limits to U.S. power and to posit a disjuncture between the structural and agential dimensions of power as a way of understanding does not suggest that the United States does not possess preponderant power of an historically unprecedented nature. Nor does it imply that we are measuring U.S. power against some preposterous benchmark which precludes any possibility of policy failure or constraint on the nature, extent or articulation of U.S. power. Rather, the argument here is that there exist a range of *intrinsic* limits to U.S. power which are sufficiently ingrained in the structures of U.S. power that we can make a strong argument, as others have done in relation to other periods, concerning the discrepancy between, in Stephen Krasner's (1977) terms, the potential and actual power of the United States or, in my own terms, the structural and agential power of the United States in the contemporary global and regional political economies. We thus need both to expose this disjuncture and to explain why it should arise in such pronounced form across the various arenas of the global and regional engagement of the United States.

It should be highlighted that the disjuncture in question is explicitly recognized "on the ground" by trade policy makers in the United States and that it permeates the design of contemporary trade strategies. It translates into a self-conscious concern with the achievement of what is usually termed "leverage."[1] This idea of leverage arises from a core perception that what has been eroded over the last several decades is precisely the degree of leverage which ensures the effective pursuit of U.S. interests and policy objectives—that is, the ability of the United States to exercise the power associated with its position of global and regional primacy in trade negotiations across the spectrum. The core argument advanced in this paper, then, is that the evolution of U.S. trade strategies, both globally and regionally, reflects attempts on the part of policy makers to mitigate and compensate the limitations of U.S. agential power. This explains clearly the shift toward bilateralism as the primary focus of trade policy, in the pursuit of the "leverage" which would facilitate the entrenchment of a global and regional commercial and economic order in line with U.S. interests and preferences. In other words, the invigoration of bilateralism in regional trade strategies is, firstly, a response to the growing challenge to U.S. power in the Americas, particularly in ideological terms and in respect of the economic and trade agenda it has elaborated and pursued. Secondly, it is a clear reflection of the limits of U.S. power in those instances in which attempts to mobilize either the attributes of structural power or agential power have failed—in this case, most clearly, in the FTAA project, but also in the difficulties surrounding the spate of bilateral agreements that have recently been submitted for congressional approval in the United States and across the region.

The task, then, is to develop this argument by attending to the reasons for the structural/agential disjuncture in U.S. power, the sources from which it arises and the implications it carries for our understandings of the politics of trade in the Americas. Before doing so, the following section offers a brief account of the evolution of U.S. trade policy.

The Evolution of U.S. Trade Policy in the Americas[2]

Throughout the post-war period, the international engagement of the United States was marked by a distinctive and largely exclusive preference for multilateralism. In trade, successive administrations consistently eschewed other modes of negotiating the construction of a (neo)liberal world order, most obviously those regionalist strategies spearheaded by the European Union (EU). Bilateralist streaks, while evident in post-war trade strategies, were limited to a collection of policy instruments that were deployed in bilateral trade *relationships*, rather than constituting encompassing bilateral trade agreements. At the same time, the historically close links between U.S. economic strategies and multilateralism have consistently been characterized by a fundamental ambivalence in state and public attitudes to multilateral institutions and the rules these institutions have established, even though these rules have been developed largely under U.S. impetus (Luck, 1999). While the United States has exercised structural dominance within the institutions of the world trading system, as in the international financial organizations, nevertheless its record of compliance with multilateral trade rules and procedures has been an increasingly unhappy one, particularly since the 1980s as the dynamism and effectiveness of multilateral trade negotiations have also declined more markedly (Bergsten, 2002: 86–98; Tussie, 1998: 183–193). At the same time, its political dominance of the process has been complicated by increasingly fractious relations with both the EU and developing countries. The result of these trends has been a much greater inclination on the part of successive U.S. governments to explore alternative avenues and arenas for advancing global trade liberalization.

The turn to regionalism in the late 1980s and early 1990s must, in this sense, be understood as arising from a growing disaffection in the United States with the progress of multilateral negotiations and, moreover, the growing political problems encountered in realizing the *particular* vision of a multilateral trading order that animated U.S. engagement in it. It was also a product of two other preoccupations. The first was that associated with perceptions within the United States of a steady erosion of its global hegemony. The "declinist" debates became prevalent from the 1970s onwards, and were epitomized by anxious concern about the apparently superior growth performances of Japanese and German models of capitalism and the steady march of integration in the EU. Regionalism became incorporated into the global hegemonic strategies of the United States largely as an attempt to counter these perceived threats to its economic dominance emerging from other regions and other powerful economies.

The second and related preoccupation was one which achieved particular salience toward the end of the 1990s, and is still deployed frequently in speeches by trade policy-makers and others as grist to the new regionalist and bilateralist mill—namely, that in the negotiation of regional and bilateral trade agreements the United States has consistently been, and remains, behind the curve. Echoed widely in political discourse, public commentary and congressional hearings on the matter (U.S. House of Representatives, 2001), Robert B. Zoellick, the U.S. Trade Representative (USTR) during the first administration of George W. Bush, frequently observed that the United States was "falling behind" the rest of the world and, moreover, its major competitors and partners: "[t]here are over 130 free trade agreements in the world; the United States is party to only two. There are 30 free trade agreements in the Western hemisphere; the United States belongs to only one" (Zoellick, 2001).

The thinking resulting from this conjunction of concerns does not signify a retraction of a ceteris paribus preference for multilateral trade negotiations. But what it does indicate is that, since the late 1980s, there has been a sustained expansion of the armoury of trade policy instruments and the arenas in which trade liberalization is negotiated. From 2000 onwards, the strategy of fostering "competition in liberalization" was elevated to the status of policy "credo" by the USTR (Zoellick, 2003b), facilitated by the granting of "fast-track" negotiating authority under the Trade Act of 2002 (which had been denied to the Clinton administration since 1998). The credo of "competition in liberalization" connoted an advance toward the negotiation of trade agreements on "multiple fronts"—multilateral, regional and bilateral—designed to place the United States "at the center of a network of initiatives" (Zoellick, 2001). The rationale was that such a strategy "provides leverage for openness in all negotiations, establishes models of success that can be used on many fronts, and develops a fresh political dynamic that puts free trade on the offensive" (Office of the U.S. Trade Representative, 2004). The element of "competition" relates to the attempt to create a series of precedents with which, in each successive trade agreement, the baseline requirements for subsequent agreements are ratcheted up, along with the incentives for trading partners to negotiate with the United States distinctively on its terms.

The trade policy credo, in other words, accelerates the momentum of global liberalization by increasing the incentives for countries to negotiate bilateral trade agreements with the United States, designed sequentially to raise the bar for subsequent negotiations (see VanGrasstek, 2000). Given that the selection of countries for these negotiations is primarily reactive in nature—it is the country (or group of countries) aspiring to a trade agreement with the United States which is required, in the first instance, to make its case for consideration (Phillips, 2007b; Feinberg, 2003)—the expectation among U.S. trade policy makers is that a competition among countries will consequently emerge to provide the most attractive set of incentives for the initiation of negotiations. By extension, as the dynamism in world trade shifts to bilateral negotiations, it is a distinctively U.S. trade agenda which is thereby facilitated as the foundation for this new playing field.

The manner in which this strategy has evolved and been deployed has been conditioned by key shifts in multilateral and regional trade politics. Most notable among these have been the gradual implosion of World Trade Organization (WTO) negotiations and the disintegration of the FTAA project in late 2003. As a result of the overriding concern with how then to establish and exercise "leverage" in its trade and economic relationships, the USTR has afforded even greater priority to bilateral negotiations. With rhetoric reminiscent of that surrounding the invasion of Iraq—leading one observer pithily to cast Zoellick as a "Donald Rumsfeld of trade policy" (Bhagwati, 2004: 52)—the strategy has been to construct a "coalition of the liberalizers": to pursue bilateral agree-ments with "willing" countries, concomitantly to exclude and isolate the "unwilling," and thereby to exert sustained pressure on "recalcitrant" countries such as Brazil. Thus, in the FTAA context, Zoellick declared in 2002 that "we want to negotiate with all the democracies of the Americas through the FTAA, but we are also prepared to move step-by-step toward free trade if others turn back or simply are not ready" (Zoellick, 2002). Precisely this occurred when the clash between Brazilian and U.S. posi-tions were deemed to have generated stalemate in late 2003. In the mul-tilateral context, again in response to the Brazilian-led G-20 coalition of developing countries formed at the 2003 WTO ministerial in Cancún, Zoellick declared his government's determination not to entertain or wait for the "won't do" countries in the multilateral system and to under-mine the G-20 by "mov[ing] towards free trade with can-do countries" (Zoellick, 2003a). The coalition splintered rapidly as the prospect of trade negotiations with the United States was held out as an incentive not to participate in this grouping, and it was precisely countries in the Americas, such as Colombia, El Salvador, Costa Rica, and Peru, that were quickest to jump ship in favor of keeping open the possibility of trade negotiations with the United States.

The cumulative result has been a rash of bilateral negotiations and agreements with partners around the world, a number of which were signed soon after fast-track authority was granted and a greater number of which were set in train following the collapse of the Cancún meetings and the original ambition for an FTAA. Notably, all the countries in the Americas that defected from the G-20 grouping have since indeed been engaged in bilateral negotiations with the United States. Agreements with Chile and six Central American countries (the latter to form a Central American Free Trade Agreement, DR-CAFTA), were ratified by the U.S. Congress in July 2003 and July 2005 respectively. In April 2004, multi-party negotiations for Trade Promotion Agreements with a number of Andean countries were initiated, and around the same time for a Free Trade Agreement with Panama. Negotiations were concluded with Peru in December 2005 and Colombia in February 2006. Ecuador was also part of these negotiations for an Andean Trade Promotion Agreement. Bilateral Investment Treaties (BITs) also exist with Grenada (1989), Panama (1991), Argentina (1994), Ecuador (1997), Jamaica (1997), Bolivia (2001), and Honduras (2001), and negotiations were concluded with Uruguay in late 2005.

It should, of course, be noted that bilateralism is not new, in the United States or elsewhere, and indeed is neither original nor unique to the United States. This much should be obvious from the statements cited earlier lamenting the proliferation of agreements that left the United States falling behind its competitors. Yet what *is* new in the United States is the pace at which such agreements have been negotiated and, indeed, the political ease with which the USTR has been able both to attract negotiating partners and successfully conclude negotiations. Each of the bilateral agreements noted above has departed only insubstantially, if at all, from the schedule of demands that U.S. negotiators would have brought to the first negotiating session, and many have been negotiated in a period of only a few months.

To recap, then: bilateralism has been pursued by the United States, in the Americas and elsewhere, as a mechanism of increasing the leverage which it has progressively lacked in both multilateral (WTO) and regional (FTAA) trade negotiations. In the terms set out at the start of the chapter, the turn to bilateralism has been a reflection of an increasingly pronounced disjuncture between the structural power that the United States possesses in the arena of trade—stemming from its structural position of dominance in the global and regional economy, as well as its dominance in the key institutions of multilateral trade— and its ability to achieve outcomes consistent with its stated objectives and interests. However, this disjuncture has also been evident in the United States' bilateral trade relationships. The passage of DR-CAFTA through the U.S. Congress was intensely fraught and considerably more difficult and acrimonious than even the USTR had envisaged,[3] even though it was eventually ratified by the narrowest of margins (217 votes to 215 in the House of Representatives). Yet DR-CAFTA has entered into force in only five of the participating countries, with the exception of Costa Rica where some demanded reforms are still pending. (The agreement entered into force with El Salvador in March 2006, Honduras and Nicaragua in April 2006, Guatemala in July 2006, and the Dominican Republic in March 2007.) Agreements with the Andean countries look likely to take on similar sorts of colors once referred for domestic ratification. At the same time, some limited progress has been made toward the establishment of a South American trade bloc—in many ways, the antithesis of what was envisaged in the FTAA, and certainly contrary to the U.S.-sponsored vision of a hemisphere-wide free trade zone.

Explaining the Structural/Agential Disjuncture in U.S. Regional Trade Relations

How then do we explain the disjuncture between the dominance of the United States in the regional economy and its trade structures, on the one hand, and on the other its ability effectively to achieve outcomes in trade policy consistent with its stated objectives and interests? I wish to explore three dimensions of a possible explanation in this chapter, all of which revolve around the central issue of the way in which U.S. power is intrinsically constituted and shaped by global, regional and domestic politics. The first is the nature of the U.S. state and the range of bureaucratic issues that impinge upon the formulation and execution of trade strategies; the second is the nature of domestic (U.S.) politics surrounding the trade process; the third is the nature of regional politics and regional structures in the Americas, revolving around the political economy of neoliberalism and contestation of the trade agenda pursued by the United States.

The Trade Policymaking Process

It has long been recognized that the particular nature of the U.S. state and political system impinges in crucial ways not only on the overall hegemony of the United States but also on the effectiveness of various policy arenas within the hegemonic project. Analyses have drawn attention to a range of characteristics of the U.S. state, ranging from constitutional provisions to coalition building by dominant political parties, the particular form of separation of powers, the presidential (as opposed to parliamentary) system and so on (see Strange, 1987). The most salient preoccupation, inevitably, has been with the ways in which all these characteristics of the U.S. political system add up to a state which is highly permeable to powerful lobbies and interest groups; consequently, much analysis, particularly in U.S. scholarship, has been imbued with a excessively narrow and determinist focus on interest group politics. Equally, there is a long-standing debate, with which space here precludes a lengthy engagement, centering on explanations for the differences in policy making processes across policy areas, particularly between trade policy and international monetary policy, and indeed in different issue areas within those policy areas. Here again, the emphasis has routinely been on contending understandings of the relationship between state and society, and specifically questions of either state autonomy in relation to societal interests or collective action within particular issue areas (Katzenstein, 1978; Krasner, 1978; Zysman, 1983; Goldstein, 1986; Gowa, 1988). Put together, all these characteristics can be taken to constitute a form of "political entropy" (Cerny, 1989), which acts to the detriment of both consistency and predictability.[4]

We will return to these issues of interest group activity shortly, along with the question of executive-congressional relations. For now, our concern is with the state and bureaucratic structures that shape particular policy areas. In trade policy making, indeed, the degree of bureaucratic and institutional fragmentation are particularly pronounced, in ways which are clearly pivotal to an understanding of the policy inconsistencies that one perceives in this policy area—policy inconsistencies that revolve around the central and long-standing tension between liberal and protectionist impulses which have manifested themselves across the gamut of U.S. trade strategies and, in particular, permeated congressional activity and public opinion surrounding trade policy.

The interagency process through which trade policy is made, along with the substantial congressional oversight and input functions developed in successive reforms since the middle of the twentieth century, have consistently made the U.S. trade policy process a strikingly unwieldy, diffuse and politically delicate one. The interagency process (consisting of the Trade Policy Review Group and the Trade Policy Staff Committee) incorporates a wide range of state agencies, most obviously the Office of the USTR and the Departments of State, Treasury, Commerce, Agriculture, and Labor, and including many Departments such as, among others, Interior, Energy, Health and Human Service, Justice, and Transportation, the Central Intelligence Agency, the National Security Council, the Environmental Protection Agency, and the Office of Management and Budget.[5] The most defining interactions lie between the first four of these agencies and represent essentially the differences (and tensions) between their guiding concerns. As is well known, the Department of State's role in the trade policy process revolves around ensuring that policy is consistent with and contributes to overarching foreign policy, security and diplomatic goals; Commerce concerns itself with the interests of specific industries; Treasury with macroeconomic issues; and so on.

The interests and concerns of these and other agencies have frequently intervened in the negotiation of trade agreements, usually in a manner which goes against the positions adopted by trade negotiators from the USTR. Perhaps the most visible case in point over recent years has been the dispute over the inclusion in trade agreements of provisions on the migration of workers to the United States, as during the negotiation of the Chile-U.S. agreement, in which various immigration agencies, the Department of Labor, Department of State and others came into conflict with the USTR, not to mention labor unions themselves. In the event, the provisions on movement of peoples, favored by Chilean negotiators and U.S. business groups but opposed trenchantly by U.S. labor unions, immigration agencies and others, were substantially watered down but still caused a firestorm and breathed further life into the longstanding and hostile debate about the relationship between trade and labor/ immigration policy. Interagency tugs-of-war over labor standards and environmental standards have also been frequent in trade negotiations with partners in the Americas, again reinforced by the activities of various environmental groups and labor unions in the broader political debate surrounding trade agreements such as DR-CAFTA.

One of the principal effects of these bureaucratic and institutional characteristics of the trade policy process has been a pronounced difficulty in formulating and executing a consistent and proactive trade strategy, beyond the broadest of commitments to a liberal trading regime in both the regional and the global setting. It is clearly the case, as many have argued, that the basic founding principle of liberal trade has remained intact in the United States over the postwar period, and is unlikely to change without a significant rupture in the nature of the U.S. political system (Gowa, 1988; Goldstein, 1986). Yet, beyond this, U.S. trade strategies are defined fundamentally by what Richard Feinberg has appositely termed "ad hoc reactivism." In the current debate about the selection of trade partners for bilateral negotiations, the USTR and others have preferred the adjectives "flexible" or "not mechanical" to "*ad hoc*," but the point remains that trade negotiations have been initiated "generally in response to an insistent external request, not as the considered unfolding of a carefully designed internally-generated strategic plan" (Feinberg, 2003: 1022). In addition, trade policy is an area which is especially vulnerable to shifts in the influence of agencies such as the State Department, as officials seek to put trade policy to the service of what may be abruptly changing foreign policy priorities. It is also more vulnerable than most policy areas to shifting patterns of congressional and public opinion, as will be discussed shortly. This is *not* to suggest that trade policy is intrinsically hostage to foreign and security policy priorities, nor indeed to subscribe to those parts of the debate that see trade policy as a blank canvas for interest group politics. Rather, it is to suggest that the elaboration of an internally generated strategic plan, to which Feinberg alludes, has been significantly complicated by the weight of multiple, and often competing, pressures that are brought to bear on trade policy through the functioning of the interagency process and the sprawling, fragmented nature of the trade policy architecture in Washington, DC.

In more general terms, the political and bureaucratic system governing trade policy gives ample expression to the aforementioned tension between liberal and protectionist impulses. The Department of Commerce is oriented around the interests of specific industries and is the agency that concerns itself most with anti-dumping actions. Indeed, for this reason domestic industry groups have pressured for a shift of authority to bring anti-dumping cases in the WTO or NAFTA from the Office of the

USTR to the Department of Commerce.[6] Likewise, protectionist impulses arise from the centrality of Congress to the trade policy–making process. Congressional scrutiny of trade policy has in fact been enhanced rather than diminished under the Bush administration, notably as a result of the terms on which fast-track authority was granted to the executive branch in 2002. In this incarnation, TPA was marked by an increase in congressional input and powers of scrutiny, and as such by an enhancement of historically substantial congressional involvement in the trade policy-making process. At the same time, it contained a raft of concessions to "sensitive" domestic economic interests, such that protectionist pressures were firmly embedded in the substance of trade negotiations. Inasmuch as TPA sets the parameters for U.S. trade negotiators, and is reinforced by particular pressures from Commerce and elsewhere, from the outset the negotiating terrain is structurally skewed toward not only U.S. interests in general but also those of specific sectors and industries (Phillips, 2005).

It is this framework, reflecting the intrinsic tension between overarching ideas in U.S. trade policy, which has generated many of the intractable tensions in trade negotiations, particularly in the FTAA process. The exclusion from these negotiations of both agriculture and trade remedies was seen by many governments and interests across the rest of the region to stand in direct contradiction with the United States' insistence on both a "WTO-plus" format and a "single undertaking" as the conditions of a hemispheric free trade agreement. The line, in essence, was that WTO-plus should prevail across the board, including in agriculture and trade remedies, and that anything short of this agreement was not acceptable to a large group of countries led by Brazil, comprising primarily member states of the Southern Common Market (Mercosur) and the Caribbean Community and Common Market (CARICOM). The way in which a turn to bilateralism facilitated the negotiation of agreements within this framework established by TPA and the surrounding bureaucratic politics is in ample evidence. In spite of the same emphasis on the WTO-plus format, the United States has excluded from the remit of bilateral negotiations the areas of trade remedies and agricultural subsidies, and sensitive sectors and products have routinely been "carved out" of bilateral agreements (sugar, for example, being a notable and controversial product exemption in the Chilean agreement).

The Domestic Politics of Trade in the United States

The historic ambivalence to free trade in U.S. public and political opinion, and the fraught politics that habitually surround free trade agreements, have been amply in evidence since the start of the 1990s.

From the time of the political battles surrounding the signing of the NAFTA agreement in the mid 1990s, the tensions between the Executive and Congress have been evident not only in the refusal to renew fast-track authority for the Clinton administration in 1998 but also in the congressional politics surrounding the vast majority of regional and bilateral negotiations into which the USTR has entered. At the start of the second Bush administration, indeed, in the words of Senator Charles E. Grassley (R-IA), "trade is more controversial than it has been for some time" (U.S. Senate, 2004). Moreover, there has been a striking decline in public support for trade since the start of the 2000s. The primary reasons for this decline are uniformly cited as the emerging "threat" from the Chinese economy, reflected in the steady annual increase in the U.S. trade deficit, and the experience of the NAFTA.[7]

Much (but not all) of this sensitivity is related to the pronounced concern about the impact of trade on the U.S. labor market. The fact that early agreements such as those with Chile, Singapore, Morocco or Australia passed through Congress with relative ease is because they represented little threat to labor and key sectors in the U.S. economy. Under the first Bush administration, indeed, early trade strategies prioritized negotiations that could be concluded and ratified relatively quickly, and this was facilitated by the fact that none of the countries concerned represented excessive threats to U.S. labor and/or the most politically sensitive parts of the U.S. economy. It must also be stressed again, however, that in each of these deals "sensitive" sectors and products were excluded from negotiation or identified as exemptions in the texts of agreements. Those agreements deemed to represent a considerably greater threat to the U.S. labor market—notably DR-CAFTA—have been subject to the same partisan and public battles as those which surrounded similarly contentious agreements in the past, such as the NAFTA.

Indeed, as noted a second ago, one frequently hears explanations of the difficulties surrounding ratification of DR-CAFTA that center on the parallels that are drawn with NAFTA. In the latter case, the political "leverage" that was mobilized for the purposes of securing its passage related to the implications that free trade would carry for dealing with many of the developmental problems that gave rise to labor migration from Mexico to the United States, and increasing the ways in which a trade agreement would enhance the—again—leverage of the United States in terms of advancing democracy in Mexico and dealing decisively with such questions as drug trafficking through Mexico to the United States. Although the infamous "giant sucking sound" never in fact materialized, neither did the developmental benefits to Mexico which were supposed (for the United States) to stem the tide of (particularly illegal) migrants or deal with other core border security issues. The reason for this is fairly clear: the absence of any significant developmental dimension to the NAFTA project that would substantially mitigate wage differentials or problems of unemployment. In fact, for many, the neoliberal project, of which NAFTA was the exemplar in the mid 1990s, generated precisely the opposite effects. Arguments similarly designed to increase political leverage relating to DR-CAFTA—and indeed the drawing of similar linkages between free trade and the war on drugs in the current negotiations with the Andean countries—have therefore gained significantly less "traction" in Congress or in public opinion more broadly.

These generalized concerns about jobs are coupled with perceptions or fears of unfair trade practices, notably dumping, and threats from freer trade to domestic producers and manufacturers. The result has been a pronounced and widespread decline in enthusiasm for existing and new trade agreements among key economic interests in the United States—notably small industries, certain agricultural sectors such as tomatoes and sugar producers (even while associations representing the wheat and corn sectors are broadly supportive), the textiles sector and a wide array of services sectors. The particular constellation of U.S. political interests opposing trade agreements has of course depended on the trade agreement in question. The agreement with Thailand featured significant problems with sugar, pick-up trucks and intellectual property, for example; in the case of DR-CAFTA, labor standards, sugar and textiles were foremost.

The primary upshot has been growing calls among such groups for much more stringent application of U.S. trade laws and opposition to the negotiation of new bilateral and regional agreements,[8] again reinforcing the tension between free trade and "protectionist" (or anti–free trade) ideas and the resulting policy inconsistencies. These pressures, channeled through such organizations as the National Association of Manufacturers, have been matched by congressional initiatives to strengthen the enforcement of existing trade agreements. Senator Max Baucus (D-MT), for example, called in March 2004 for a thorough review by the General Accounting Office (GAO) of current enforcement practices in response to such concerns as software piracy in India and the lax enforcement of intellectual property rights in trade partner countries around the world (U.S. Senate, 2004). But what this increasing pressure on the trade agenda means, in essence, is that those elements of U.S. trade policy that are already most controversial and already complicate trade negotiations in the region and outside it are being substantially strengthened, and are likely to continue to be strengthened over the coming years. Put the more stringent application of trade remedies together with ongoing agricultural protection, more forceful enforcement mechanisms on matters of intellectual property and labor issues (the latter particularly in the context of a bitter debate surrounding immigration reform in the United States), and it appears that trade politics over the rest of this decade are likely to become more rather than less tense. By extension, the clash of overarching ideas governing trade policy is likely to be sharpened, exacerbating many of the institutional and political obstacles not only to the effective design of trade strategies, but also to the exercise of U.S. agential power in the arena of trade.

The Regional Politics of Trade in the Americas

Finally, then, what can we say of the regional politics of trade which shape, define and, indeed, limit the agential power of the United States in this arena? The first and most obvious point to make is that the political economy of the Americas can no longer be understood, if it ever could be, in the simple terms of a north-south structure of economic and political dependence, on the one hand, or, on the other, the clear-cut and indisputable dominance of the United States. In general terms, the structural power that the United States possesses in the region could be said to have remained intact, but the methods by which it is exercised shifted away from the coercive, interventionist foreign policies of the Cold War period toward an approach based on the building of ideological "consensus" around the transitions to democracy and market economics, and on the elaboration of regionalist projects.

One interpretation of these trends sees their result to be a "relational delinking" between the United States and Latin America, in which relations have come to be characterized by the increasing political and economic independence of Latin America from the United States, on the one hand, and on the other the diminishing political and diplomatic interest of the United States in the Latin American region (Muñoz, 2001: 73–90). To an extent, this idea captures something of the changing nature of U.S.-Latin American relations, and becomes persuasive in the context of the increasing global presence of Brazil, Mexico, and other countries, and indeed the increasing challenge mounted by a range of countries—notably Brazil—to the unilateral assertion of U.S. primacy in the region. In the issue of trade which concerns us here, the manner in which both Brazil and Chile have come to articulate global trade strategies and profiles, rather than ones dominated by either the region or the U.S. market, is certainly indicative of a reduced degree of straightforward dependence on the United States.

However, the same cannot be said for the majority of the countries of the region, which have continued to be characterized by a pronounced dependence on the United States. Indeed, as global competition has intensified under the impact of globalization, as well as multilateral and unilateral processes of liberalization, many countries in the Americas have found competitive participation in global markets to be more, rather than less, remote as a strategic option. Furthermore, the emergence of China in the global economy has been pivotal in reinforcing and sharpening the profound obstacles to competitiveness in Latin American economies, including in the U.S. market (Dussel Peters, this volume; Jenkins et al., 2006; Phillips, 2007a). Notably too, this new political economy of dependence features not only dependence on the U.S. market as a destination for exports and a source of investment, but also dependence on the U.S. economy as a source of jobs for hundreds of thousands of people who migrate each year to the United States from Latin America and the Caribbean (LAC).

It is to be expected, then, that yawning differences across the region in terms of levels of dependence on the United States and associated issues of political and economic "weight" should yield considerable variation in the nature of participation in trade and trade politics. Yet, even in cases in which dependence is pronounced, there have been clear limits to the extent to which the United States has been able to dominate the trade agenda—that is, there has been a clear disjuncture between the structural power that arises from its position of primacy and the nature of regional dependence on the U.S. economy, on the one hand, and, on the other, the ability of U.S. governments to secure outcomes consistent with stated preferences. In part, this disjuncture stems from a changing regional politics, in which coalitions of countries have been able to mount challenges to the particular strategies pursued by the United States. In other part, it arises as a result of profound regional- and domestic-level rejections in various contexts of both U.S. power and the particular trade agenda through which the United States has sought to entrench its hegemony in the region.

The first of these—a changing regional politics—was manifest in the FTAA negotiations. A Brazilian-led coalition, comprising essentially Mercosur and CARICOM countries (along with Venezuela) and opposing the U.S.-sponsored vision of the FTAA, contributed to the trenchant politics that ultimately led to the breakdown of the negotiations in late 2003, even while some Latin America countries, notably Chile and Mexico, remained more or less fervent supporters of an FTAA. Of course, the collapse of the FTAA negotiations gave way to the bilateral thrust of U.S. trade strategies that has accelerated particularly since 2003 and, as noted earlier, contributed to a reinforcement rather than diversion of U.S. power and the distinctive agenda of the United States in the region. Nevertheless, these shifting regional politics were central to the inability of the United States either to push forward the FTAA negotiating process or, through it, to set in place a trading and wider economic order that was distinctively consistent with its interests and priorities.

"Success" in diverting an FTAA based on the articulation and extension of U.S. power breathed new momentum into the process of constructing a South American trade bloc, which, in its aspirations, stands in direct contradiction with both the priorities of hemispheric free trade and U.S. dominance of the regional political economy. Yet one should clearly not be inappropriately optimistic about the prospects for this bloc, particularly in view of the apparent tensions that have come to prevail between participation in the South American project and conducting bilateral negotiations with the United States for the majority of Andean countries. Most significantly, Venezuela abandoned the Andean Community in April 2006 in protest at the Peruvian and Colombian deals with the United States, even though it remained committed to becoming a full member of the Mercosur. The prospects for the consolidation of a "South American" bloc as a coherent political force were also thrown clearly into doubt in mid-2007 as the putative alliance between Venezuela and Brazil—and in a wider sense Venezuela and the Mercosur—began visibly to wane, Mercosur governments (including the Brazilian government) becoming uncomfortable with the vision of this alliance being touted by Caracas and, moreover, developments in Venezuela after the re-election of President Chávez in December 2006 that were widely (internationally) interpreted as contrary to democratic principles. Similar arrangements for Bolivia's full membership of Mercosur were also frustrated in early 2007, as the other Mercosur countries objected to Brazilian support for this prospect. It would therefore appear that this regional politics of opposition to an FTAA is unlikely to have yielded a significant, long-term political force which acts to the detriment of the agential power of the United States in the region, and certainly it has done little to dilute the forms of structural power that the United States continues to possess.

In this light, the more intriguing and potentially important dimension of regional politics relates to the second area mentioned above—the domestic-level rejections of the U.S. trade agenda. This is evident primarily in the tortuous course of bilateral agreements, particularly in the politics surrounding DR-CAFTA and the emerging politics surrounding the Andean agreements. As noted earlier, the politics of DR-CAFTA in Costa Rica have been particularly contentious. The focal points of opposition have been the provisions on intellectual property (particularly in the area of pharmaceuticals), investment and agriculture—precisely those that generated most tension and acrimony in the FTAA negotiations. The prospects for ratification improved after the election of President Oscar Arias, who took office in May 2006 and is a proponent of DR-CAFTA. But his victory over Otton Solis, vocally opposed to the agreement, was a very slim one, and Arias took office without a legislative majority. This fact, as well as ongoing active opposition from labor unions and other popular groups, indicated clearly that opposition to DR-CAFTA was extensive. There was an aggressive media campaign in favor of free trade, supported by the big transnational pharmaceutical companies, the president's office and other pro-DR-CAFTA groups, but this did not prevented the steady growth of social protest culminating in a march by tens of thousands of people in early 2007 against the ratification of the agreement. At the same time, concerns were raised about the use of force to repress this social opposition. In the end, DR-CAFTA was approved in a referendum in October 2007, but by just three percentage points and in the midst of continued political polarization.

Political tensions have also emerged forcefully in the Andean countries. At the "official" level some governments are unwavering proponents of the trade agreements and others hold out prospects of a resounding rejection of them, rhetorically at least. The political panorama for ratification of these bilateral agreements in the Andean countries themselves looks rather like that of DR-CAFTA countries, with the extra twist of the elections of left-wing governments in Ecuador and Bolivia and the deterioration in both cases, for various reasons, of relations with the United States. Social protest has accompanied the negotiations also in this subregion, the protagonists here including Ecuadorian indigenous groups and Peruvian farmers' groups.

The central issue in these regional politics of trade is thus linked directly with broader questions about the structural/agential disjuncture in U.S. power, and concerns the declining *legitimacy* of both U.S. power and the particular trade and economic agenda it has pursued, both regionally and globally. In this respect neo-Gramscian conceptions of hegemony become rather useful, centering as they do on the question of legitimate and consensual power: hegemony constitutes a condition in which the governed accept or acquiesce in authority without the need for the application of force. Hegemony, as Robert Cox puts it, "meant leadership rather than domination" (Cox, 2004: 311). Consent is therefore crucial to the exercise of power, not in the sense that there needs to be active consent before power can be exercised (the United States can and does act unilaterally and coercively), but rather that the increasing difficulty in the exercise of agential power is linked, I suggest, to the erosion of the legitimacy of U.S. power.

In the arena of trade in the Americas, this erosion of legitimacy has been particularly marked, and has taken three principal forms. The first is as a rejection of neoliberalism and, in particular, the Washington Consensus as a template for political and economic organization in the region. The prevalent disillusion with developmental performance under neoliberalism has found expression in the election of a rash of center-left or left-wing presidents in countries such as Brazil, Venezuela, Bolivia, Ecuador, Venezuela, and Argentina, and a surge of left-wing political currents in countries like Mexico. In some of these cases, such as Brazil and Argentina, there has not been a rejection of market economics per se, but rather a rejection of the neoliberal orthodoxy embedded in the Washington Consensus. Some would, of course, argue that this is hardly significant in as much as the Washington Consensus has rarely been pursued in a "pure" form and as such fairly minor deviations from it, while the thrust of a market-led development model is preserved, are not especially noteworthy. In others, notably Bolivia and Venezuela, the reaction against neoliberalism has been much more pronounced as a rejection of the tenets of market-led development, even though a clear alternative policy model has not emerged in any concrete sense.

However, what must be noted in this context is that a widespread rhetorical rejection of neoliberalism, whether of the "softer" or "harder" variety, has not significantly infected Latin American *trade* strategies. Indeed, the drive to negotiate trade agreements, build trade relationships, capitalize on the trade opportunities presented by China or else, in cases such as Mexico and Central America where the emergence of China has thus far posed severe difficulties in the area of trade (especially as a result of direct competition in key sectors), put in place measures to shore up key trading relationships in a "defensive" manner has been undiluted by the region-wide acknowledgement of the failures of more than a decade of neoliberal development strategies. Even on its own, the enthusiasm for bilateral negotiations with the United States in the majority of countries of the region provides ample illustration of this point, notwithstanding the difficulties encountered in some cases once legislation was passed for domestic ratification.

Rather than as a rejection of trade per se, then, the second form that the erosion of the legitimacy of U.S. power has taken, has been that of a reaction against the particular type of trade strategy pursued by the United States in both the FTAA and bilateral negotiations. In a nutshell, the "trade" agenda for the United States is essentially an agenda for the entrenchment of a much wider range of economic disciplines, focusing on such areas as intellectual property, investment rules, liberalization of trade in services, labor and environmental standards, competition policy, and so on. Put together with the exclusion of trade remedies and agricultural subsidies from the remit of negotiations, the cursory attention paid to special and differential treatment for smaller and poorer economies, and the routine "carving out" of sectors deemed "sensitive" by the United States (and usually of profound importance for trade partners in Latin America and the Caribbean), the characteristics of U.S. trade strategies have been seen to add up to an agenda which is prejudicial to the development prospects of the region and designed to serve a set of distinctively U.S. priorities. The degrees of dependence on the U.S. market that obtain in the vast majority of the countries of the region, coupled with the challenges posed by the emergence of China to Latin American exports in the U.S. market, have ensured that in most cases this reaction has not translated into a rejection of trade relations or new trade agreements with the United States—indeed, as we have seen, quite the opposite has occurred, except in countries such as Brazil and Venezuela. Yet the legitimacy of the U.S. trade agenda and the manner in which the U.S. government has pursued it have been called fundamentally into question, particularly as dimensions and indicators of its overall strategy for maintaining primacy in the region, and certainly popular forms of contestation and resistance have been increasingly notable features of the landscape of trade politics. The domestic rejection of free trade agreements evident in the problems associated with their ratification, as in Central America, is noteworthy as a dimension of a broader reaction against the U.S. economic and trade agenda in the region.

The third form that the erosion of legitimacy has taken, which needs only brief mention, is that of a cruder variety of anti-Americanism, the trade agenda providing a useful focal point but not necessarily the crux of the political issue at stake.

In this way, it is the broad erosion of the legitimacy of U.S. hegemony, as it is expressed through both the neoliberal project and particular economic and trade strategies, that forms the foundation of the regional politics which have acted to limit the agential power of the United States in the Americas. Notwithstanding continuing forms of dependence on the United States, increasingly strident ideological and political challenges in Latin America and the Caribbean have permeated the politics of both hemispheric and bilateral trade, to the extent that the United States has been quite strikingly constrained in its ability to secure its preferred outcomes in trade negotiations.

Conclusions

Mainstream debates about U.S. power understand it essentially as an "input" in world and regional politics. Hegemony, in the bulk of IR and IPE debates, is taken largely as a given, whether referring to structural or relational power, and the only task is apparently to measure it and establish whether it is declining in either absolute or relative terms. What I have tried to suggest here is that we need to focus not on the amount of U.S. power and not on hegemony as an "input" or "public good" in the global political economy, but rather on the ways in which the *nature* of U.S. power is forged by politics and political interactions, at the domestic (U.S.), regional and global levels (although the latter has not been the focus here). In other words, the appropriate debate about U.S. power (or hegemony) is not a debate about resources or attributes, but rather a debate about *politics* and the way that hegemony is constituted and shaped both domestically and regionally or globally. This point about politics is not trivial—in fact, it suggests a very different approach to understanding power and hegemony from the one which currently prevails, which not only focuses on hegemony as an attribute of a given state and as an input in world or regional politics, but is also characterized by a curious "apoliticism." Part of the problem here is that U.S. hegemony is habitually analyzed in a manner consistent with wider trends in U.S. social sciences, which Anatol Lieven has identified as "increasing isolationism, determinism and dogmatism" associated with dominance of rational choice models (Lieven, 2004: 66). U.S. hegemony is conceived essentially in isolation from the rest of the world (the notion of hegemony as an "input" in world politics) and as existing curiously independently of any form of constitution by domestic political economy. Furthermore, when, in a theoretical sense, politics *have* been injected more centrally into the analysis, the tendency has been again to conceptualize politics distinctively as domestic politics, as in the work, mentioned earlier of Krasner, Goldstein, Gowa, Katzenstein, and others. The notion of U.S. power as an input into world politics thus remains essentially intact— U.S. power is shaped and constituted by *domestic* politics and then projected outwards.

This emphasis on the political constitution of power in the domestic, regional and global contexts is central to explanation of the structural/ agential disjuncture, both in general and in trade politics. Linking to the core issue of the legitimacy of U.S. power and fracturing of "consensus" or "soft power" in the trade arena, the argument here has been that it is the nature of both domestic politics and an emerging regional politics of trade that have complicated the effective, agential, mobilization of the structural power that the United States possesses in the regional political economy and in the arena of trade more specifically. Furthermore, consistent with this line of argument, bilateralism may be seen as a response to the consequent limitations of U.S. agential power and the underlying weaknesses of U.S. power in general terms, not a reflection of unprecedented strength, as is assumed in much of the over-excited analysis of contemporary U.S. power.

In this light, then, our discussion of trade in the Americas has revealed an arena which is increasingly dominated by a U.S. political landscape that is more hostile to new trade agreements than it has been for some time, particularly to those which are perceived to carry implications for the US labor market. At the same time, there are considerable political constraints on, and opposition to, the trade agenda in other parts of the region, emerging in the main from a larger and more fundamental rejection of both neoliberalism and the forms of U.S. power that are put to the service of its regional entrenchment. These trends, and their reinforcing consequences for the core disjuncture between the structural and agential power of the United States, seem set to become much more central to both the regional political economy and the arena of trade within it.

Notes

I would like to thank the participants at the conference at the LSE in mid-2006, from which this volume arises, for their reactions and comments on the preliminary draft of this paper, along with the editors of this volume for their very helpful suggestions.

1. The issue of "leverage" and mechanisms for achieving it permeated extensive discussions and interviews concerning foreign economic policy with U.S. government officials, representatives of congressional offices and committees, trade policy makers, representatives of key state agencies, representatives of business and labor organizations, and others. All interviews to which I refer in this chapter were conducted in Washington, DC, during September and October 2004, and all were conducted on a "not for attribution" basis.
2. This section borrows from Phillips (2007b).
3. There is clear evidence that the administration miscalculated how vigorously the labor movement would oppose DR-CAFTA and was taken by surprise by the extent of difficulty encountered in the ratification process. Author's interviews.
4. This emphasis on the inconsistency of U.S. policy and the greater space in the U.S. system for political "U-turns" has not gone unchallenged: G. John Ikenberry (1998/1999), for example, sees the transparency of the U.S. political system as acting to reduce surprises and allay concerns that partners may have about abrupt changes in policy.
5. The third layer of the interagency process is the National Economic Council, which is chaired by the president. For an overview, see http://www.ustr.gov/Who_We_Are/Mission_of_the_USTR.html; also Heunemann (2002: 67–73).
6. Interviews, representatives of congressional committees.
7. Interviews, members of Congress, representatives of business associations, and representatives of labor unions.
8. Interviews, representatives of the National Association of Manufacturers and representatives of various congressional offices.

References

Bergsten, C. F. (2002) "A Renaissance for U.S. Trade Policy?" *Foreign Affairs,* 81 (6): 86–98.
Bhagwati, J. (2004) "Don't Cry for Cancún," *Foreign Affairs,* 83 (1).

Cerny, P. G. (1989) "Political Entropy and American Decline," *Millennium: Journal of International Studies*, 18 (1): 47–63.

Cox, R. W. (2004) "Beyond Empire and Terror: Critical Reflections on the Political Economy of World Order," *New Political Economy*, 9 (3): 307–324.

Feinberg, R. E. (2003) "The Political Economy of United States' Free Trade Arrangements," *The World Economy*, 26 (7): 1019–1040.

Goldstein, J. (1986) "The Political Economy of Trade: Institutions of Protection," *American Political Science Review*, 80 (1): 161–184.

Gowa, J. (1988) "Public Goods and Political Institutions: Trade and Monetary Policy Processes in the United States," *International Organization*, 42 (1): 15–32.

Heunemann, J. E. (2002) "On the Trade Policy-Making Process in the United States," in Inter-American Development Bank (ed.) *The Trade Policy-Making Process: Level One of the Two Level Game: Country Studies in the Western Hemisphere*, INTAL-ITD-STA Occasional Paper 13, March.

Ikenberry, J. (1998/1999) "Institutions, Strategic Restraint, and the Persistence of American Postwar Order," *International Security* 23 (3): 43–78.

Ikenberry, J., D. A. Lake, and M. Mastanduno (eds.) (1988) *The State and American Foreign Policy*. Ithaca, NY: Cornell University Press.

Jenkins, R., E. D. Peters, and M. M. Moreira (January 18–19, 2006) "The Economic Impact of China on Latin America—An Agenda for Research," paper presented at the Seventh Annual Global Development Conference, pre-conference workshop on *Asian and Other Drivers of Global Change*, St Petersburg.

Katzenstein, P. J., ed. (1978) *Between Power and Plenty: Foreign Economic Policies of Advanced Industrialized States*. Madison: University of Wisconsin Press.

Krasner, S. D. (1977) "US Commercial and Monetary Policy: Unravelling the Paradox of External Strength and Internal Weakness," *International Organization*, 31 (4): 635–671.

Lieven, A. (2004) *America Right or Wrong: An Anatomy of American Nationalism*. London: HarperCollins, 2004.

Luck, E. C. (1999) *Mixed Messages: American Politics and International Organization, 1919–1999*. Washington, DC: Brookings Institution Press.

Muñoz, H. (2001) "Good-Bye USA?" in Joseph S. Tulchin and Ralph H. Espach (eds.) *Latin America in the New International System*. Boulder, CO: Lynne Rienner.

Office of the United States Trade Representative (2004) *2003 Annual Report and 2004 Trade Policy Agenda of the President of the United States on the Trade Agreements Program*. Washington, DC: USTR.

Phillips, N. (2005) "US Power and the Politics of Economic Governance in the Americas," *Latin American Politics and Society*, 44 (4): 1–25.

Phillips, N. (2007a) "Consequences of an Emerging China: Is Development Space Disappearing for Latin America and the Caribbean?" Centre for International Governance Innovation (CIGI), working paper no. 14, January.

—— (2007b) "The Limits of 'Securitization': Power, Politics and Process in US Foreign Economic Policy," *Government and Opposition*, 42 (2): 181–212.

Strange, S. (1987) *States and Markets*. London: Pinter.

Tussie, D. (1998) "Multilateralism Revisited in a Globalizing World Economy," *Mershon International Studies Review*, 42: 183–193.

U.S. House of Representatives, Committee on Ways and Means (March 29, 2001) *Free Trade Deals: Is the United States Losing Ground as Its Trade Partners Move Ahead?*, Hearing before the Subcommittee on Trade of the House Committee on Ways and Means, 107th Congress, first session (transcript).

U.S. Senate, Committee on Finance (March 9, 2004) *The Administration's International Trade Agenda, Hearing before the Committee on Finance of the United States Senate, 108th Congress, second session*, (transcript).

VanGrasstek, C. (2000) "US Plans for a New WTO Round: Negotiating More Agreements with Less Authority," *The World Economy*, 23 (5): 673–700.

Zoellick, R. B. (September 24, 2001) "American Trade Leadership: What Is at Stake?" Speech to the Institute for International Economics, Washington, DC.

—— (2002) "Trading in Freedom: The New Endeavour of the Americas," *Economic Perspectives: An Electronic Journal of the U.S. Department of State*, 7 (3).

—— (September 22, 2003a) "America Will Not Wait for the Won't-Do Countries," *Financial Times*.

—— (July 10, 2003b) "Our Credo: Free Trade and Competition," *Wall Street Journal*.

Zysman, J. (1983) *Governments, Markets, and Growth: Financial Systems and the Politics of Industrial Change*. Ithaca, NY: Cornell University Press.

Chapter 7

State and Society: The Political Economy of DR-CAFTA in Costa Rica, the Dominican Republic, and El Salvador

Diego Sánchez-Ancochea

Following the steps of its Northern neighbor, Central America has increased its integration with the U.S. economy by signing the Dominican Republic-Central America Free Trade Agreement (DR-CAFTA).[1] With the agreement, the Central American countries aim to respond to the increasing competitive threat from China and other Asian countries by locking in their preferential market access to the United States. They also expect to expand their exports to the United States, receive new foreign direct investment (FDI) inflows, and make state institutions more transparent.

The agreement was enthusiastically supported by all governments in the region, but has later followed different paths in each of the countries. While El Salvador introduced the required reforms before schedule, in the Dominican Republic key reforms were only implemented in November 2006 and in Costa Rica the agreement was not approved until a referendum in October 2007.

This chapter explores the meaning of DR-CAFTA in light of the profound changes in the region in the last two decades. It also explains different responses to the agreement by focusing on the changing pattern of state-society relations in Costa Rica, the Dominican Republic and El Salvador. The chapter makes two basic claims. First, DR-CAFTA should be primarily understood as deepening and "locking in" the neoliberal model that has been dominant in the region since the mid-1980s. By furthering the process of trade liberalization, increasing protection of foreign investors, expanding the economic links with the United

States and reducing the policy space available to promote capacity-enhancing development strategies (see Abugattas and Paus, this volume), DR-CAFTA will reinforce some of the key changes that all countries have experienced since the mid-1980s. The treaty will likely result in further concentration and transnationalization of capital and the weakening of the state as employer and promoter of equitable development. Central America's support of the agreement should thus be seen as a new step in the neoliberal project that all governments have been following.

Second, the specific characteristics of state-society relations and their evolution over time go a long way in explaining country differences in the political dynamics of regional integration with the United States. While all countries face similar external constraints and are equally dependent on the U.S. market, differences in long term policies and class relations have determined different responses. The difficulties to approve the agreement in Costa Rica are the result of the opposition from social movements and trade unions, who are stronger than in the rest of the region. These groups fear that an unequal new economic model (NEM) is rapidly replacing the successful social-democratic consensus that characterized Costa Rica's development during the 1960s and 1970s. El Salvador's rapid approval of DR-CAFTA is the natural corollary of the political and economic dominance of a small elite, that is increasingly dependent on the United States. In the Dominican Republic, the treaty has been enthusiastically supported by domestic exporters from the export processing zones (EPZs), but not as much by traditional business groups who still depend on the domestic market and the support of the state for their success.

Three caveats should be made before concluding this introduction. The chapter concentrates on the macro-patterns of state-society relations, paying relatively little attention to the way they play out in the political arena (i.e., in the national legislatures and in the interaction between political parties). In many ways, this is a reductionist approach, since class interests and demands do not have automatic translations into specific positions in political discussions. The policy process is always more complicated and generates unexpected alliances. Yet identifying the structural patterns of state-society relations remains useful. Doing so provides a general background for the daily, more problematic interaction between politicians and various economic actors.

The chapter will discuss general trends in Central America but will make no specific reference to the cases of Guatemala, Honduras, and Nicaragua. The addition of each of these countries would offer a richer picture of the political dynamics within the region, but would not alter the main arguments in any significant way. In Guatemala, Honduras, and Nicaragua, social movements and trade unions are relatively weak and domestic capital is highly influential and dependent on the U.S. market. Despite differences in patterns of state-society relations, the three countries are thus more similar to El Salvador than to Costa Rica and the Dominican Republic. Not surprisingly, DR-CAFTA had entered into force in all three by the middle of 2006.[2]

The discussion concentrates on explaining differences in the process of approval of DR-CAFTA. Yet at the end even Costa Ricans supported the agreement. The most relevant question is then whether the three countries will experience convergence to similar economic models with similar patterns of state-society relations. In the conclusion I offer some preliminary reflections on this matter. I will suggest that differences between the three countries are likely to diminish over time, unless Costa Ricans are able to recuperate their historical ability to build effective consensus.

The chapter is divided into five sections. It starts with an explanation of the main characteristics of the agreement. The next section places DR-CAFTA within the recent changes in the region and shows how it will consolidate trends that began in the late 1980s. The fourth section illustrates the differences between Costa Rica, the Dominican Republic and El Salvador in the implementation of the NEM, explaining them in terms of asymmetric state-society relations. The fifth section will use the same independent variable to explain the reasons behind different responses to the project of economic integration with the United States. The chapter finishes with some reflections on the likely impact of DR-CAFTA in state-society relations and the economic model in the long run.

The Meaning of Regional Integration with the United States within the Central American Context

As Shadlen (2005) argues and the introductory chapters to this volume further develops, regional and bilateral trade agreements (RBTAs) between the United States and various Latin American countries imply a basic economic bargain. The United States offers preferential access to its large domestic market in exchange for an opening of the agricultural sector and the introduction of significant institutional reforms in areas such as government procurements and intellectual property rights.[3] RBTAs are thus a costly way of securing high exports to the U.S. market and promoting an expansion of foreign direct investment.

In Central America's case, DR-CAFTA will primarily institutionalize the unilateral trade incentives granted in the Caribbean Basin Recovery Act (CBRA) of 1983, which was part of the broader Caribbean Basin Initiative (CBI). The CBRA established duty free access to the U.S. market to numerous goods, including electronic assembly, handicrafts, wood products, fresh and frozen seafood, tropical fruit and ornamental horticulture. The main condition that the CBRA imposed was that 35 percent of the total value added of exports was generated in the Caribbean Basin.

The CBRA explicitly excluded most textiles and footwear from the list of beneficiary articles. Textile assembled for export into the U.S. market, however, had benefited from a special access clause since the early 1960s.[4] Provision 807 was aimed at increasing the competitiveness of the U.S. clothing sector by facilitating the creation of assembly operations abroad (Mortimore and Zamora, 1998). The provision established that all apparel assembled from U.S.-formed and -cut textiles would only have to pay duties for the value added generated outside the United States. In 1986 the CBI textile program further facilitated the access of textiles assembled in Central America and the Caribbean by eliminating most quotas applicable to the countries in the region (Kaplinsky, 1993). In 2000 the United States finally passed a provision that gave apparel exports from countries in the CBI similar treatment to Mexico under the North American Free Trade Agreement (NAFTA). The new provision expanded the amount of duty-free activities that these countries could perform, including cutting United States made fabric. The 2000 provision also allowed countries to export a limited amount of items made from knit fabric produced in the domestic economy with U.S. yarn (World Bank, 2006).

In addition to locking in preferential access, with DR-CAFTA the U.S. government will have to liberalize the few sectors (with the exception of sugar) that did not have zero tariffs. The United States will also adopt regional rules of origin, which imply that all the inputs produced in the region are exempted from tariffs. In the specific case of apparel, the new rules of origin will allow Central American countries to use cloth and other inputs produced in Mexico, Canada and within their own countries, without being penalized for it.

In exchange for these benefits, Central America will gradually eliminate all restrictions to U.S. imports of goods and services. In the case of agricultural goods, tariffs will be progressively reduced in periods of five to twenty years. Only a few sensible products like potatoes and onions in Costa Rica and corn in the rest of the countries will remain protected. In the case of manufacturing goods, the process of liberalization will be faster: 80 percent of the goods will have a zero tariff immediately and only 4 percent will benefit from long transition periods of 12 to 15 years.

DR-CAFTA will also institutionalize and deepen other nontrade related reforms with the aim of securing a favourable and stable regulatory environment for foreign firms:

- The agreement eliminates all norms and regulations that discriminate against firms from other member countries, thus prohibiting the establishment of conditions in areas like local content and technology transfers. The agreement goes further than the World Trade Organization regime in this area because it is applied to all laws and not just to trade-related ones and affects both goods and services;

- It requires the liberalization of most services, including banking and finances, telecommunications and insurance (the last two particularly important in the Costa Rican case);
- It further strengthens protection of intellectual property rights. DR-CAFTA requires member countries to sign all agreements in this area (including those related with the management of biodiversity). It also extends the duration of patents and copyrights, as well as the period of confidentiality of data used in applications for marketing authority of medicines and other chemicals. End user piracy will also be criminalized and governments are expected to improve enforcement of all their laws in this area;
- Creation of a more transparent system of government procurement, requiring a tendering process for large contracts and eliminating the possibility of discriminating in favour of domestic firms;
- Creation of a system of international arbitration in case of conflicts between a firm from a member country and a government. Following NAFTA's Chapter 11, foreign firms can resort directly to an arbitrator if they believe that their interests have been harmed in any way (see Van Harten, this volume);
- Commitment by all participants to maintain and protect all labor and environmental laws that already exist at the time of signing the agreement.

DR-CAFTA and the Consolidation of the NEM in the Region

The signing of DR-CAFTA comes in the midst of a dramatic transformation in the region. Starting in the early 1980s and accelerating in the 1990s, Central America has witnessed the consolidation of a NEM based on neoliberal principles. In addition to implementing standard measures of liberalization, deregulation and privatization, Central American countries focused on the creation of EPZs to promote new exports. Export expansion was facilitated by preferential access to the United States.

The NEM has resulted in similar changes in the structure of production and exports in the three countries under consideration. More importantly for the current discussion, it has also triggered similar alternations in the characteristics of the private sector—including growing concentration and transnationalization of capital—and in the influence of the state in the economy. These changes in the class and institutional structures partly explain why all countries embraced DR-CAFTA enthusiastically as a tool to consolidate and strengthen the new model.

The Components of the NEM in Central America

The implementation of the NEM in Central America, like in the rest of Latin America, was driven by the diffusion of the Washington Consensus. The new policy package had three dominant pillars:

- Liberalization of the trade and capital accounts. Starting at different times and moving at different speeds, all countries in Central America eliminated non-tariff protection measures like quotas and reduced their tariffs. Of the three countries discussed in this chapter, Costa Rica was the first to begin the process of trade liberalization in the second half of the 1980s. According to Herrera (1992), the result of this measure was a reduction in the average tariff rate from 27 percent in 1986 to 19.7 percent in 1990 and in the standard deviation from 24.4 to 16.5 percent at the end of the period (cited in Lizano, 1999: 77). Trade liberalization did not start in the Dominican Republic and El Salvador until the 1990s, but then accelerated to reach similarly low tariff levels.
- Domestic deregulation, particularly in the financial sector. In Costa Rica, the banking sector was opened to private banks, while in El Salvador the banks that had been nationalized during the early 1980s went back to private hands. In all three countries, financial repression and other types of intervention were eliminated and universal banking promoted.
- Privatization of key public corporations and reduction in the state's involvement in the economy. Costa Rica began earlier this process, with the privatization of the Costa Rican Corporation for Development (CODESA), a conglomerate of industrial firms, and the freeze in public employment. The Dominican Republic and El Salvador did not start their privatization program until the second half of the 1990s, but proceeded more radically. Privatization was particularly intense in El Salvador with the selling of the only telecommunication company, the privatization of the electricity and banking sectors and the reduction in the state's involvement in other areas.

The process of neoliberal transformation in Central America had some regional particularities as a result of the geopolitical relevance of the Isthmus during the 1980s. The region received ample support from the United States through the CBI. The objective of this program was the conversion of these economies into export platforms of labor intensive manufactures to the United States, thus helping U.S. firms to reduce costs simultaneously.

The creation of new comparative advantage in light manufactures was further enhanced by the creation of EPZs. Within the region, the regime was first introduced in the Dominican Republic in 1969 and expanded rapidly during the late 1980s and 1990s. The EPZ regime involved generous tax incentives as well as duty-free imports of inputs and capital goods to all goods produced in the industrial zones and exported to the rest of the world.

Economic Consequences of the NEM

The new policy package triggered significant changes in the economic structure and in the way the region is inserted in the global economy. Both the promotion of EPZs and the preferential access to the U.S. market contributed to the creation of new comparative advantages in manufacturing exports. The EPZs grew rapidly during the 1990s: between 1993 and 2004, exports from the export processing zones grew by an annual average of 17 percent in Costa Rica, 18 percent in El Salvador and 4 percent in the Dominican Republic, where the expansion had began earlier. As a result, the share of exports from EPZs (which concentrate on light manufacturing) in total exports also grew significantly: in El Salvador, the contribution of EPZs to total exports went from 28.1 percent in 1993 to 55.3 percent in 2004 (table 7.1). The expansion of EPZs also had positive consequences on employment. In 2000 the export processing zones provided employment to nearly 50,000 workers in El Salvador and 34,000 in Costa Rica. In the Dominican Republic, employment in the free trade zones multiplied by more than ten in the period 1980–2002, going from 16,400 to 170,883.

Table 7.1 Exports from EPZs as Percentage of Total, 1993–2004

	Costa Rica	Dominican Republic	El Salvador
1993	26.0	84.1	28.1
1994	19.8	81.3	34.4
1995	13.6	76.9	39.2
1996	10.0	76.7	42.7
1997	31.2	78.0	43.3
1998	25.7	82.3	48.3
1999	22.8	84.3	52.6
2000	29.7	83.2	54.3
2001	39.1	84.9	57.1
2002	39.6	83.9	58.2
2003	37.0	80.9	59.5
2004	43.3	78.5	55.3

Source: Author's calculations using data from the Economic Intelligence Unit.

This move away from primary exports toward light manufactures produced in EPZs was one of the central characteristics of the new insertion of Central America in the global economy. A second important feature of the new Central American model was the increasing dependence on remittances from abroad.[5] Table 7.2 reflects remittances in absolute values and as a percentage of exports of goods. Between 1997 and 2005, remittances grew from US$1,088 million in the Dominican Republic and US$1,200 million in El Salvador to US$2,410 million and US$2,830 million respectively; the latest amount represents 40 percent of total exports in the Dominican Republic and an astonishing 83 percent in the Salvadorian case. This large expansion is the result of the growth of migrants from the Dominican Republic and El Salvador to the United States (and some European countries) during the 1980s and 1990s. The number of people born in the Dominican Republic and living in the United States, for example, doubled between 1980 and 1990 and again from 1990 to 2000, going from 169,000 people in 1980 to 688,000 in 2000.[6] Costa Rica is an exception in this area as it is a net receptor of migrants and receives a negligible volume of remittances.

Central America is no longer predominantly rural, as the importance of the agricultural sector slowly decreased. As table 7.3 shows, a common trend in the three countries since the early 1980s has been the reduction in the share of the primary sector in gross domestic product (GDP). As a result, agriculture represented less than 12 percent of GDP in 2005.

Table 7.2   Remittances from Abroad (US$ Millions and Percentage of Merchandise Exports), 1997–2005

	DR		El Salvador	
	Total	% of exports	Total	% of exports
1997	1088.9	23.6	1199.5	49.4
1998	1326.0	26.6	1373.8	56.3
1999	1518.7	29.6	1373.8	54.7
2000	1689.0	29.4	1750.7	59.5
2001	1807.8	34.3	1910.5	66.7
2002	1959.6	37.9	1935.2	64.6
2003	2060.5	37.7	2105.3	67.3
2004	2230.2	37.6	2547.6	77.2
2005	2410.7	39.3	2830.2	83.5

Source: Banco de Reservas del Salvador (http://www.bcr.gob.sv/estadisticas/se_remesas.html, accessed September 15, 2006) and Banco Central de la Republica Dominicana (http://www.bancentral.gov.do/estadisticas_economicas/sector_externo/remesas.xls, accessed September 15, 2006).

Table 7.3   GDP in Constant Local Currencies per Sector (Percentage of the Total), 1980–2005

	Costa Rica			Dominican Republic			El Salvador		
	A	M	S	A	M	S	A	M	S
1980	13.1	21.7	65.1	16.4	22.7	61.0	19.0	23.2	57.9
1985	12.7	22.4	64.8	16.3	21.0	62.7	18.6	21.0	60.4
1990	12.9	22.8	64.3	13.4	21.2	65.3	16.5	22.6	60.9
1995	12.7	23.3	64.0	12.6	20.9	66.5	13.6	21.6	64.8
2000	11.7	26.3	62.0	11.2	18.7	70.1	12.3	23.0	64.7
2005	10.4	25.6	63.9	11.5	16.3	72.2	11.8	23.5	64.6

Notes: A = agriculture, M = manufacturing and mining, S = services.
Source: For Costa Rica, Instituto de Investigaciones en Ciencias Económicas (UCR) and Banco Central de Costa Rica (http://indicadoreseconomicos.bccr.fi.cr/indicadoreseconomicos, accessed ¿September 16, 2006). For the DR, Banco Central de la Republica Dominicana (http://www.bancentral.gov.do/estadisticas.asp?a=Sector_Real, accessed September 17, 2006). For El Salvador, Segovia (2002) and Banco de Reservas de El Salvador (http://www.bcr.gob.sv/estadisticas/sr_produccion.html, accessed September 17, 2006).

The main beneficiary of the NEM has been the service sector with a growing share of GDP in all countries with the exception of Costa Rica. The growth of transport and communications, trade, tourism and finance has been substantial in all countries; in the Dominican Republic it has gone together with an expansion of construction. Costa Rica's exceptionality comes from the expansion of the manufacturing sector, which has grown as a result of the attraction of high tech foreign investment as well as the success of large firms in the regional market.

New State-Society Relations: Concentration, Transnationalization, and the Weakening of the Activist State

Behind changes in the structure of production and exports lay significant alterations in the characteristics of the private sector and in the role of the state. These changes contribute to explain the evolution of income distribution and other variables. They can also help to predict the likely evolution of the political economic structure in the long run.

One of the most evident effects is the increasing concentration of economic power among a relatively small number of large family groups. Measuring capital concentration in the contexts of small, developing countries is nearly impossible as statistics on primary distribution of income are scarce and public companies practically non-existent. Household surveys on income distribution are not particularly useful either, as they notoriously understate the income share of the rich. Therefore, it becomes necessary to rely on specific examples to illustrate the importance and diversification of large firms (see, in particular, Robinson, 2003; Sánchez-Ancochea, 2005; Segovia, 2005; and Sojo, 1995).

Segovia (2005) identifies some of the largest groups in each of the Central American countries (including Panama but not the Dominican Republic) and follows its strategy of diversification and regional expansion. Ten of the twenty-eight groups he identifies come from El Salvador. It is, for example, the case of the Grupo Poma with interests in real estate, tourism, automobile imports and distribution, banking, manufacturing and other services; Grupo Taca (familia Kriete), who owns the main regional airline and has also interests in tourism, banking and agro-industry, and Grupo Siman (storage, real estate, construction, banks, and apparel production).

In Segovia's account of the regional groups, there are only four Costa Rican groups, one of which is a cooperative. The list includes the owner of the main newspaper and a media emporium (La Nacion), whose main shareholders also have a majority stake in the main producer of beer, water and juices; one of the largest manufacturing groups (Durman Esquivel), as well as the owner of the largest supermarkets, Supermercados Unidos, which also has agro-business interests.

Sánchez-Ancochea (2005) presents similar findings for the case of Costa Rica and also discusses the Dominican experience. Based on some quantitative analysis of the firms in Costa Rican stock market, secondary sources and interviews with managers from large firms, the study concludes that in both Costa Rica and the Dominican Republic domestic capital became increasingly concentrated and linked to transnational corporations (TNCs), while financial capital increased its economic and political influence. In the Dominican Republic, the study identifies ten large groups with interest in banking, media and other services and, in some cases, manufactures as well. The group Corripio, one of the largest and most successful, constitutes an illustrative example of the effect of the neoliberal model in large Dominican groups. This economic group began operating in the 1930s and expanded successfully for several decades, becoming a small emporium with interests in many industrial businesses. During the 1980s and 1990s the growth of the group and its expansion into new sectors accelerated. Between 1997 and 2002 the number of Corripio's employees increased from 5,600 to 7,100. At the beginning of the current decade, the company owned the morning daily Hoy, the evening daily *El Nacional*, the free newspaper *El Día*, the magazine *Ahora*, several television channels (including Teleantillas and Channels 2, 11, and 30) as well as the editing company Editora Corripio.

It also expanded its involvement in the industrial sector with the creation of a joint venture to produce concrete and another to produce PVC products.

At the same time as Central American domestic groups became larger and more influential, they strengthened their links to TNCs as subordinate but important partners. The ways in which this relationship has been organized has varied. In the maquila sector, a significant number of domestic producers have become suppliers of large foreign apparel companies and department stores. While many of these producers are relatively small and have struggled to compete, a selected number of domestic capitalists in the maquilas have become the new business elite in Central America. As we will see in the next section, this has been particularly the case in the Dominican Republic, but there are also some examples in El Salvador and Honduras.

Traditional domestic groups have built different ties with TNCs. In many cases, they have become importers, representing some of the largest global brands within the country. MercaSID, the largest Dominican agro-business group, combines domestic production of juices, water, butter, oil, and many other food products with the representation of many of the largest global food companies such as Haagen Daas, Danone, or Kellogs. Other large groups like Corripio and Leon Jimenes are also some of the largest importers in the country. In Costa Rica, Supermercados Unidos is both one the largest supermarkets, an important agro-business producer and one of the largest importers.

The creation of joint ventures with foreign capitalists and the sale of a minority stake in their companies is the third way in which large domestic groups have built links with TNCs. These types of collaboration show the dependent character of domestic firms in Central America, yet, they also demonstrate that domestic partners have been fundamental for TNCs. They help them to secure political contacts, distribution networks and provide them with knowledge of the domestic market.

The strengthening of large domestic groups with growing ties with TNCs has coincided with a weakening of the influence of the state in the economy. As expected, neoliberal reforms reduced the capacity of the public sector to influence production directly, as protection went down and subsidies were lowered. While the state is still influential in securing new areas of accumulation for the private sector (Segovia, 2004a), it can no longer favor specific sectors through the adjustment of tariffs or the concession of loans at favorable rates.

The weakening of the state has been evident in other areas as well. The increasing emphasis on macroeconomic stability and low fiscal deficits severely constrained the role of the public sector as employer. The contrast with the previous period was particularly striking in Costa Rica, where the public sector had been one of the drivers of job creation during the 1970s. The debt crisis of the early 1980s, which affected Costa Rica earlier than any other country, modified this trend sharply; public employment was frozen at around 155,000 employees and decreased from 19.1 percent in 1985 to 15.9 percent in 1991 as percentage of total employment. In 2005, public employment represented 14.2 percent of the total.

State institutions remained weak and relatively little efforts have been made to increase the capacity of the bureaucracy. In the Dominican Republic, for example, turnover in public employment has remained high and dependent on the political cycle. According to an incomplete census of public employment published in 1997, more than one fourth of the more than 300,000 workers employed by the Dominican government had been working in the public sector for less than a year and nearly half have been working for less than four years (ONE, 1997). At the same time, the influence of civil servants at the top of the public administration has decreased, even in Costa Rica, as the number and power of political appointees and outside advisers increased significantly during the 1990s (Sánchez-Ancochea, 2005).

It is in the contest of these characteristics of the NEM that DR-CAFTA should be analyzed. In many ways the agreement is no more than a consolidation of current economic trends and state-private sector interactions (Segovia, 2004b). By securing a TNC-friendly regulatory environment permanently and opening up the economy even more, it is likely to result in a growing transnationalization of the economy. By making preferential market access to the United States permanent, it will link Central America with that country even more. By introducing institutional reforms on government procurements, intellectual property rights and other areas, DR-CAFTA may further diminish the ability of the state to implement different kinds of interventionist policies (Sánchez, 2004).

State-Society Relations and Differences in the Implementation of the NEM

The previous section illustrated the extent of the socioeconomic changes that the neoliberal policy package triggered. The NEM altered the production structure of all Central American countries and led to similar changes in state-society relations, including the concentration and transnationalization of capital and a reduction in the influence of the state in the economy (Robinson, 2003). Despite these common trends, the region should not be treated as a monolithic whole. Neither policies nor outcomes have been the same in all Central American countries. Thus, for example, while Costa Rica has still not privatized its telecommunication and insurance sectors, El Salvador is at the forefront of neoliberal reforms in Latin America. Understanding these differences and identifying its causes is important in order to later explain different reactions to DR-CAFTA and forecast future development paths.

This section shows how the particularities of the NEM in each country can be explained by differences in the historical patterns of state-society relations and institutional development. While some of these differences have their roots several centuries back, I start the discussion in the late 1950s. In this period—when the importance of the urban sector grew and countries focused on production for the domestic market—new social coalitions emerged. They shaped the patterns of production and growth during two decades and influenced how each country reacted to the debt crisis and to the subsequent challenges of globalization.

Differences in Leading Coalitions under Import-Substituting Industrialization (ISI)

Table 7.4 summarizes the basic characteristics of the leading coalitions that shaped public policy and influenced economic performance in Costa Rica, the Dominican Republic, and El Salvador during the 1960s and 1970s. Costa Rica represented one of the most successful cases in the developing world in achieving economic growth combined with equity and formal democracy (Rovira, 2004). According to statistics from the World Bank, between 1965 and 1980, GDP per capita in constant U.S. dollars grew at an annual average of 3.3 percent compared to 3.0 percent in Latin America as a whole. The country used these growing resources

Table 7.4 Leading Coalitions and Development Outcomes, 1960s and 1970s

	Costa Rica	Dominican Republic	El Salvador
State-Society Relations	Broad leading coalition rule	Exclusive leading coalition (state-large family groups)	Authoritarian coalition army-agricultural oligarchy dominant, but weakened by ISI
Economic Performance	High economic growth with high social spending and increasing wages	High economic growth with low social spending and stagnant real wages	Moderate growth with low social spending and increasing instability

to expand social spending considerably: public spending in health, education and other social services as percentage of GDP increased from 8.7 percent in 1958 to 16.4 percent in 1971 and 23.6 percent in 1980. While it is harder to obtain indicators of income distribution, sustained growth of wages and low unemployment signal a positive outcome in this regard, reinforcing the social democratic model which underpinned political and economic stability.

The consolidation of a broad leading coalition, which included cooperatives, an active middle class and large capitalists, was behind these positive outcomes. The influence of all these groups took place directly, through their participation in the Council of Management of public institutions, and indirectly through the electoral process. Between 1950 and 1980, more than 200 new public institutions were created in diverse areas from transportation to social policy and industrial development. Most of these institutions were independent and had representatives from both business associations and trade unions.

The interactions between an expanding public sector and the increasing influence of public workers played a central role in the deepening of the Costa Rican social democratic model and the strengthening of a broad leading coalition. Higher government spending led to more public servants, who, in turn, demanded more public spending and (as part of the urban middle class) better public services. Between 1950 and 1980 the government was responsible for a large share of middle-class jobs: by 1980, for example, 75.4 percent of professionals and technicians worked in the state. Public employees represented at that time 25.9 percent of total wage earners (data from Rodríguez, 2004) and had higher levels of unionization than workers in the private sector. In the mid-1970s an estimated 43 percent of public sector employees were unionized, as opposed to only 5 percent of private sector workers (Rottenberg, 1993). Not surprisingly, the leading confederations of workers represented primarily the interests of civil servants.

The National Liberation Party (Partido Liberación Nacional, PLN) was also important in providing a political platform to the emerging leading coalition. It represented the interests of the new industrialists who benefited from the protection of the state and also of the urban middle class who demanded the expansion of the public sector (Rossenberg, 1993; Rovira, 2000). Due to the support of these different groups, the PLN became the dominant force in Costa Rica's politics and shaped its particular welfare-oriented development model (Sánchez, 2004). Between 1949 and 1978, five of the eight administrations came from the PLN, which also maintained permanent control of the Legislative Assembly since 1953.

The Dominican Republic experienced even higher rates of growth than Costa Rica during this period. Between 1965 and 1980, GDP per capita in constant U.S. dollars more than doubled, growing at an annual average of 4.7 percent. The fruits of economic growth, however, were distributed differently than in Costa Rica with public social spending and real wages growing less than profits. Public social investment, stagnated between 1966 and 1980 at levels below 6 percent of GDP, while average real wages grew slowly and minimum real wages actually decreased (Lozano, 2001).[7]

Behind the Dominican model of unequal growth lied a particular alliance between the Balaguer administration and a small number of family business groups from Santo Domingo and, to a lesser extent, from Santiago de los Caballeros. Between 1966 and 1978, Balaguer promoted the growth of these new groups, making the expansion of profits the primary objective of economic policy. High investment in infrastructure, protection of the domestic market and a systematic policy of wage repression contributed to accelerate profits and sustained a high level of economic growth. The relationship between his administration and the new industrialists was based on personal contacts and also on the lobbying of the Association of Industrialists (Moya Pons, 1992).[8]

The situation in El Salvador during this period was much more complex. In many ways, the country became the best example of what Bulmer-Thomas (1987) has called "the hybrid model": regionally-based import substitution industrialization took place on top of and delinked from agricultural development. The traditional oligarchy maintained its influence on economic policy, preventing the exchange rate and relative prices from moving against primary products. The hegemonic position of the army in the political arena was not questioned either. Between 1961 and 1979 the party of the military, the National Conciliation Party, remained in power as a result of repression of the political opposition and of electoral fraud. Yet, the basic oligarchic coalition became increasingly unsustainable, as the volatility of traditional export prices increased and new fractions with more interest in industrial development emerged within the elite (Acevedo, 1996; Segovia, 2002). They were more modern, less dependent on wage repression and unequal land distribution and more willing to support the liberalization of the political regime than the traditional agrarian elite (Paige, 1997).

The model was less successful than in the other two countries in terms of economic growth. As figure 7.1 illustrates, El Salvador had a sluggish performance during the second half of the 1960s and, despite accelerating growth in the early 1970s, was left behind when compared to Costa Rica and the Dominican Republic. In absolute terms, GDP per capita in constant U.S. dollars went from US$1,858 in 1965 to US$2,325 in

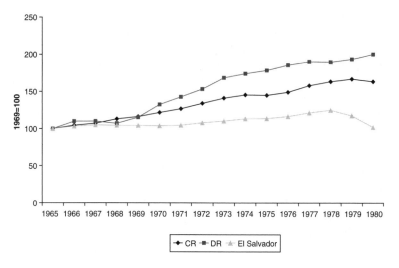

Figure 7.1 GDP per Capita (Constant U.S. Dollars of 2000), 1965–1980 (1965=100)

Source: World Bank. World Development Indicators electronic database (accessed September 1, 2007).

1978, while in Costa Rica it grew from 1,971 to 3,235 and in the Dominican Republic from 749 to 1,422 during the same period.

Economic growth thus could not compensate the unequal distribution of income in the same way as it did in the Dominican Republic. Inequality in the distribution of income and land became extremely high, further fuelling social tensions. According to data from Dunkerley (1991), by 1977 the richest 6 percent of the population had the same income than the poorest 63 percent. In the rural sector 41 percent of the families were landless and an additional 34 percent had less than 1 hectare. Urban workers were better paid and constituted an emerging, small middle class, but many were still unable to meet its basic needs. They became a major force for political and economic change, with its higher level of education and opportunities to organize and its desire for a more open political regime (Acevedo, 1996).

The comparative analysis of state-society relations during ISI has shown that there were significant differences between Costa Rica, the Dominican Republic and El Salvador, many of which emerged during this period. In Costa Rica, a broad and stable leading coalition contributed to high social spending, a relatively equal distribution of income and high rates of economic growth (by regional standards). In the Dominican Republic, an exclusive coalition between the Balaguer administration and large economic groups generated high economic group together with high inequality and low social spending. In El Salvador, a traditional oligarchic coalition between the army and agriculture landowners, while still dominant, was slowly eroded. Economic growth was low and social instability mounted.

The Impact of the Debt Crisis and the NEM, 1980–2005

A key argument of this chapter is that the differences in the leading coalitions just described are essential to understand the diversity in responding to the debt crisis of the 1980s, the changing global environment of the 1990s and the approval of DR-CAFTA. Let's now review the evolution of each of the countries since 1980 to illustrate this causal link.

In El Salvador, the economic crisis of 1979, when GDP per capita in constant U.S. dollars decreased by 13 percent, was the ultimate trigger of a latent social conflict caused by inequality in the distribution of income and wealth, increasing population density and a violent military dictatorship. In October 1978, a relatively progressive segment of the military organized a coup d'etat against the more conservative Romero administration. The new government, however, failed to restructure the economy and reduce political tensions. By mid-1980 all the leftist opposition movements united around the Farabundo Marti National Liberation Front (Frente Farabundo Marti para la Liberación Nacional, FMLN). In January 1981, the FMLN launched a military offensive, resulting in the beginning of a bloody civil war (Acevedo, 1996; Dunkerley, 1991).

In parallel to the civil war, a less dramatic struggle took place within the Salvadorian economic and political elite to decide the best way to transform the economy. Segovia (2002) shows how the conflict between reformists and neoliberal factions of the elite emerged and evolved over time. The Christian-Democrat Party (in power from 1980 to 1982 and again in 1984) initially proposed a communitarian model with pillars in state intervention and the growth of cooperatives. By 1984 its position had evolved towards the defence of a social market model. Most of the large capitalists, together with the U. S. Agency of International Development (USAID), pressured the government for a Neoliberal agenda concentrated on liberalizing trade and promoting non-traditional exports.

A combination of factors resulted in the consolidation of the radical neoliberal model during the 1990s. In 1989, Alfredo Cristiani, the candidate of the right wing Republican Nationalist Alliance (Alianza Republicana Nacionalista, ARENA) won the presidential elections. During the negotiation of the Peace Accords between the government and the left-wing opposition, the discussion concentrated on the consolidation of democracy, with economic issues playing a secondary role.

With the traditional parties virtually disabled and the former guerrillas reorganizing as a political force and pushing for the consolidation of democracy, the Christiani administration faced virtually no opposition to its neoliberal approach. The lack of strong trade unions with the strategic capabilities and political strength to participate in policy debates also worked at the government advantage.

During the early 1990s a new consensus emerged within the economic elite regarding the role of the state in the economy. Led by capitalist groups with interests in new sectors like banking and maquilas, and facilitated by ARENA's political dominance, El Salvador consolidated a model based on a small state, large business groups and heavy dependence from the United States. The prominence of the remittances coming from the United States contributed to reduce the levels of poverty, but made the United States even more important and increased the influence of the banking sector (Segovia, 2002).

The Costa Rican experience offers a striking contrast to that of El Salvador. Costa Rica also implemented some neoliberal reforms since the mid-1980s with support from the World Bank and other international financial institutions. Yet, its pace was always slower, contradictory and incomplete. Costa Rica has simultaneously been a regional leader in the signing of preferential trade agreements and a reluctant privatizer. It has deregulated its financial sector substantially, but still maintains large public banks. The country has a larger welfare state and more equitable income distribution than the rest of the region, but it has experienced a notable growth in inequality in the last few years.

Costa Rica's contradictory record in the last two decades is a result of at least two factors: the elite's inability to build a dominant coalition in support of a free market model and the unequal character of many of the reforms implemented. By freezing public employment, reducing real wage growth and expanding political appointees, neoliberal reforms have weakened trade unions and reduced its involvement in policy design. At the same time, however, trade unions and other social movements still maintain some veto power. They have succeeded in mobilizing social opposition to key neoliberal proposals and in building stronger ties with other institutions like public universities and the Catholic Church. Together with the opposition Citizen's Action Party (Partido de Acción Ciudadana, PAC), they have also made alternative proposals for economic development in the country.

Costa Rica's social impasse has also become clear in the formal political arena.[9] Since 1994, the results of the Presidential elections have been increasingly close, culminating in 2006 with a practical tie between two candidates.[10] No party has been able to obtain a majority in the National Assembly either. The political stalemate, together with the traditional culture of consensus, has forced the successive administrations to adopt gradualist approaches that avoid radical changes and try to compensate the losers of economic interventions.

The failure to liberalize the telecommunication sector in 2000 represents the best illustration of the impasse in Costa Rican society. The reform of the telecommunication and electricity sectors had long been in the agenda of the two dominant parties, but real advances had never taken place. In March 2000, the PLN government finally sent a proposal to liberalize both sectors to Congress. The government aimed to modify the structure of the Costa Rican Institute of Electricity, the single provider of both services. In first reading the project had forty-five votes in favor and only ten against.

The project was enthusiastically supported by much of the Costa Rican elite, including the Union of Chambers (the peak employer organization), the Board of Directors of the Costa Rican export promotion agency, the Chambers of Industry and Trade as well as some of leading TNCs like Intel. A very significant share of the population led by trade unions did not share the same enthusiasm. Only three days after the approval of the law, massive street protests began, and two weeks later the government backed down and desisted from liberalizing the telecommunication sector.

In many ways the Dominican Republic represents a middle case between Costa Rica and El Salvador. In the Caribbean island, neoliberal reforms have taken place more gradually than in El Salvador. Yet, the reason has not been the existence of popular movements with informal political influence like in Costa Rica, but the combination of careful governments and divisions within the economic elite.

The most notable characteristic of the Dominican response to globalization has been the changes within the capitalist class. Traditional business groups oriented to the domestic market have remained influential in the economic and political arenas. During the 1990s, they used their influence on the state to set the pace of the liberalization agenda and broaden their economic interests into new sectors. These changes within the old economic elite have coincided with the emergence of a small number of powerful entrepreneurs in the EPZs (Schrank, 2005; UNDP, 2005). Companies like Grupo M, D'Clase Corporation and Interamericana Products have used their links to foreign clients (that provide them with know-how and capital) and generous tax incentives to expand and gain political influence.

The two groups at the top have different political interests. Traditional groups are still concentrated in the domestic market as producers and importers, demanding protection, some subsidies and an overvalued exchange rate. The new groups, however, are a result of globalization and have pressured for a more radical reform agenda. For a long time the existence of the EPZ regime, which promoted export expansion without affecting domestic producers, prevented any serious conflict between the two. Yet DR-CAFTA and other elements of the globalization agenda have made this equilibrium harder to sustain in more recent times.

Synthesis

Many critics of neoliberalism in Central America emphasize the convergence of all countries towards a similar model based on the growing strength of large domestic capitalists, their increasing dependence on TNCs and the lack of autonomy of the state (see, e.g., Robinson, 2003). This view is partly correct: there is little doubt that neoliberal globalization has resulted in dramatic shifts in Central America's political economy and that the alliance between TNCs and large domestic groups is real all over the region.

This section, however, has tried to show how differences in patterns of state-society relations developed during the ISI period have led to a variety of responses to the neoliberal project. In Costa Rica, the previous existence of a broad leading coalition has resulted in the slow and irregular implementation of the new policy package. Much of the political and economic elite have supported market-friendly reforms enthusiastically, but trade unions and social movements, while increasingly weak, have maintained some veto power.

In the Dominican Republic, the leading coalition between the state and traditional business groups remains influential, but has added the more dynamic group of domestic capitalists from the EPZs as new partner. As a result of tensions and interactions between the two segments of the domestic capitalist class, neoliberal reforms have been relatively rapid in some areas (e.g., privatization, external financial liberalization) but not in others. Finally, in El Salvador, the civil war and its aftermath resulted in the substitution of the exclusive coalition between the army and the traditional oligarchy for a new exclusive coalition led by the large domestic groups with interests in new sectors such as finance.

No Surprise: Different Responses to DR-CAFTA in Central America and the Caribbean

The differences in state-society relations discussed in the previous section are fundamental to understand why El Salvador embraced DR-CAFTA with enthusiasm, why the Dominican Republic approved it but has taken a long time in implementing some complementary reforms and why Costa Rica's Legislative Assembly failed to take a decision and the government opted for a referendum. In many ways, DR-CAFTA constitutes an excellent laboratory to observe how country-specific characteristics remain important to explain reactions to a changing environment. It also allows us to see how countries still maintain a certain level of autonomy in the global economy.

El Salvador lost little time in approving DR-CAFTA. Only seven months after the agreement was signed by all governments, it was approved by the National Assembly in December 2004. While the main opposition party, the leftist FMLN, was always against the treaty, DR-CAFTA was approved rapidly without much discussion or analysis. This step was followed by supplementary laws to secure that El Salvador met all the requirements and stipulations set in the agreement. All these new laws simply reinforced the neoliberal character of the Salvadorian model, which had been established long before.

The combination of strong domestic groups linked to the U.S. economy, an Executive committed to a free market model and weak social participation in policy making help to explain the rapid approval of DR-CAFTA in El Salvador. As we have previously discussed, a small number of economic groups has become particularly influential within the business sector, crowding out small and medium firms in the political process. These large groups no longer concentrate their interests in manufacturing production for the domestic market and primary exports, instead specializing in maquilas, trade, real state and banking. Of all these sectors, only the Salvadorian banks could be negatively affected by DR-CAFTA-led competition, but they succeeded in negotiating key benefits. They have been allowed, for example, to open subsidiaries in the United States, thus having the potential of profiting more than before from remittances.

While the opposition to DR-CAFTA in El Salvador is large among the general public, resistance has been disperse and relatively disorganized. Opposition in the streets was not significant until the treaty's entry into force in early 2006, and even then it only amounted to a few hundred people. Salvadorian universities are weak and did not have the resources and expertise to elaborate critical evaluations of the agreement. Trade unions and other social movements have also limited capabilities and have proven incapable of designing independent strategies or elaborating new models.

The weakness of the institutional structure, including a dysfunctional National Assembly, and the particularities of Salvadorian politics reinforced the outcome (Spalding, 2006). A highly polarized electorate with strong party identification makes the discussion of fundamental issues hard. ARENA had little incentive to negotiate, as most of its electorate was in favor of DR-CAFTA and little gains could be obtained from a more consensual approach.

The Dominican Republic represents again an intermediate case. The approval of DR-CAFTA has never been questioned: the Dominican Congress overwhelmingly voted in favour of the agreement in

September 2005 with only 2 opposing votes. DR-CAFTA, however, did not enter into force until March 2007 because the country was slow in completing all the supplementary reforms required.

This outcome reveals the relatively weak nature of the Dominican state as well as the fractured character of the Dominican elite. The Dominican Republic was slow in entering into negotiations with the United States. Only when it became clear that Central America would obtain preferential access to the United States did the Dominican government attempted to bandwagon into the negotiations. Despite benefiting from an excellent team of negotiators funded with resources from the Inter-American Development Bank, the Dominican Republic was ill equipped for the negotiation.[11] According to a business leader who was involved in the negotiation, the U.S. team often knew more about the Dominican economy than the government representatives themselves.[12] UNDP (2005) argues that there were not serious studies of the impact of DR-CAFTA and that the government made many mistakes during the process of negotiation.

The Dominican business elite was more divided than the Salvadorian counterpart with regard to the impact of DR-CAFTA. The emerging capitalists from the EPZs were the biggest supporters of the agreement because it would allow them to secure preferential access for their goods permanently and expand production into new tasks. The traditional family groups from Santo Domingo had a more ambivalent position. While acknowledging the importance of the U.S. market and the need to maintain export growth, they are also worried about their potential loss of market share in key sectors. This is the case, for example, of large agrobusiness producers that face growing competition, as well as that of large construction companies that will have more obstacles to obtain public contracts.[13]

Participation of other groups in the discussion was limited with no real social mobilization on the subject. Studies on the long term impact of DR-CAFTA are also scarce and the most influential have been prepared by international organizations (see UNDP, 2005; World Bank, 2005). At the same time, the government has been slow in preparing the required reforms and Congress in approving them. This is the result of institutional weakness, as well as the government's desire to adapt slowly to the changing environment and the lobbying of different business groups.

The reform of the system of public contracts and tenders constitutes a good illustration of the delays in implementing the supplementary reforms and the forces behind these delays. The Dominican government has traditionally used government procurements and public constructions to support the growth of specific Dominican firms. Legal controls were relatively weak and the tendering process, when implemented, lacked transparency. A Decree approved in 1998 introduced some reforms, but the discretionary role of the government in this area remained (Participacion Ciudadana, 2006). Despite pressures from the U.S. government demanding a more transparent system that did not discriminate against foreign firms, no new reforms were discussed in Congress for nearly six years.

The signing of DR-CAFTA forced the Dominican Republic to introduce a new Law of Public Contracts. Yet the approval of new legislation was slow, contradictory and subject to numerous external pressures. The law was not approved until July 2006 after more than a year of discussions. The version approved—after lobby from the construction sector and others—still contained some clauses that would have allowed the government to discriminate in favor of selected domestic firms.[14] After pressures from the U.S. Embassy, a second law was introduced in November 2006, which met the foreign investment-friendly requirements of DR-CAFTA.

The Costa Rican experience contrasts sharply with that of the rest of the region. Costa Rica is the only country where DR-CAFTA has faced major obstacles. The combination of intense opposition to the agreement by a significant share of the population and a fragmented party system resulted in political paralysis for several years. Months of discussion in the Legislative Assembly failed to lead to a vote. In May 2007 the Electoral Court allowed a group of social movements to collect signatures for a referendum on DR-CAFTA, and the government was forced to respond by calling a referendum of its own that took place on the 7 October. The yes vote won by just 3 percentage points after a tough campaign in which the government was accused of abusing power and the opposition was heavily outspent. The result showed the growing polarization and the difficulties that the proponents of DR-CAFTA will face to pass all the associated reforms in the upcoming months.

Costa Rica has also been unique in the level of analysis and social debate about the consequences of free trade in general and DR-CAFTA in particular. The two main universities have promoted several studies (see, e.g., Florez-Estrada and Hernandez, 2004; Weisleder, 2004; Universidad Nacional, 2003) as well as taking official positions on the subject. Prominent think tanks such as Estado de la Nacion (see Alonso, 2005), trade unions and the government have also prepared their own evaluations and participated in multiple forums to discuss the future of the country. Social movements, trade unions and also the PAC, the main opposition party, have not only developed sophisticated arguments against the agreement, but have also elaborated alternative proposals to better integrate Costa Rica in the global economy and promote economic development.

While most studies carefully analyze all the dimensions of the agreement including the environment, the system of international arbitration and the reduction in agricultural protection, social debate has primarily concentrated on the changing role of the state. In particular, disagreement with regard to the provision of social services and, more importantly, to the liberalization of the telecommunication sector has been at the heart of the conflict on DR-CAFTA.

The treaty constitutes the most recent battle over the direction of the Costa Rican model and some key social actors view it as a particularly important one. In fact, both the president of the Costa Rican Union of Chambers, Samuel Yankelewitz, and the head of one of the trade unions confederations, Albino Vargas, believe that the approval of DR-CAFTA will have a major impact on the consolidation of an export oriented, neoliberal model (each with opposing evaluations of this result).[15] While these views may be exaggerated and Costa Rica will still keep some of its unique features (e.g., high social spending, consensual politics, slow reforms) no matter the final result of the process, there is little doubt about the polarizing effect of DR-CAFTA. The close result of the recent elections is the best demonstration of this trend.

Conclusion

The comparative analysis of Costa Rica, the Dominican Republic and El Salvador has shown that long term state-society relations are important to understand the different responses to DR-CAFTA. In particular, Costa Rica's extreme polarization around the agreement is the result of the frontal opposition from influential segments of the labor movement and the middle class, groups that benefited from the successful social-democratic model of the 1960s and 1970s. Yet are the differences described really relevant? Since even Costa Ricans has supported the treaty, will state-society relations converge all over the region?

This is a vital question since differences in state-society relations give rise to different policy choices and development outcomes. Higher social spending in Costa Rica, for example, has been partly the result of relatively influential trade unions demanding better public services. The evolution of state-society relations is also fundamental to evaluate the prospects of active industrial policy in the future. Even if, as Abugattas and Paus (in this volume) or Amsden (2001) convincingly show, industrial policy is required to expand domestic capacities and knowledge assets, it will never be implemented without support from the domestic capitalist elite.

Leaving aside the poorest countries (Honduras, Guatemala and Nicaragua) and concentrating on the three that we have been studying, I would argue that some convergence to a similar economic model is likely to take place. A small number of successful domestic groups may become even more powerful, controlling both the import and commercialization of goods and the export of labor intensive manufactures. New manufacturing exports and remittances will grow even more and will further strengthen the ties between Central America and the U.S. economy. Trade unions will remain weak (and will weaken in Costa Rica), but will build transnational coalitions with U.S. trade unions (Murillo and Schrank, 2005). This may result in better labor standards, but it is unlikely to alter distributional patterns between wages and profits.

Economic outcomes in the post-CAFTA are thus likely to be similar than in the recent past. Economic growth will be steady but not spectacular and income inequality will remain high. While social spending is likely to increase as a proportion of GDP in both El Salvador and the Dominican Republic, it will still remain low by regional standards. Costa Rica will maintain higher levels of social spending, but some of its current problems (insufficient resources and unequal distribution of some services) will not be resolved.

This vision assumes that Costa Rica will slowly become more similar to the Dominican Republic and El Salvador due to different factors. My analysis assumes that the liberalization of telecommunications and other public services will weaken the political influence of trade unions and social movements. The consolidation of the export-led model focused on assembly of high tech products and the production of services will generate further inequality, thus questioning basic components of the traditional Costa Rican social-democratic model. The country is also unlikely to build new linkages between the export sector and the rest of the economy and will thus witness the consolidation of a "two-engine" economic model.

There is a chance that Costa Rica can overcome some of the constraints imposed by DR-CAFTA and outperform the other two countries. Paus (2005) argues that an optimistic future of high tech export expansion and rapid economic growth a la Ireland, while difficult, is not impossible. Achieving this kind of success, however, will require that Costa Ricans recognize their specific competitive assets. In particular, the unique ability of the country to build consensus and incorporate many actors in the process of policy design should be strengthened. These "social assets" were important in Costa Rica's ability to expand social spending rapidly during the 1960s and 1970s and also in its success in adapting more rapidly and less costly to the debt crisis of the 1980s than other countries.

I am not suggesting a return to the status quo in which many policy discussions go on for years and ultimately end up with little results. The experience of the recent fiscal reform, which was not even voted in Congress after more than three years of debate, is pernicious and should be avoided at all costs. Yet all actors in Costa Rica (from the two dominant political parties to the economic elite to the trade unions and other social organizations) could relearn to collaborate more actively and abandon their current all-or-nothing strategies. They could perhaps build new institutional spaces to discuss their preferred economic model and the most effective way to insert in the global economy. Unfortunately, neither the process of discussion of DR-CAFTA nor its implementation is moving the country in that direction.

Notes

I would like to thank Eva Paus, Rafael Sánchez, Aaron Schneider, Andrew Schrank, and Ken Shadlen for comments on a previous version of this chapter. All errors and omissions are of course only mine.

1. In this chapter Central America will refer to the countries that are part of DR-CAFTA: Costa Rica, Dominican Republic, El Salvador, Guatemala, Honduras, and Nicaragua.
2. For a comparison of Nicaragua's leading coalitions and development outcomes from those of Costa Rica and the Dominican Republic, see Sánchez-Ancochea (2007).
3. The RBTAs are also part of the U.S. strategic agenda, aimed at maintaining its influence in the region and increasing the number of allies that will support its positions in international forums like the Doha Round of the WTO. See Phillips (this volume) and Vizentini (2004).
4. In 1989 Provision 807 shifted into Provision 9802.00.80 in the Harmonized Tariff Schedule (Mortimore and Zamora, 1998).
5. Tourism has been the third key pillar on the new insertion of Central America in the global economy, particularly in Costa Rica, the Dominican Republic, and Guatemala.
6. Data from the U.S. census based on a sample (see http://www.census.gov/population/www/socdemo/foreign.html, last accessed on February 11, 2008). If illegal migrants are taken into consideration, the number of Dominican-born population living in the United States is likely to be much higher, well above 1 million people.
7. For a discussion of the difficulties in measuring the evolution of real wages in the Dominican Republic, see Sánchez-Ancochea (2004).
8. Information also comes from an interview with one of the leading entrepreneurs in Santo Domingo (Santo Domingo, September 2005).
9. The following paragraph is based on ideas from Rovira (2004). See also Estado de la Nacion (various years).
10. Oscar Arias from the PLN won the February 2006 elections by less than 30,000 votes (just 1.1% of the electorate) more than its opponent, Otton Solis from the PAC.
11. According to three of the negotiators (interview in Santo Domingo, September 2005), the fact that the Dominican Republic entered late

into the process and reached an agreement rapidly was positive for the country. They used the Central American agreement as reference point and concentrated only on specific areas of interest. According to UNDP (2005), however, the small period of negotiation was imposed by the U.S. Trade Representative and did not allow the country to do an adequate evaluation of its effects.

12. Interview with a highly influential business leader (Santo Domingo, September 2005).

13. This ambivalent position was clear when interviewing two business leaders from the traditional elite from Santo Domingo in September 2005.

14. Article 3 Point 8 of the original law, for example, established that public contracts "will try to encourage the creation of new local companies with financial and technological capabilities to promote national development." In the new law of November 2006, this clause was modified. The new version only established that the government "will promote the participation of small and medium firms, while recognizing their limited financial and technological capacity."

15. Interviews in San Jose, July 2005.

References

Acevedo, C. (1996) "The Historical Background to the Conflict," in J. Boyce (ed.) *Economic Policy for Building Peace. The Lessons of El Salvador*, Boulder, CO: Lynne Rienner Publishers.

Alonso, E. (2005) *Aportes para el análisis del Tratado de Libre Comercio Centroamérica, República Dominicana y Estados Unidos*, San José, Costa Rica: Programa Estado de la Nación.

Amsden, A. (2001) *The Rise of the Rest. Challenges to the West from Late-Industrializing Economies*, New York: Oxford University Press.

Bulmer Thomas, V. (1987) *The Political Economy of Central America since 1920*, Cambridge: Cambridge University Press.

Dunkerley, J. (1991) "El Salvador since 1930," in L. Bethell (ed.) *Central America since Independence*, Cambridge: Cambridge University Press.

Estado de la Nación (various years) *Informe del Estado de la Nación en Desarrollo Sostenible*, San José, Costa Rica: Proyecto Estado de la Nación.

Florez-Estrada, M. and G. Hernandez, eds. (2004) *TLC con Estados Unidos: contribuciones para el debate.¿Debe Costa Rica aprobarlo?* San José, Costa Rica: Instituto de Investigaciones Sociales, UCR.

Herrera, C. (1992) "La apertura gradual de Costa Rica a partir de 1983," *Pensamiento Iberoamericano*, 21: 147–164.

Kaplinsky, R. (1993) "Export Processing Zones in the Dominican Republic: Transforming Manufactures into Commodities," *World Development*, 21 (11): 1851–1865.

Lizano, E. (1999) *Ajuste y crecimiento en la economía de Costa Rica, 1982–1994*, San José, Costa Rica: Academia de Centroamérica.

Lozano, W. (2001) *Los trabajadores del capitalismo exportador*, Santo Domingo, Dominican Republic: Banco Central de la República Dominicana.

Mortimore, M. and R. Zamora (1998) "The International Competitiveness of the Costa Rican Clothing Industry," *Desarrollo Productivo*, no. 46 Santiago, Chile: Economic Commission for Latin America and the Caribbean.

Moya Pons, F. (1992) *Empresarios en conflicto. Políticas de industrialización y sustitución de importaciones en República Dominicana*, Santo Domingo, Dominican Republic: Fondo para el Avance de las Ciencias Sociales.

Murillo, V. and A. Schrank (2005) "With a Little Help from My Friends: Partisan Politics, Transnational Alliances, and Labor Rights in Latin America," *Comparative Political Studies*, 38 (8): 971–999.

ONE (1997) *Censo del sector público de la República Dominicana, 1997*, Santo Domingo, Dominican Republic: Oficina Nacional de Estadística.

Paige, J. (1997) *Coffee and Power. Revolution and the Rise of Democracy in Central America*, Cambridge, MA: Harvard University Press.

Participación Ciudadana (2006) *El Sistema de Compras en la Administración Publica: Propuestas para su transformación*, Santo Domingo, Dominican Republic: Participación Ciudadana. Movimiento Cívico No Partidista.

Robinson, W. (2003) *Transnational Conflicts. Central America, Social Change, and Globalization*, London: Verso.

Rodríguez, C. (2004) "Estratificación y movilidad sociooupacional en Costa Rica en la segunda mitad del siglo XX," in C. Castro and A. Gutiérrez (ed.) *Transformaciones en la estructura social en Costa Rica: estratos sociooupacionales, educación y trabajo*, San José, Costa Rica: Instituto de Investigaciones Sociales, Universidad de Costa Rica.

Rottenberg, S., ed. (1993) *The Political Economy of Poverty, Equity and Growth. Costa Rica and Uruguay*, Oxford: Oxford University Press for the World Bank.

Rovira, J. (2000) *Estado y política económica en Costa Rica, 1948–1970*, San José, Costa Rica: Editorial de la Universidad de Costa Rica.

—— (2004) "El nuevo estilo nacional de desarrollo de Costa Rica 1984–2003 y el TLC," in M. Florez-Estrada and G. Hernandez (eds.) *TLC con Estados Unidos: contribuciones para el debate.¿Debe Costa Rica aprobarlo?* San José, Costa Rica: Instituto de Investigaciones Sociales, UCR.

Sánchez, R. (2004) *Estado de bienestar, crisis económica y ajuste estructural en Costa Rica*, San José, Costa Rica: Editorial Universidad Estatal a Distancia.

Sánchez-Ancochea, D. (2004) "'Leading Coalitions' and the Structures of Accumulation and Distribution in Small Countries. The Cases of Costa Rica and Dominican Republic under Globalization," Ph.d. dissertation, New York: New School University.

—— (2005) "Domestic capital, Civil Servants and the State: Costa Rica and the Dominican Republic under Globalization," *Journal for Latin American Studies*, 37: 693–726.

—— (2007) "La globalización en países pequeños en desarrollo. Nicaragua en perspectiva comparada," *Revista Mexicana de Sociología*, 69 (2) (April–June): 199–242.

Schrank, A. (2005) "Entrepreneurship, Export Diversification, and Economic Reform: The Birth of a 'Developmental Community' in the Dominican Republic," *Comparative Politics*, October: 43–62.

Segovia, A. (2002) *Transformación Estructural y Reforma Económica en El Salvador*, Guatemala: DyD Consultores-F&G Editores.

—— (2004a) "Centroamérica después del café: el fin del modelo agroexportador tradicional y el surgimiento de un nuevo modelo económico," *Revista Centroamericana de Ciencias Sociales*, 1 (2): 5–38.

—— (2004b) "El Impacto del CAFTA en el Modelo de Desarrollo Centroamericano," *Proyecto Centroamérica en el Siglo XXI*, ASIES-IDRC.

—— (2005) *Integración real y grupos de poder económico en América Central: implicaciones para el desarrollo y la democracia de la región*, San José, Costa Rica: Friedrich Ebert Foundation.

Shadlen, K. (2005) "Exchanging Development for Market Access? Deep Integration and Industrial Policy under Multilateral and Regional-Bilateral Trade Agreements," *Review of International Political Economy*, 12 (5): 750–775.

Sojo, C. (1995) "En el nombre del padre: patrimonialismo y democracia en Costa Rica," in C. Sojo and M. Rojas (eds.) *El malestar con la política*, San José, Costa Rica: FLACSO.

Spalding, R. (2006) "Free Trade and Democratic Processes: A Comparative Analysis of CAFTA Negotiation and Ratification in El Salvador and Costa Rica," paper presented at the 26 International Congress of the Latin American Studies Association, San Juan.

Spar, D. (1998) *Attracting High Technology. Intel's Costa Rican Plant*, Washington, Occasional Paper 11, Washington, DC: Foreign Investment Advisory Service, World Bank.

UNDP (2005) *Informe nacional del desarrollo humano. República Dominicana 2005*, Santo Domingo, Dominican Republic: Programa de Naciones Unidas para el Desarrollo.

Universidad Nacional (2003) *Diálogo Ciudadano sobre el TLC entre Centroamérica-Estados Unidos*, Heredia, Costa Rica: Cátedra Víctor Sanabria of the Universidad Nacional.

Vizentini, P. (2004) "The FTAA and U.S. Strategy: A Southern Point of View," in P. Vizentini and M. Wiesebron (eds.) *Free Trade for the Americas? The United States' Push for the FTAA Agreement*, New York: Zed Books.

Weisleder, S., ed. (2004) *Tratado de Libre Comercio Centroamérica-Estados Unidos: procesos y resultados*, San José, Costa Rica: EUNED.

World Bank (2005) *Dominican Republic: Review of Trade and Labor Competitiveness*, Washington, DC: World Bank Caribbean Country Management Unit, Latin America and the Caribbean Region.

—— (2006) *DR-CAFTA: Challenges and Opportunities for Central America*, Washington, DC: Central American Department and Office of the Chief Economist, Latin America and Caribbean Regions.

Chapter 8

FTAA Trade Negotiations: A View of the Brazilian Co-chairmanship

Adhemar G. Bahadian and
Mauricio Carvalho Lyrio

In 1998, Bahadian and Vieira Vargas (1998) alerted to the risks of excluding social issues from the integration effort as proposed in the Summit of the Americas, and of an excessive emphasis on the Free Trade Area of the Americas (FTAA) negotiations alone, without considering the need to create a less asymmetric reality in the western hemisphere. Unfortunately, a decade after the publication of that article, divergences in regional trade negotiations have deepened. The FTAA remains far from becoming a real free trade area; instead of bringing together our countries' economies, negotiations have revealed the persistence of protectionist measures both in traditional areas, such as agriculture, and in new areas, such as intellectual property rights. In this latter area, the attempt to create rules that go beyond those that have been negotiated in the World Trade Organization (WTO) could have highly negative impacts on developing countries—Brazil included—such as escalating the costs of social security and restraining access to generic drugs by poorer sectors of our societies.

This chapter reflects the experience of one of the authors as Brazilian co-chair of the FTAA negotiations between 2003 and 2005. Its objective is to discuss the development of the negotiating process and the involved parties' perceptions regarding the gains and losses that the formation of a regional free trade area in the Americas could bring.

The publication of this testimony derives from the same conviction that has motivated the actions of the Brazilian government in the negotiations, that the debate on the FTAA should be as wide and transparent as possible. It is essential to have a public and well-informed debate on these negotiations, on the different possibilities of agreement, and their probable consequences. This is particularly so because the issues addressed in the FTAA affect fundamental elements for each country's social and economic development. Only with an open and frank dialogue will it be possible to signal opportunities and risks, correct wrong or biased perceptions and, above all, reconcile and express the expectations and interests of all segments of society in the different countries of the hemisphere.

Since the beginning of the FTAA negotiations, Brazil has put its maximum effort into reaching a balanced agreement, aimed at promoting development.[1] We should not assume beforehand that the FTAA initiative is, in and of itself, negative. We should certainly, as Brazil and the other Mercosur countries have been trying to do, improve the direction of the negotiation process, removing from it extraneous propositions and topics that favor only a few specific groups and governments and which move away from achieving social and economic development. What inspires Brazil and its Mercosur partners is the goal of giving an eventual FTAA a focus that is clearly centered on development, with an emphasis on market access, including that of agricultural products to developed countries.

It is not possible to assess the current state of the FTAA negotiations without an analysis of the evolution of negotiations since they began at the Miami Summit in December 1994. We will present here an overview and an evaluation of the negotiations from the Miami Summit to the most recent developments, including the Vice-Ministerial Meeting in Puebla, in February 2004, and the informal consultations following that meeting. Based on this evaluation of what happened throughout the whole negotiation process, we will examine the current stalemate that is impeding the parties from reaching an agreement satisfactory to all countries involved in the process. At the end, we will present our assessment of where we are today and to where the FTAA process may be going.

To explain what has transpired (and what may still transpire) in the FTAA negotiations, we present two main lines of argument. The first is that, for the past ten years we have had a distortion of the original propositions agreed at the Summit of the Americas, in 1994, which established the goal of creating the FTAA. We knew, by then, that the liberalization of markets would not be a panacea for all development problems of the countries in the region; hence we could also anticipate, at that time, an entire agenda that would transcend and complement the FTAA initiative. We could anticipate then the need to address such diverse and essential aspects as political and financial support for social development projects, strengthening education and health cooperation programs and the need to have financing for infrastructure projects in transportation, energy and communication. What has occurred during the past ten years, since that moment when the initiative was launched, has been the virtual abandonment of the agenda items involving *social progress and infrastructure, and financial support* that constituted a crucial part of the Declaration and Plan of Action agreed at the Miami Summit. As a result of a lack of engagement by those countries that could contribute more to benefit others, that initial promise proved to be no more than rhetoric. In reality, what has survived is a limited FTAA initiative, without a comprehensive focus on how we could—and should— foster development in the Hemisphere.

The second—and related—argument is that the current proposals suffer as a consequence of the distortion of the original objectives. The proposed agreement has been transformed into a proposition that is increasingly unbalanced and, in many aspects, harmful not only to national development projects but also to its own central goal of free trade in the region. Under pressure from specific countries, the FTAA initiative, as it has come to evolve, would exclude trade liberalization in essential sectors, such as agriculture, while also limiting the ability of governments to act in areas such as investment policies, intellectual property rights and public sector procurement. The very essence of a free trade agreement—trade liberalization in all sectors—has been evaded and what has been conceived is an FTAA intended to regulate aspects of economic operations that are not directly related to trade. Beyond abandoning the social aspects, financial support and infrastructure of the original initiative for hemispheric integration, as a result of straying away from the Declaration and 1994 Plan of Action, the initiative has lost the core of what should have been a genuine free trade area, that is, the main goal of dismantling customs tariffs and nontariff barriers.

Imbalanced Negotiations and Mercosur's Response

The view that the FTAA negotiations suffer from fundamental imbalances is now almost unanimous. Some of these imbalances arose from the very structure of the hemispheric negotiations, while others are more related to the process itself, how it developed in the past and the arrangement of topics on the agenda of negotiations.

The more structural imbalances are related to the inevitable differences in a process that involves 34 countries with immense disparities in economic, social and political development, as well as in size and population. As one might expect, this is reflected in distinct interests, priorities and expectations, which are quite difficult to reconcile. We have in our Hemisphere a wide range of countries, from the small islands of Saint Kitts and Nevis to nations of almost continental size, such as Brazil and Canada; from the largest economy in the world, the United States, to some of the most impoverished, such as Haiti. No other trade integration initiative in history has involved such a heterogeneous set of countries as have the FTAA negotiations. This fact illustrates the real magnitude of the difficulties and challenges inherent in the process.

Other imbalances have arisen from circumstances related to the nego-tiating process itself. Two of those imbalances were the most significant: 1) the then-existing disproportion between a very broad agenda and the lack of time to complete the negotiations by January 2005 as initially scheduled; and 2) the imbalance between an agenda that was ambitious in aspects such as the preparation of hemispheric rules in areas of no interest to countries like Brazil and its Mercosur partners and an agenda that was very restrictive in the areas of most immediate interest to us, such as agriculture and antidumping.

Both the disproportion and the paralysis resulting from it can be attributed to different causes. The main cause appears to be an inappro-priate attitude on the part of some of the parties involved—the United States in particular—which combined a lack of realism in evaluating the difficult framework of negotiations and an excessively maximalist approach in pursuit of results that had already proven themselves to be impracticable. Since 1994, the evolution of international trade negotia-tions and the domestic context in almost all countries involved in the FTAA have revealed the existence of significant national sensitivities in many of the negotiating areas. Due to the resistance from some parties, these sensitivities were not seriously addressed in the FTAA negotiating process. In other words, the specific difficulties that countries have in certain areas of the negotiations were not being translated into an effec-tive restructuring of the FTAA negotiating architecture. This explains the stalemate and the paralysis that was to occur.

The best example of this attitude was the behavior of the United States, the country that launched the FTAA negotiations with the con-vocation of the Miami Summit. Since 1994, the evolution of U.S. trade policy has shown us that country's difficulty in negotiating specific top-ics on the FTAA agenda. This difficulty is reflected in the oft-repeated American reference to the so-called "systemic matters" that allegedly could only be addressed under the WTO, but not in a hemispheric frame-work, such as domestic support payments to agriculture and antidump-ing policies. At the Trade Negotiations Committee meeting in Trinidad and Tobago, in September 2003, the American delegation even recog-nized explicitly that it is impossible for the United States to negotiate those two matters within FTAA, using the argument that they are "global matters."

It only takes a reading of the U.S. government's limited constitutional authority over trade issues, under the "Trade Promotion Authority," (TPA) to have an idea of the virtual veto power the United States exer-cises over negotiations on such matters as agriculture and antidumping. Under the TPA, any proposal to eliminate tariffs on "sensitive products" (almost 500 being agricultural products) must go through a series of dif-ficult steps in the U.S. Congress, in terms of winding its way through

Congressional Committees and the preparation of impact studies. In practice, this process gives the U.S. Congress a significant capacity to block progress, thus obstructing any regular negotiation of such matters. In the case of antidumping issues, the U.S. government is prohibited from negotiating any international agreement that "weakens" the country's legislation, that is to say, anything that imposes limits to the arbitrary power of national authorities in trade protection.

This fact demonstrates that even the country with the largest economy in the Hemisphere and in the world and the one that was responsible for launching the idea of creating a FTAA also had—and still has—profound national sensitivities, to the point of demanding the exclusion of some topics from the final FTAA package.[2] The critical mistake here was failing to recognize that these difficulties would lead to a rearranging of the negotiations as a whole. By excluding these two key aspects from the round of negotiations, the United States broke the already fragile balance of gains and losses for the other countries and made a rearranging of the negotiating process inevitable. The contradiction was that a country presented its national sensitivities and tried to exclude some matters from the negotiating round, while seeking to impede other countries from doing the same. Nevertheless, it sought to maintain merely rhetorical support for a broad and ambitious agreement, which, by definition, was no longer possible from that point onwards.

There was no greater imbalance within the FTAA process than the contrast between the pressure that more developed countries—the United States and Canada—applied towards establishing a set of regulations more comprehensive than those of the WTO in areas such as services, investments and intellectual property, in contrast with their refusal to accept regulations more comprehensive than those of the WTO in areas such as antidumping and agriculture. They sought—and continue to seek—an advanced FTAA in the so-called new aspects of the trade agenda—which for the most part have no genuine trade aspects—while at the same time they attempted to solidify barriers against agricultural products and also against those manufactured goods in which we had become more competitive, such as shoes, textiles and steel. They act as if the more developed countries, but not the poorer ones, deserved special and differentiated treatment.

Thus the FTAA agenda lacked both balance and proportion, and this was what Mercosur's proposals tried to restore. Without rearranging its architecture to reflect the changes that had occurred after 1994, the FTAA initiative was seriously at risk—and today remains at risk—of remaining merely a plan. The widely cited 7,000 brackets in the agreement, representing the "pending points" in the chapters negotiated among the 34 countries, would not have been so significant if they merely reflected minor differences, natural in any trade negotiating process. However, these brackets reflected substantial differences among the participants, not related to marginal topics, but almost always constituting contradictory and incompatible views of the depth and scope of negotiations in each and every one of the main areas. In other words, the bracketed text did not point to aspects of the agreement that would have to be "fine tuned," but rather they reflected the deadlocked state of negotiations.

Upon taking office at the beginning of 2003, President Lula's government encountered this situation of imbalance and stalemate in the FTAA negotiations. We faced a dilemma: the United States refused to make any more significant concessions in the areas in which we had the greatest interest, such as agricultural trade and antidumping regulations, and exerted pressure seeking advances in areas in which we had a so-called "defensive interest," such as services, investments, government procurement and intellectual property.

The most shocking example of this imbalance was the fact that in the first six months of 2003 all of the countries negotiating FTAA had to present market access offers in five areas (tariffs on agricultural and industrial goods, commitments in services, investments and government procurement), without any commitments on subsidy reductions in agriculture, or in reform of what we regard as unfair and discriminatory antidumping obligations. In other words, we had to present market opening offers in three areas of great sensitivity for Brazil (services, investments, and government procurement) without any return in the two areas of most interest to us, reducing the subsidies that governments of more developed countries give to their agricultural sectors and disciplining the deployment of antidumping measures, which, arbitrarily applied as they have been, would most likely cancel the benefits we could obtain from tariff reduction on our products. The barriers to our exports of steel products to the American market, and most recently, even to shrimp exports, illustrate how the elimination of tariffs can be useless without disciplining the use of antidumping measures.

As the negotiations proceeded, they seemed to point towards reaching an unbalanced agreement, contrary to the interests of Brazil and its neighboring countries. Furthermore, evasiveness and optimistic expectations that all would end well, or turn out to be satisfactory as time passed, were unconvincing. As scheduled deadlines drew nearer—Brazil's new government took office only two years before the previously established final deadline—the urgent need to rebalance the negotiating agenda became increasingly clear.

Facing the firm position of Brazil and Mercosur, the American negotiators themselves began to assume that it would not be possible to achieve a final agreement under those terms. This is why, during a visit to Brasilia in May 2003, the United States Trade Representative Robert

Zoellick presented to Brazilian foreign minister Celso Amorim a proposal to condense the FTAA agenda, which was called the "Baseline Agreement."

At the Vice-Ministerial Meeting in El Salvador, in July 2003, Mercosur presented its first proposal to negotiate FTAA in "three tracks." Although encountering great resistance from other countries, it was, at the same time, a response to the existing imbalance and a call for pragmatism, as would become evident months later. Its great merit was to recognize that all countries, not only the Mercosur countries or the United States and Canada had national sensitivities in particular areas of the negotiations, which needed to be taken into account when restructuring the FTAA architecture. The virtue of the Mercosur proposal was to acknowledge the reality expressed by the State Parties and to translate it into a negotiation framework that would contemplate each country's difficulties. Therefore, the idea of a "possible FTAA," was developed as opposed to the idea of an unbalanced FTAA, ambitious only in those aspects that interested the wealthy developed countries. Following the position advocated by the United States, according to which agricultural subsidies and antidumping measures could only be negotiated within the WTO, we proposed the same for those matters in which we had great difficulties, such as the negotiation of new regulation of services, investments, intellectual property and government procurement.

The Brazilian resistance to negotiate hemispheric regulation in these areas was not simply a reaction to the American attitude. We had—and we still have—an overriding interest in avoiding a Hemispheric disciplining of specific areas that would limit our ability to formulate and implement public policies in our interest. The Uruguay Round left us with the lesson, learned through the reality of the implementation of its agreements, that we cannot accept commitments that limit the liberty of each country to act in fundamental areas—as it was the case, for example, of patent policy and public health (affected by the TRIPS agreement) and the policy of incentives and offsets to the installation of foreign firms in the country (affected by the TRIMS agreement). As noted by Dani Rodrik (2001), the multilateral trading system has often been used to channel rich countries' demands that not only do not help the development process in poorer countries but even hurt it. The desire to regulate and to create Hemispheric regulations in areas such as services, investments, intellectual property and government procurement pointed in the same undesirable direction, and therefore we were trying to avoid accepting commitments that could incur great future costs for us.

We do not refuse to negotiate "market access" agreements in areas such as services and investments. Mercosur even received and presented offers in both of these areas. What we vehemently refuse is to negotiate, in those sensitive sectors, new regulations that transcend national legislation and undermine our ability to promote national government policies.

Besides this pragmatic view that takes into account national sensitivities in specific topics, the Mercosur proposal also endorsed another important modality of negotiation already practiced in the FTAA process: the bilateral negotiation—4+1, for Mercosur—to exchange market access offers. When presenting its initial offers, the United States decided to distinguish between groups of countries that would receive differentiated offers, giving Mercosur the least favorable tariff elimination set for market access into the country. What the Mercosur proposal did was to extend to other countries this same possibility of differentiating what to offer to one or another partner in the FTAA negotiations.

It did not—and does not—make any sense that Mercosur is required to offer to wealthy developed countries, namely the United States and Canada, the same set of offers extended to less developed countries with lower competitiveness and less export penetration, such as our South American neighbors. In just the same way as the U.S. government made distinctions between the poorer Caribbean, Central American, and Andean countries, to the detriment of the Mercosur countries, it is also appropriate for us to offer smaller countries a tariff elimination timetable that is different from those offered to the United States or Canada.

The Success at the Miami Ministerial

Apart from representing a necessary adjustment in the negotiating agenda to rebalance losses and gains among the thirty-four countries, the Mercosur proposal was a call for pragmatism and for a more realistic approach to the negotiations. What the many bracketed texts in the proposed agreement showed us was the enormous distance between countries in crucial areas. The Mercosur proposal, as a response to this stalemate, demonstrated that it was possible, with realism and a practical approach, to find inspiration in measures already adopted by the main countries, with the goal of reducing existing differences and reorganizing topics and the scope of negotiations.

In all of the Trade Negotiation Committee's meetings, Brazil and Mercosur aimed to introduce the principle of flexibility into the FTAA negotiations. This was true in El Salvador, in July 2003; in Trinidad and Tobago, in September 2003; and in Miami, in November 2003. We advocated the principle that nothing should be restricted to, nor imposed on, any State. Countries would define, by mutual agreement, a minimum set of common obligations in various areas, applicable to all thirty-four countries. Those that would wish to go further, each in its own interest areas and with those parties they may wish to negotiate, could do so with no restrictions or impositions.

That was the proposal that Minister Celso Amorim, with the support of his Mercosur partners, presented at the Virginia Mini-Ministerial and at the Miami Ministerial Meeting itself, in November 2003, the first FTAA meeting under the new Brazilian government. This was a practical solution, based on the notion that we had to negotiate a nucleus of commitments that would safeguard each country's interests—itself a very complex task—and that each country could seek, in its own priority areas to establish what we call "plurilateral agreements" with other countries within FTAA.

Mercosur's idea to propose such "plurilateral agreements," on a voluntary basis, as was done, for example, under the Tokyo Round of the old GATT, was—and is—intended to add flexibility to the negotiating process, to accommodate national difficulties. We achieved this flexibility in Miami due, in large part, to the firm defense of Brazil's and Mercosur's interests. Miami culminated a course of action that had the goal of correcting the path of negotiations, as well as redefining of the FTAA architecture, making it more pragmatic and feasible.

As a result of the Miami Ministerial, the Vice Ministers received a set of tasks to complete during the Puebla Vice-Ministerial Meeting, in February 2004. The goal was to translate decisions taken by the Ministers into instructions to negotiators in all of the several areas involved. Two of them, in particular, were to be tasks assigned to all countries to allow for the continuation of the negotiations: the development of the so-called "common and balanced set of rights and obligations applicable to all countries," mentioned above, and to the definition of procedures for the negotiation of multilateral agreements, such as the requirements for the participation of members and observers.

The topic that dominated the Puebla meeting, on which we had not yet reached agreement, was precisely the drawing up of a common set of rights and obligations for all countries. We did not reach a consensus, at least not as of July 2007, for two reasons. The first is the fact that to redraw the FTAA architecture, in order to adapt it to what countries can effectively—and not only in theory—do is not an easy task. To advance in this area, a series of consultations and informal meeting with different countries have taken place since the suspension of negotiations consultations; yet this process was affected, in the second half of 2004, by the U.S. presidential elections. The second reason is that some countries still resist the spirit and text of the Miami Ministerial Declaration. Although we were not going anywhere before the Ministerial Meeting, drowned in brackets and in meetings with no advances, some negotiators still resist adapting themselves to new circumstances—to the natural idea that all countries, and not only a few, must defend their interests and sensitivities.

The Current Stalemate, Ten Years Later

What is preventing us from reaching an agreement? What are the points where differences remain, impeding advances? Among the many differences confronted by countries in the Hemisphere, two appear to be the most fundamental ones. Both of them express, in a symbolic way, the asymmetries of the negotiating process, and the gap that separates the priorities of the developed countries from those of the developing countries. These are agriculture and intellectual property. Let us consider both.

Agriculture is the most ancient sector of international trade and is still the one subject to most protectionist measures. It is the permanent taboo of the international trade agenda, an agenda that has been incorporating, during the last few decades, noncommercial topics of interest to developed countries without ever addressing agricultural issues. What happens in the FTAA negotiations faithfully reflects the trade negotiations, including the multilateral ones, of recent decades: rich countries refuse to negotiate the reduction of subsidies and the reduction of the highly distorted trade mechanisms, which affect both poorer countries and those with efficient agricultural sectors, such as Brazil and its Mercosur partners.

We need not reiterate the scope of billions of dollars of subsidies granted to agriculture in the rich North American, European, and Asian countries, with their devastating effects on income and livelihood prospects for poor populations, in Latin America, Africa and Asia and other parts of the world. Those subsidies affect us in three main ways: by impeding access to richer markets; by provoking unjust competition in third markets; and by reducing international prices of the main export products of poorer countries.[3]

Although it is particularly dangerous to combine free trade with subsidies, as Mexican farmers could see when subsidized U.S. products entered their country as a result of the North American Free Trade Agreement, wealthy Western Hemisphere countries, conniving with narrow-minded domestic lobbies, have always resisted negotiating agricultural subsidies in the FTAA. Oddly enough, these same countries, today, give signs that they will also refuse the total elimination of customs tariffs, a basic aspect and defining element of a free trade area. They are beginning to signal their intention to apply exceptions and restrictive measures, such as quotas, rather than advancing under the previous commitment of tariff liberalization for all goods, industrial and agricultural. The fact that the WTO historically permitted the adoption of quotas in agriculture does not imply we will accept this same trade-distorting mechanism in the FTAA negotiations, since it is a process that should establish a free trade area. On the other hand, we cannot deny that there have been some advances that we consider auspicious, although still quite preliminary, in recent WTO meetings in Geneva, in discussions on eliminating export subsidies and reducing domestic support for agricultural production. Only future negotiations may confirm—or fail to confirm—this trend.

The idea of general tariff elimination in the FTAA is an old and basic one in the negotiations. The attempt to exclude the agricultural sector, or part of it, from the elimination program illustrates that self-respect has been lost and rhetoric has prevailed in these negotiations. The countries that most vehemently advocate the creation of a free trade area in the Hemisphere are precisely the ones that continue to envisage regulated agricultural trade, seeking to deny liberalisation of a crucial sector for most of the thirty-four countries of the Hemisphere. Recent WTO condemnations of cotton and sugar subsidies demand from us additional caution in the FTAA, so as to not undo or minimize victories already conquered at the multilateral forum.

Adding to the refusal of any significant opening in the most ancient sector of international trade, developed countries, also under pressure from domestic lobbies that have great concentrations of power and operate as oligopolies, have also been strongly pushing for the creation of new disciplines in this Hemisphere, in an area that is not exactly a trade issue, namely intellectual property (IP).

The awkwardness of dealing with the topic of IP in trade agreements derives from the fact that the complex and broad perspective that the issue always merited has now been completely abandoned. According to Jagdish Bhagwati (2002), for example, a free trader and one of the most respected experts in international trade, the incorporation of the topic into the trade agenda is itself illegitimate, "a cancer" in the multilateral system of trade.

The historical treatment of the topic, within the scope of the Paris Convention, has always tried to balance monopoly rights for patents with the necessary offsets, such as technology transfer and the social impact of patent rights. In return for any significant licensing—monopoly over commercial exploitation—there was a naturally corresponding obligation to provide compensation that could result in some benefit for the country that protected foreign patents, such as technology access or, at least, some prevention for abuses of monopolistic power.

What has happened over the past two decades has been the accelerated rupture of this balance. The recognition of the importance of technology transfer and the socially responsible use of monopolistic patent rights have been abandoned. The result is obvious: many poor countries now have difficulty in providing minimum access to medicines to their populations, as proven, for example, by the particularly tragic context of the spread of AIDS on the African continent. The outrageous prices of medicines condemn whole populations to agony and increase the risk and velocity of contamination. In this sense, they affect—and can affect even more in the future—the very solvency of States, less and less able to assume the costs of unsustainable public health and social welfare systems due to the incorrect appropriation of monopolistic rights by a few pharmaceutical conglomerates. This is already evident in the wealthy countries, beginning with the country that most strongly defends this kind of international agreement. The question of the difficulty of access to medicines gained such significance and urgency in the United States that it became one of the main topics in the presidential campaign of 2004.

There is increasing evidence—pointed out not only by international organizations such as the World Health Organisation (WHO), but also by nongovernmental organizations (NGOs) such as Oxfam—that bilateral trade agreements signed by the United States have strong negative impacts in the production capacity and commercialization of generic medicines. The bilateral trade agreements proposed by the United States of America, as well as its intentions in the FTAA, tend to ruin already achieved social progress and to replace rights attained within the WHO, thus creating unjustified mechanisms of protection for some few groups.[4]

As if the already unfavorable status quo of developing countries and poor populations in the Hemisphere were not enough, the United States wishes to strengthen restrictive disciplines in IP through the introduction of new obligations regarding the terms of patents, confidentiality of information and compulsory licensing in the FTAA agreement—following what has been done through bilateral agreements.[5] These disciplines would constrain even more our ability to promote public health policies, such as local production of medicines and generics, already hurt in the WTO by the TRIPS agreement.

Such resistance to new obligations should not, however, be confused with acceptance of intellectual property theft. Brazil has always supported enforcement actions against intellectual property theft, of any kind, particularly because Brazil is, as most countries are, directly affected by its pernicious effects, as in the case of copyright violation of Brazilian popular music. We are willing to join any effort to efficiently combat this universal phenomenon. What we cannot accept is that, with the excuse of combating intellectual property theft, the FTAA is used to legitimize trade retaliation mechanisms against our exports, thus transforming a matter that demands cooperation and international coordination into one more excuse to impose trade barriers motivated by protectionist impulses. This would be harmful to the goal of promoting trade itself and would also compromise, in advance, market access concessions on agricultural and industrial goods, since those concessions could be suspended at any time based on the excuse of an alleged inefficiency in applying IP legislation.

Prospects for the Negotiation Process

The fundamental contradiction between crystallizing the ubiquitous protectionism in agricultural trade and the search for strict regulation and new disciplines in IP that could guarantee the technological supremacy of a few countries in high-technology sectors demonstrates the huge gap between different national interests in the FTAA negotiations and also explains the paralysis and stalemate that we currently face in the negotiation process.

This contradiction also shows, as we mentioned at the beginning of this chapter, that we have distanced ourselves from the original proposal for the creation of FTAA. The 1994 Miami Summit had as its broadest goal the economic and social development of the Hemisphere. The creation of the free trade area was one of the instruments to achieve that goal, not a means to consolidate differences between countries and consolidate market access and technology access barriers for poorer countries.

We are living, in fact, a paradoxical moment in international economic relations. While at the WTO, in great part due to the catalyzing power of the group of 20 (G-20), we are witnessing what could be the beginning of the dismantling of agricultural protectionism, in bilateral trade agreements and, indirectly in the FTAA, we observe an opposite phenomenon. This situation reminds us of the importance of the balance of power in the negotiations. The disproportionately asymmetric bilateralism allows for the reversion of the most legitimate expectations of the relatively weaker less developed countries, leading them to accept regulations that do not represent a consensus within the framework of multilateral negotiations. The fact that these asymmetrical negotiations had been accepted based on a rhetoric favoring free trade and supporting economic development illustrates how the U.S. integration proposals became distant from the social demands and necessities of the people.

Brazil and Mercosur have stressed that their priority in FTAA is to negotiate market access. We are ready to negotiate a significant improvement in market access conditions both for goods and services. Therefore, we are being more faithful to the principles of free trade than other countries involved in the process, because free trade means, most of all, the elimination of tariff and nontariff barriers and this is what Mercosur has emphasized as the essence and core of the FTAA.

However, we can not accept the illusion that in exchange for market access to wealthy countries we should accept disciplines that impede our ability to act in fundamental areas in our own countries. All countries will present offers in market access for goods and services and it is through weighing all of these offers that we must find the equilibrium between concessions and advantages for all of us. The United States cannot accept ambitious regulations in sensitive areas, and nor can we. There is no prejudice, reluctance or ideology in this position: disagreements in trade negotiations reflect national priorities and interests that are both distinctive and legitimate. What we cannot do is to sacrifice the instruments that promote development. To cite Kenneth Shadlen, referring critically to the recent negotiations of bilateral and regional agreements by countries like the United States, "the price to be paid for increased market access under regionalism-bilateralism is that countries must relinquish many of the very tools that historically have been used to capture the developmental benefits of integration in the international economy" (Shadlen, 2005: 752). This is certainly not acceptable for countries such as ours. Moreover, in general, countries that recently signed bilateral free trade agreements with the United States have not been able to obtain significant advantages in agricultural trade, even after having paid the price of having made important concessions in areas of obvious interest to the U.S. government.

What the FTAA negotiation process lacks is not ambitious goals, but a grand view, especially by the developed countries. Latin America as a whole is going through an extremely delicate period, with higher poverty indices, increased unemployment rates, proliferation of drug trafficking and weakened political institutions. Agricultural protectionism in wealthy countries or their attempts to impose inflexible and unbalanced disciplines in new areas, can only aggravate the state of economic, political and social fragility in the region. Only market opening in developed countries, as well as a constructive reexamination of the treatment of noncommercial matters, could help poorer countries in the Hemisphere to overcome this moment of crisis and advance towards the common goal of development.

The Brazilian government is not opposed to FTAA. That is a myth we must fight against, since it only suits those who wish to distort facts and protect minority interests. What the Brazilian Government is trying to do is to redirect the FTAA process towards a balanced agreement while simultaneously rejecting those aspects that would be negative for Brazil's economic and social development. There is no opposition to the United States either based on principle or based on ideology. What we combat are those proposals made by protectionist and conservative forces in the United States and in other countries, mainly in agriculture and the intellectual property industries. These economic sectors are subject to criticism and opposition even from the more progressive streams of thought in the United States. What we intend, therefore, is to restore the FTAA initiative born at the Summit of the Americas and its central goals of increasing employment rates, promoting economic development and improving social conditions. In other words, what we aspire to achieve is an FTAA that is fully compatible with the rhetoric that launched it.

The development agenda cannot be ignored any longer. In recent decades, developing countries have accumulated a "fatigue" regarding the incorporation of new and strict regulations in areas of interest to developed countries, without effective offsets or compensation in market access to those same countries. A liability of incorporated regulations, with variable costs, was created without any significant increase in exports in those sectors in which poorer countries are more competitive, such as agriculture and low-tech manufactured goods (e.g. textiles and shoes).

Moreover, we cannot ignore the fact that, even in a process of effective integration, in which a dismantling of tariff and nontariff barriers occurs, it will be necessary to create mechanisms and measures to support developing countries, especially the poorer countries of the Hemisphere. We cannot maintain the illusion that in this Hemisphere we will introduce compensation and adjustment mechanisms similar to those created within the European Union (EU), with the goal of making the integration of economies and societies in distinct stages of development more equitable and fair. It is important not to ignore, however, the fact that it will need to create instruments within the FTAA process to avoid the trauma of sudden competition between some of the wealthier and some of the poorer countries of the Americas, which is a Hemisphere characterized by much deeper social and economic heterogeneity than Europe.

A trade integration process between such distinct and asymmetric economies should necessarily anticipate a set of adjustment and compensation measures that could guarantee a minimum balance in taking advantage of the opportunities that accompany trade integration. In other words, there is an imperative, evidenced both at the Plenary Meetings and in the meetings of the FTAA Negotiating Groups, to find trade and financial mechanisms that can contribute to the preparation and adaptation of poorer countries to the process of integration with two of the wealthiest economies in the world. It is thus of the utmost importance that the developed countries of the Hemisphere have the necessary sensitivity to create and promote instruments, including financial ones, to benefit the poorer countries of the region.

We need caution and tranquility to evaluate what Brazil and Mercosur will be able to negotiate in the very complex context of the resumption of the FTAA negotiations. The Brazilian government continues to be firmly engaged in pursuing its goal that the FTAA negotiations are brought to completion according to the flexible architecture that all 34 countries agreed to establish in Miami. Some steps were taken on the path towards a balanced trade agreement, satisfactory to all countries: we reformulated the FTAA architecture by introducing the principle of flexibility; we established the principle of positive lists for market access negotiation in services and investments; we refused market access negotiation in government procurement, which would harm our ability to use state resources to foster national projects; and we limited the scope of negotiations on regulations regarding services, investments and government procurement (areas that should be conducted under WTO rules and/or under principles of transparency). There are, nonetheless, many tasks to complete to consolidate the architecture of the agreement and the exchange and evaluation of offers. As we saw, crucial differences must be overcome—with agriculture and IP being the most important.

We cannot, however, lose sight of the essential goals. The formation of a free trade hemispheric area is not an end in itself, to be achieved at any cost and by all means. It is not acceptable to create an FTAA founded on propositions that frustrate basic social goals, especially in the area of public health. As in any other trade negotiation in which Brazil has participated, the FTAA should be evaluated on its benefits and costs—both economic and social—taking into consideration the interests of society as a whole and the goal of development in its broader sense. The appropriateness of FTAA should be measured, therefore, through the contributions that a possible agreement could make, or fail to make, to prosperity and the reduction of social and economic inequities in the Hemisphere.

Conclusion

In Europe there seems to be a dangerous trend in which one country's protectionist measures justify more protectionism in other countries. It is hard to say if that constitutes a long term movement or is just an occasional phenomenon. It is clear, however, that these days are not particularly favorable for the negotiation of free trade agreements. Recent agreements signed by the United States have faced significant resistance in the U.S. Congress, not to mention resistance in countries that happen to be their counterparts in those agreements. On the multilateral side, the Doha Round of trade negotiations is in danger, largely because of Europe's reluctance to make significant reforms to its Common Agricultural Policy. That same stumbling block hinders the advance of an agreement between the EU and Mercosur, while the FTAA seems unlikely to become a reality in the foreseeable future. In this context, it is time rich countries start to realize that their current attitude of fiercely protecting their markets—especially in agriculture—while making outrageous demands of liberalization in new areas—such as services, investment, intellectual property and government procurement—will only create more resistance in developing countries, which will probably be attracted to protectionism themselves.

Notes

The authors thank Keila Evangelista and Davi Augusto Oliveira Pinto for their assistance in preparing this chapter.

1. Ideally, an agreement aimed at promoting development might be *unbalanced* in favor of poorer countries. What we were facing in the FTAA negotiations was the opposite situation, however, in that the proposals were actually unbalanced in favor of rich countries. Our realistic goal therefore was to reach a balanced agreement, which took into consideration the interests and needs of all countries.

2. See Nicola Phillips (this volume).

3. Some analysts suggest that agricultural subsidies are beneficial for developing countries because they lower the prices of imported food and inputs. However, while this does provide a temporary benefit for consumers, we maintain that this is not a good thing for developing countries, since that effect actually damages their economies by discriminating against local producers, who are unable to compete—sometimes in their own internal markets—against subsidized prices.

4. A press released from Oxfam, titled "U.S. Free Trade Agreements Block Access to Medicines" and dated August 16, 2006 (available at http://www.oxfam.org/en/news/pressreleases2006/pr060816_aids, last accessed February 23, 2008) summarizes the dangerous provisions included in agreements recently negotiated by the United States:

    U.S. bilateral trade agreements include provisions to:
    – expand the scope of pharmaceutical patents to include new indications, new formulations, and other minor changes;
    – limit grounds for issuing compulsory licenses to emergencies, government non-commercial use, and competition cases only;
    – bar parallel trade of on-patent drugs sold more cheaply elsewhere;
    – extend patent monopolies for administrative delays; and
    – enhance protections for clinical trial data by providing at least five years of data exclusivity and by linking drug registration rights to patent status.

    Oxfam has published in the past years a series of Policy Papers in which these issues are examined in detail. They are all available at http://www.oxfam.org/en/policy, last accessed February 23, 2008.

5. The latest draft chapter of FTAA on Intellectual Property Rights, which can be found in the official FTAA Web site (http://www.ftaa-FTAA.org/FTAADraft03/ChapterXX_e.asp, last accessed February 23, 2008) includes several "TRIPS-plus" proposals, as the

two examples below, extracted from the Subsection on "Undisclosed Information." As most of the draft agreement, the proposals are between brackets, meaning that not all countries support them:

[If a Party requires the submission of information concerning the safety and efficacy of a pharmaceutical or agricultural chemical product prior to permitting the marketing of such product, such Party shall not permit third parties not having the consent of the party providing the information to market the same or a similar product on the basis of the approval granted to the party submitting such information for a period of at least five (5) years from the date of approval.]

[If a Party provides a means of granting approval to market products specified in paragraph 1.2 on the basis of the grant of an approval for marketing of the same or similar product in another Party, the Party shall defer the date of any such approval to third parties not having the consent of the party providing the information in the other Party for a period of at least five (5) years from the date of approval in the Party or the date of approval in the other Party, whichever is later.]

References

Bahadian, A. G. and E. Vieira V. (1998) "O Brasil e a Cúpula das Américas," Política Externa, 7 (2) (September–November), 90–116.

Bhagwati, J. (2002) *Free Trade Today*, Princeton, NJ: Princeton University Press.

Rodrik, D. (2001) *The Global Governance of Trade As If Development Really Mattered*, New York: United Nations Development Program.

Shadlen, K. C. (2005) "Exchanging Development for Market Access? Deep Integration and Industrial Policy under Multilateral and Regional-Bilateral Trade Agreements," *Review of International Political Economy*, 12 (5) (December): 750–775.

Chapter 9

Canada and the Politics of Regional Economic Integration in the Americas

Laura Macdonald

As a key actor in two intersecting regional integration projects, Canada's position can arguably reveal much about the complex dynamics of economic integration in the Americas. Canada has undergone a fundamental shift in its economic and foreign policy priorities since the late 1980s that has brought it closer to the hemisphere. After a long history of rejection of a comprehensive free trade relationship with the United States, the Canadian government first sought, and later signed, the Canada-U.S. Free Trade Agreement (CUSFTA), which entered into effect in 1989 (against much popular opposition). Canada was a less willing participant in the North American Free Trade Agreement (NAFTA) after Mexico decided to imitate Canada's success in gaining preferential access to the U.S. economy, but the Canadian state has since become a proud NAFTA booster. As well, after belatedly entering into inter-American politics by joining the Organization of American States (OAS) in 1990, Canada has become one of the most active and prominent countries in promoting a Free Trade Area of the Americas (FTAA). As discussed elsewhere in this volume, the prominent role of the United States is one of the most controversial aspects of the ongoing process of regional economic integration in the Americas. Can Canada present a "kindler, gentler" face to the economic integration project?

Daudelin and Molot argue in a 2000 article that Canada has been the "single most important driving force behind the [FTAA] process as it has evolved over the last five years, since the process was initiated at the Miami Summit of the Chiefs of States of the Americas in 1994. We have also been a leader in the formal negotiations on the agreement that began

18 months ago" (2000: 48). More recently, the Conservative minority government of Stephen Harper announced in May 2007 that Latin America and the Caribbean would be one of Canada's main foreign policy priorities.

Canada's entry into the CUSFTA and, to a lesser extent, the NAFTA, were extremely controversial domestically in Canada because of long-standing fears of U.S. dominance over the much smaller Canadian economy and corresponding fears of loss of sovereignty and identity. In retrospect, though, Canada's formal embrace of North American regional integration reflects a long-standing process of gradual integration of the U.S. and Canadian economies. Canada's role as an enthusiastic and prominent promoter of the FTAA seems more surprising, given Canada's minimal trade and investment ties with FTAA countries other than the United States and, to a much lesser extent, Mexico.[1] Given the fact that Canada has little to gain in economic terms and something fairly significant to lose, that is, being forced to share with more countries its privileged access to its most important trading partner and the world's largest market, how do we explain Canada's position? Revealingly, Canada's posture differs significantly from that of its NAFTA partner Mexico, which has adopted a low-profile position of support for the FTAA. This posture reflects Mexico's lack of desire to break openly with the United States, but its distinct lack of enthusiasm for the prospect of sharing its preferential access to the U.S. economy with its neighbors in Latin America and the Caribbean.[2] Although there are several possible explanations of why Canada might support the FTAA initiative, I argue that only a constructivist approach, which emphasizes the importance of ideas and identity in the construction of regional spaces, adequately explains the fervor of Canada's support for the FTAA and its reluctance to actively pursue bilateral trade agreements with individual Latin American countries.

In this chapter, I offer an explanation of Canada's role in the process of inter-American regional integration, drawing upon recent theories of the "new regionalism" and constructivist approaches. In particular, Peter J. Katzenstein's (2005) theory of world politics as dominated by "porous regions" embedded within an "American imperium" provides a convincing analysis of the global context in which regional integration is occurring. I argue that this approach captures the stark asymmetries that characterize the process of regional integration in the Americas, and takes into account both the structural and the inter-subjective dimensions of regionaliza-tion. A constructivist approach suggests Canada's commitment to the project of hemispheric integration is best understood not as a misguided illusion of state elites or as a project to counterbalance U.S. power, but as a technique by which policy actors are able to simultaneously embrace and resist U.S. power. Thus, as discussed in the chapter by Bahadian and

Carvalho Lyrio in this volume, Canada remains a strong supporter of some of the more controversial aspects of U.S. positions in continental negotiations, such as its support for inclusion of intellectual property rights.

Theoretical Approaches to Regional Integration

There are several existing explanations of Canada's role in the FTAA, all of which focus primarily on domestic determinants of Canada's position. Given that there are few domestic actors that have enthusiastically endorsed the FTAA, this is a difficult position to sustain. Like in the United States and other states of the hemisphere, non-business civil society actors actively oppose the FTAA, as an extension of their opposition to the CUSFTA and NAFTA, as well as new ties with hemispheric civil society actors in the Americas. Business actors, while not opposed to the FTAA, have not made support for the FTAA a priority, reflecting their overwhelming interest in the U.S. market that accounts for 87 percent of Canadian exports (Goldfarb, 2004: 7). Lacking a compelling domestic constituency to which to attribute Canada's position, most analysts refer to classic liberal institutionalist explanations of Canada's position. Traditional interpretations of Canadian foreign policy argue that Canada has traditionally pursued middle-power politics in support of multilateral institutions because of its desire to offset U.S. dominance and restrain U.S. unilateralism.

Along these lines, in the context of the Americas, some argue that while Canada's economic interests in Latin America may be minor, as a relatively small economy, Canada has an interest in a rules-based system of trade in the region. Others refer to the Canadian state's interest in an orderly hemisphere, and thus to Canada's desire to promote a community of the Americas, what former Prime Minister Jean Chrétien referred to as *una gran familia* (Gecelovsky, 2002: 745). Gordon Mace maintains, "Ottawa's overriding goal [in promoting the FTAA framework] was to balance the asymmetrical Canada-U.S. relationship in the context of the Americas" (Mace, 2007: 112). A 1998 *Toronto Star* editorial argued, rather surprisingly: "The great benefit for Canada of getting involved in Latin America is that it gets us out of the U.S. backyard" (quoted in Goldstein, 2001: 194). John Graham, the chair of the Canadian Foundation for the Americas (FOCAL) states that the timing is good for Canada to revitalize its role in the hemisphere: "The U.S. is so focused on Iraq, and its influence in the region has never been as low as it is now" (*Globe & Mail*, April 24, 2006).

Nevertheless, as Mace points out, Canada has been unwilling to depart significantly from U.S. trade policy or to compromise with some of the Latin American actors in the FTAA negotiations such as Brazil and Argentina that have resisted a "WTO-plus" agreement. The Canadian government has insisted in the need for the FTAA to cover new trade issues like rules on investment, services, subsidies and intellectual property rights which were included in the NAFTA (Mace, 2007: 113–14; Lofthouse, 2004: 827). It is unclear how involvement in the FTAA could result in any real balancing of the role of the United States if Canada fails to shift away from the NAFTA model of trade policy to incorporate some of the critiques made by southern partners and civil society actors.

A realist response to these positions argues that given Canada's minimal economic ties with FTAA countries other than the United States and Mexico, the Canadian state's enthusiastic pursuit of the FTAA is highly misguided. Alexander Lofthouse, senior policy analyst for the Canadian Chamber of Commerce, rejects traditional Canadian goals of diversification of Canadian trade in order to avoid "dependence" on the U.S. market: "Canada's top trade priority is, and must remain, its relationship with the United States" (Lofthouse, 2004: 815). Canada should not "pull the plug" on the FTAA, but it should not lose sight of "priority one: enhancing Canada-U.S. and NAFTA-zone trade" (Lofthouse, 2004: 816). The implication is that the FTAA should be put on the trade policy back burner.

From a somewhat different perspective, Jean Daudelin and Maureen Molot argue: "the hemisphere is not a real option for Canada's trade strategy; an FTAA is not likely to serve the region well in the short or medium term, or to bring Canada closer to key hemisphere players; and finally, focused bilateral efforts rather than regional negotiations would better serve Canadian interests." Daudelin and Molot review the justifications that have been given for Canadian participation in the FTAA, and find them all wanting. They maintain that given the strain on Canadian foreign policy capacity, a more sensible policy would involve focusing on more realistic priorities: first, the fledgling WTO trade architecture, and, within the Americas, developing a stronger relationship with Brazil, a country with which Canada has been drawn into unproductive trade disputes. While raising many important critiques, Daudelin and Molot fail to explain convincingly why Canada has pursued its quixotic quest of support for the FTAA. It could be argued from a realist perspective that, as with the case of the negotiation of NAFTA, the Canadian government recognized that the U.S.-led process of regional integration in the Americas was a freight train they could not stop, and that it would have an affect on Canadian interests, so Canada should support the process in order to have some control over the outcomes. Or, alternatively, it could be argued, as Daudelin does in his article "Foreign Policy at the Fringes," that the fact that Canada has little at stake in the FTAA discussions means that policy can quite easily be hijacked by a single player, as, he maintains, occurred with the case of Bombardier and Brazil (Daudelin, 2003: 659).

In the case of the FTAA, it is possible that either narrow sectoral interests like mining companies with a strong interest in liberalized investment rules, or fervent pro-free trade bureaucrats within the trade division of Foreign Affairs, hijacked the FTAA process.

Nevertheless, I contend that these explanations, while adequate to explain Canada's support for the FTAA, fail to explain the fervency and enthusiasm with which Canada has supported the FTAA project. Nor do they explain why Canada has not enthusiastically pursued bilateral trade agreements that might achieve the same objectives and lower political costs, particularly in the past couple of years when the FTAA project has faltered. In the Americas, since the signing of NAFTA, Canada has only negotiated trade agreements with Chile (1997) and Costa Rica (2001). The Harper government recently announced that it is attempting to con- clude trade pacts with the "Central American four" (CA4)—El Salvador, Guatemala, Honduras, and Nicaragua, negotiations that have languished for years, and plans to launch negotiations with Colombia, Peru, the Dominican Republic, and other Caribbean states (MacKay, 2007). Nevertheless, Canada lags well behind the United States in establishing regional and bilateral trade agreements.

While both realist and liberal institutionalist approaches illuminate some dimensions of Canadian policy in the hemisphere, they both have conceptual weaknesses. Liberal institutionalist approaches fail to address the growing ties with the U.S. economy and the qualitative shift in the nature of Canadian integration with the U.S. economy. As Daudelin and Molot put it, "Canada is now part of a North American financial and industrial unit that includes the US and Mexico, but no one else. For better or worse, NAFTA has an economic basis that an FTAA utterly lacks" (Daudelin and Molot, 2000: 49) An approach based on "balancing" U.S. power fails to recognize the overwhelming nature of U.S. power, particularly within the North American region, and clings to outdated notions of state autonomy. Liberal institutionalist approaches are derived from a cold war context that ignores the fundamental shifts that have occurred in global power relations since the end of the cold war and, in particular, the rise of a U.S. unilateralism that is apparently oblivious to the maneuverings of erstwhile "middle powers" (Macdonald, 2004). On the other hand, realist accounts underestimate the importance of intersubjective factors as drivers of state policy. The fact that Canada's economic ties with Latin America are minimal in contrast with its ties with the United States does not mean that Latin America is unimportant in Canadian policy. However, Canada has played a role in the FTAA not as a way to balance U.S. power, but as an extension of its entrenched position within the NAFTA region.

As suggested above, dominant explanations of Canada's role in the FTAA are rooted primarily in explanations based on domestic determinants of state policy. I suggest here, however, that a more convincing explanation requires a sophisticated analysis of the intersection of the forces at work in the global economy with the domestic politics of identity construction. In particular, how do we understand the strong forces promoting the complementary but also contradictory forces of globalization and regionalization? Most theories of regionalization are based on the experience of the European Union (EU), an experience that is not particularly helpful for explaining either the global dynamics of regionalization, or the internal dynamics of non-European regions. Despite the failure of Europe-based integration theories to examine the dynamics of regional integration in other settings, these are the conceptual tools that have been largely adopted by theorists of the "other regionalisms" (see Hettne, 1997; Larner and Walters, 2002; Wallace, 1994).[3]

Nevertheless, one of the more useful approaches to come out of recent theorizing on the process of regional integration in Europe is constructivism. Constructivist scholars have argued for the importance of ideas, norms, institutions and identities, in the emergence of the European Community (Diez and Wiener, 2004: 9; Rosamond, 2001). Constructivists do not deny the importance of interests, but contend that there is no such thing as a "real" interest independent from the discursive context in which they emerge (Diez, 2001: 86). Andrew Hurrell thus contends,

> There are no "natural regions," and definitions of "region" and indicators of "regionness" vary according to the particular problem or question under investigation.
>   Moreover it is how political actors perceive and interpret the idea of a region and notions of "regionness" that is critical: all regions are socially constructed and hence politically contested. (1995: 38–39)

Constructivist approaches to the North American region are relatively rare. Stephanie Golob presents one constructivist reading of Canada-U.S. border politics after 9/11. As she argues, constructivist accounts help to account for a variety of state behaviors that might otherwise be viewed as unlikely or irrational: "States…delineate and judge their options for international action based upon criteria that may advance symbolic or identity-inscribed values as opposed to material interests" (2002: 8). Canada and the United States thus share not only a geographic but also a symbolic space that makes asymmetry a "defining feature of their relationship. . . . While Canada's foreign policy apparatus is almost entirely geared either to deal with the U.S. or to symbolically distinguish Canada from the U.S., Canada barely registers on the U.S. foreign policy radar screen" (2002: 15; see also Gilbert, 2005). Francesco Duina also argues that regions are socially constructed, and emphasizes that neoliberalism is a relatively generic ideology that manifests itself differently in different locations, depending on the preexisting norms, ideologies, and institutions of that area. In the case of NAFTA, he maintains, the dominance of a common-law tradition in the United States and Canada led to a minimalist form of region-building, compared to the more interventionist style that has emerged in areas such as the EU where civil law traditions hold sway (2006).

International Political Economy scholar Peter Katzenstein also offers useful theoretical tools for interpreting regionalism and its global context. In his recent book, *A World of Regions*, Peter Katzenstein argues that the best way to understand the world after the end of the cold war and after September 11 is: "ours is a world of regions, embedded deeply in an American imperium" (2005: 1). Like the constructivists, Katzenstein understands regions as comprising both material and symbolic dimensions and underlines the contributions of critical theories of geography: "regions are politically made." As Ruggie argues, in the modern state system, "Space is not given in nature. It is a social construct that people, somehow, invent" (Ruggie, 1999: 235, cited in Katzenstein, 2005: 9). He makes four main arguments: (1) the American imperium has been having a profound effect on regions through a mix of territorial and nonterritorial powers; (2) these regions differ in their institutional form, type of identity and internal structure; (3) complementary processes of globalization and internationalization are making this "a world of *porous* regions"; and (4) the porosity of regions is enhanced by vertical relations linking core regional states to the American imperium, to smaller state and non-state actors in the regions, and to subnational areas (Katzenstein, 2005: 1–2). The United States both shapes, and is shaped by, its relations with global regions. The construction of a North American region, for example, is a highly political and symbolic process. Similarly, Canada's recent turn to the hemisphere has not occurred because it has physically shifted locations, but as the outcome of long-standing economic and political processes, and resulting shifts in national identity. This is also, of course, a highly contested process.

Katzenstein emphasizes the porosity of regions to counter traditional geopolitical constructions of regions as bounded, inward-directed trading blocs. International and global exchanges push contemporary regions toward links with other regions and global institutions and actors. Regional and Bilateral Trade Agreements are thus "stepping stones, not stumbling blocks, for porous regions" (Katzenstein, 2005: 24–25). The distinctive form of regionalism in the Americas, according to Katzenstein, is shaped by the intensity of the exercise of both territorial and nonterritorial power by the United States, and the absence of a regional power like Germany in Europe or Japan in Asia, that can act as an interlocutor between the U.S. imperium and the region (between the NAFTA and the Mercosur models).

Canada and Mexico cannot play this role (similar to the role envisioned for Canada by the liberal institutionalists) because they are too close to, and dependent on, the United States. In the absence of such a dependable ally in the region, U.S. policy in the region "oscillates widely between disengagement and unilateralism" (Katzenstein, 2005: 228). The porosity of regions means, however, that the stalling of the FTAA has resulted in the proliferation of bilateral trade agreements throughout the region, an outcome that is not likely to have positive outcomes either in promoting Latin American development or in reducing U.S. hegemony in the region (Phillips, 2004). The current impasse in the FTAA negotiations thus presents a major dilemma for Canada's strategy toward the Americas.

As this brief review of the literature has suggested, explanations of Canada's role in promoting economic integration in the Americas is not clearly explained by traditional realist or liberal institutionalist accounts. The case of Canada displays that an adequate understanding of the current process of regional economic integration requires an approach that is sensitive to the role of ideas, institutions and identity as well as interests in the formulation of policy.

Canada and Economic Integration in the Americas: From CUSFTA to NAFTA

As discussed above, the construction of a North American economic region is a relatively recent historical process. Canada and Mexico historically had little consciousness of each other, and few commercial or political interactions, despite their common physical location on the North American continent, because of the looming presence of the United States in between and in the national imaginary of each. For example, in the postwar period the term "North American" was (and is) most commonly used in English to define the bilateral relationship between Canada and the United States, while in Mexico the term *norteamericano* signifies a citizen of the United States. NAFTA provided a reminder to many Canadians that Mexico was a part of the continent as well.

Nevertheless, the United States has historically relied upon geographic location on the North American continent as a basis of its rise to global power. Throughout much of the nineteenth century, the United States' drive to expand its territorial control westward, southward, and northward throughout the North American continent created anxiety among both Mexicans and the British colonies that became Canada, not to mention the Aboriginal peoples who were often violently displaced or extinguished. U.S. right to territorial expansion into Aboriginal lands was justified by the (specious) argument that Indians were nomads and that the land could be considered empty (Stephanson, 1995: 25). Expansion throughout the whole North American continent was justified in the name of the concept of "manifest destiny," a term coined in 1845 by John O'Sullivan. O'Sullivan used this term to refer to the mission of the United States, as a nation chosen by God, to "overspread the continent allotted by Providence for the free development of our yearly multiplying millions" (Stephanson, 1995: xi). Throughout the twentieth century, once continental borders were firmly established, the United States was able to extend its global reach, secure in the notion that neither neighboring country would present a military challenge, and that they would also insulate the United States from more hostile nations and peoples (Gabriel and Macdonald, 2007). Distrust toward the United States remained strong in both Canada and, especially, Mexico, and successive Canadian governments resisted the lure of formalizing its economic ties with its partner to the south through a free trade agreement. It was not until the signing of first the CUSFTA and then the NAFTA that North America shifted from being a continent, to being an economic region.

The CUSFTA was the outcome of several converging factors. First, the deep economic recession of the 1980s destroyed confidence in the prevailing economic model. Second, years of Canadian participation in the General Agreement on Tariffs and Trade (GATT) negotiations had resulted in gradual reduction of tariff barriers, weaning Canadian business from its traditional reliance upon protectionist state barriers. Third, the rise in protectionist U.S. trade policy led business and government leaders to view with favor an arrangement that they hoped would guarantee Canada preferential and secure access to the U.S. economy. And finally, the election of a business-friendly Conservative Party government under Prime Minister Brian Mulroney, as well as the shift of several Canadian provinces toward support for free trade, created the political opening necessary for the negotiation of a free trade agreement. The trade agreement was heavily contested in the so-called "free trade election" of 1988, and was actively opposed by a coalition of trade unions, women's groups, environmentalists, and other social movements, as well as the Liberal Party of Canada. However, the Conservative Party's victory in that election paved the way for the implementation of the agreement.

Canada was less than enthusiastic about Mexico's pursuit of its own agreement with the United States, but eventually agreed to the negotiation of a trilateral agreement in the hopes of avoiding the formation of a hub-and-spoke arrangement, with the United States dominating the region through a series of bilateral accords. The process of negotiation and signing of the NAFTA apparently signified the formal equality of the three North American partners, as each country had a seat at the table. Canada and Mexico hoped that establishing a rules-based system for the management of regional trade would diminish the historical asymmetries between the United States and its two neighbors, and restrain U.S. unilateralist behavior in the region.

Critics of NAFTA would argue that continued trade disputes, such as
the one over softwood lumber, and the failure of Canadian negotiators
to achieve its main objective in the negotiations, a subsidies code,
demonstrate that U.S. unilateralism continues unabated. Nevertheless,
the CUSFTA (and to a lesser extent the NAFTA) has had a dramatic
effect on the Canadian economy and has increased historic patterns of
Canadian dependence on the U.S. economy (see figures 9.1 and 9.2).
Alan Rugman notes that the increase in regional integration under the
CUSFTA and NAFTA has been achieved mainly through trade, not
through investment. He notes that virtual free trade exists in merchandise
trade between Canada and the United States, although significant tariff
barriers exist in trade in services (services exempted in the CUSFTA and
NAFTA include cultural services, health, education, social services,
transportation, and financial services) (Rugman, 2004: 93). Intraregional
trade in NAFTA has risen to 55.7 percent from 33.6 percent in 1980 and
49.19 percent in 1996, largely as a result of the increasing dependence of
both Canada and Mexico on the U.S. market (Rugman, 2004: 93). As of

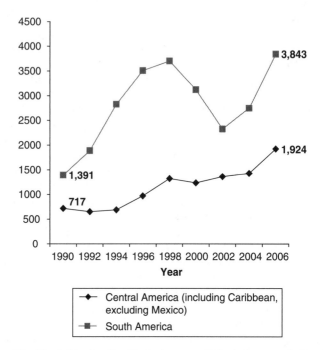

Figure 9.1 Total Merchandise Trade between United States and Canada (in
Million C$)

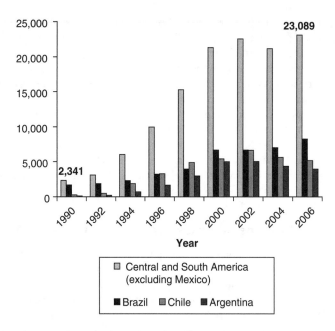

Figure 9.2   Canadian FDI (Stocks) in United States and Mexico

2005, 84 percent of all Canadian exports went to the United States, up from a very high level of 75 percent in 1990 (Statistics Canada, 2006).

The figures for foreign direct investment (FDI) integration are less dramatic. Rugman notes there was a decrease in intraregional FDI as a percentage of total FDI from 30.3 percent in 1986 to 21.1 percent in 1997 to 18.2 percent in 1999. The main reason for the decline in intra-NAFTA investment is the decrease in the percentage of U.S. FDI going to Canada. At the same time, Canadian investment in the United States (and to a lesser extent, in Mexico) has increased (see figure 9.2). These figures contradict the fears of Canadian nationalists that NAFTA would increase the high levels of U.S. investment in Canada, which was historically a major concern. Rugman argues that the main cause of the decrease in U.S. investment in Canada is the CUSFTA, which eliminated existing barriers to trade between the two countries, "reducing the need for FDI to overcome trade barriers." U.S. businesses "can access the Canadian market better than before from production bases in the United States, so less FDI is required to overcome regulatory barriers to traded goods" (Rugman, 2004: 96). It is important to note that manufacturing trade between Canada and the United States is heavily concentrated in the automobile sector (about 50% according to Rugman), and that much of this trade is intra-firm. The trade data thus reflect the increased integration of production across borders as a result of just-in-time production processes. Thus, U.S. domination over the continental economy is shifting in character, not declining.

Rugman's data confirms the arguments made by Katzenstein about the nature of a "world of regions." We see that the NAFTA region is simultaneously being increasingly integrated, while at the same time remaining porous, as intraregional FDI is declining, not only in NAFTA but also in Asia and the EU. Trade data also confirms the extreme asymmetries in the NAFTA region and the predominance of the United States, as the Canadian and Mexican economies have become increasingly dependent on the U.S. market, while both Canada and Mexico are of far less importance in the U.S. economy.

Canada in the Americas: From NAFTA to the FTAA

As we have seen, Canada's engagement with North American regional economic integration has thus far not acted as a barrier to, but as an impetus for, its pursuit of a role in the Western hemisphere, also confirming Katzenstein's argument about the porosity of regions. Up until 1990, Canada resisted joining the OAS, first because Canada's colonial ties to the United Kingdom precluded its joining an organization that resisted external intervention in the hemisphere, and later because of its reluctance to get caught up in the cold war politics of the United States' role in Latin America. According to Richard Gorham, former Canadian permanent observer to the OAS, "the traditional explanation for not joining was that we would have to oppose Washington on particular issues or else run the risk of becoming a U.S. puppet" (Tittemore, 1995). Mulroney chose to apply to join the OAS (after eighteen years as a permanent observer) after signing the CUSFTA, in belated recognition of the fact that Canada was a nation of the Americas. After joining the OAS, Canada became an active member, with major emphasis on such areas as democratic development, environmental protection and institutional reform (Tittemore, 1995). Canada was the major supporter of the creation of the Unit for the Promotion of Democracy. Canada hosted the OAS General Assembly in Windsor in June 2000 and the Summit of the Americas in Quebec City in April 2001. Canada has also been a major actor in establishing a Democracy Charter and in pushing for resolution of the Peruvian political crisis (Randall, 2002). As former Minister for International Trade, Pierre Pettigrew, stated to a multistakeholder consultation on Canada and the FTAA, "We are the ones who decided to put democracy and good governance at the centre of the hemispheric agenda" (DFAIT, 2003: 6).

In the economic domain, Canada's involvement in the hemisphere has been gradually increasing. As figures 1 and 2 show, both trade and investment have been rising at a healthy rate in absolute terms. However, Canada remains a relatively small player, and overall levels of trade with Latin America and the Caribbean (outside of Mexico) remain stagnant. While Canada's total exports to the United States increased 228 percent between 1990 and 2004, and a dramatic 393 percent to Mexico in the same period (on a very low base), exports to Latin America outside of Mexico increased only 138 percent. This figure actually represents a decline in Latin America's share of Canada's total exports, which went from 1.41 percent in 1990 to 1.15 percent in 2004. Daudelin and Molot argue that Canadian·government rhetoric about the FTAA promise of access to a market with a total population of 800 million people and a combined GDP of $15 trillion is utterly misleading:

> What the FTAA would add to NAFTA is closer to 400 million people and $2.4 trillion of GDP. That's big, but hardly what is advertised. Moreover, half the new market is made up of Brazil—the country least enamoured of an FTAA—and more than 70 percent is Mercosur; the trade group Brazil leads. (Daudelin and Molot, 2000: 49)

Moreover, investment figures (in figure 2) are misleading, because more than half of Canadian stock of investments in the region is located in a few Caribbean banking centres (Daudelin and Molot, 2000: 49). Jean Daudelin argues, starkly: "in economic terms, Latin America and the Caribbean can in no way be conceived as [an] important or even relatively significant region for Canada, not now, not in the future" (Daudelin, 2003: 641).

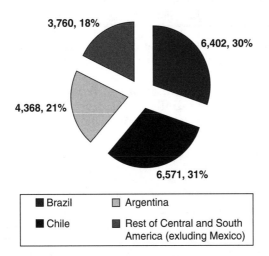

Source: DFAIT, 2007.

Despite the relatively minor nature of Canadian economic interests in the Latin American and Caribbean, Canada has played an energetic role in promoting an FTAA. After launching the FTAA project, the United States appeared to become indifferent to its success. Particularly after the attacks of 9/11, the United States shifted its attention to the war on terror and military engagements in Afghanistan and Iraq. Thus, paradoxically, once having decided that economic integration in the Americas was proceeding and it was in Canada's interests to join in, Canada found itself as one of the only states actively promoting it (Daudelin, 2003: 649).

Instead of displaying a real openness to the region, however, Canada's strategy has reflected a desire to extend the provisions of the NAFTA to the FTAA, rather than an incorporation of the interests and concerns of its major Latin American counterparts, especially Brazil. The Canadian government has thus insisted on the inclusion of not just tariff reduction but also the elements of the "new trade agenda" such as rules on investment, services, subsidies, and intellectual property rights that were part of the NAFTA agreement (Mace, 2007: 112).[4] In 2000, a FOCAL policy paper argued:

> ... looking at Canada's increasing integration into NAFTA, its basic interests may lie in the spreading of the "NAFTA Model" both at the regional and global level. Fortunately, the trends in this regard are already apparent and Canada only needs to help push them forward. At the global level, agreements negotiated or proposed in the past few years appear to be heavily influenced by the nature and structure of NAFTA. At the regional level, the influence of the "NAFTA Model" is even more apparent in the structure adopted for the FTAA negotiations. (FOCAL, 2000: 6)

It was, however, perhaps this similarity to the NAFTA model, so heavily promoted by Canada and the United States, which was responsible for the stalling of the FTAA.

Former Canadian trade negotiator and executive director of FOCAL, Donald Mackay, argued that the formula developed in the 2003 Miami Declaration, which threw out the "single undertaking," was prejudicial to Canadian interests:

> Undeniable is the fact that the US has now sent the signal that it is prepared to entertain the prospect of granting much-desired access to its market in exchange for a less than comprehensive price. That is to say, Canada, Mexico and Chile all had to agree to deep and broad disciplines in order to achieve preferential access to the US market. If the US eventually exchanges similar levels of access to Brazil at a lower "price," then the US will have effectively discounted the efforts of its larger and more important trading partners. (Mackay, 2003: 11)

Following Mackay's logic, Canada had an interest in enforcing the NAFTA model on other countries, rather than in allowing the FTAA to adapt to the interests of the Mercosur countries.

Canada's role in the hemisphere has also been limited by its rocky relationship with Brazil, the other country that could possibly serve as intermediary between U.S. and Latin American interests. Canada has failed to develop a strong relationship with Brazil, despite the fact that Brazil is an obvious candidate for trade diversification. As the Brazilian ambassador to Canada noted in 2004,

> here are two large hemispheric neighbours reaching out to the world and yet failing to find ways to cooperate with each other more closely. What is more, they tend to share similar perceptions of, and favour similar approaches to, some of the most significant issues currently featuring high on the international agenda but, for the most part, fail to coordinate their endeavors. (Leão Neto, 2004: 3)

Trade disputes over aircrafts and beef have undermined the relationship. But Jean Daudelin argues the differences are more fundamental, related to the two countries' very different trajectories: "While Brazil was going global, Canada was turning North American; in both cases, it meant that the bilateral relationship was becoming increasingly irrelevant" (Daudelin, 2002: 266). So closely tied to their neighbor and largest trading partner, Canadian leaders were unable to look beyond the North American mindset to permit real dialogue and compromise. The comments in the chapter by Bahadian and Carvalho Lyrio in this volume about Canada's close supportive role of the United States in the FTAA negotiations reflect the skepticism of the Brazilian government about Canada's hemispheric ambitions.

Nevertheless, the Canadian government has felt compelled to venture out into the hemisphere at the same time as it becomes ever more closely linked with the U.S. economy. This desire is not merely "symbolic," as Daudelin terms it (2002: 268). Rather it reflects deeply felt anxieties among the Canadian population and governors about the country's close ties with the United States (particularly under the country's current unilateralist leader), and Canadians' strong attachment to the image of themselves as global (or at least regional) "consensus-builders" and "facilitators."[5] Canada's engagement with the politics of regional economic integration thus allows the country to simultaneously embrace and resist the powerful forces of economic and political integration with the United States.

Conclusion

Canada's enthusiastic pursuit of a leading role in the FTAA can thus tell us much about the broader dynamics of integration in the Americas.

Peter Katzenstein's work suggests that regions are not autarchic and inward-looking, but porous and interconnected. All global regions, the Americas in particular, are shaped by the dynamics of the imperial role of the United States. And regions are shaped by a combination of material and ideational forces. This ideational aspect imbues nations with meaning beyond their merely economic dimensions. As Wendy Larner and William Walters point out, analysts' understanding of the "new regionalism" is generally impeded by long-standing intellectual habits that tend to naturalize or "inevitablize" the region. These modes of interpretation thus overlook what is novel about regions in the contemporary period:

> Not only is regionalism about place, making agreements, and the work the subjects of those agreements must do to fulfill them—it is also about "clubs." Inclusion and exclusion are not derivative or incidental features of regionalism, but are intrinsic to the way regions govern. As the enlargement process of regions shows, regions govern in part by implicating their members in projects (perhaps "missions") of reform, rationalization and national improvement. This is how the process of inclusion works, backed always by the possibility of exclusion should requisite standards not be met. (Larner and Walters, 2002: 418)

Membership in regions is pursued not just because of the economic motivations of powerful actors, like multinational corporations, but also because they carry with them connotations of prestige and progress, and contribute to national processes of identity formation.

As this interpretation suggests, Canada has sought leadership in the FTAA "club" as an outcome of its successes and its dilemmas as charter member of the NAFTA club. The FTAA thus takes on importance out of proportion to the hard facts as revealed in trade and investment statistics. Former Canadian trade minister Pettigrew was thus quoted as saying, "If the FTAA stumbles, Canada could be left by the wayside. . . . We will lose some of our place in the world" (Mace, 2007: 108). As this chapter has demonstrated, despite the fact that Canada lacks important economic interests in the region of Latin America and the Caribbean, and despite a long history of engagement in the region, since joining NAFTA, Canada has consistently sought to carve out a leadership role in the process of inter-American economic integration. Its strong stake in the NAFTA mission precludes it, however, from transcending its identity as NAFTA club member and assuming a true intermediary role between the U.S. imperium and the states of Latin America and the Caribbean.

The crisis of the FTAA project thus poses important challenges to Canada. The United States' pursuit of bilateral trade agreements throughout the Americas may help promote the NAFTA model, but thrusts us back into the hub-and-spoke model of U.S. dominance that Canada had hoped to avoid with the signing of NAFTA. And while Canada has signed its own trade agreements with Chile and Costa Rica, and has talks ongoing with other countries, these are not grand schemes that can fulfill the desire for diversification and engagement outside of North America promised by the FTAA. The other clear alternative available to Canada is the path towards deeper North American integration, an alternative that has been heavily promoted by business associations and some academics. The signing of the Security and Prosperity Partnership of North America (SPP) in Waco Texas in March 2005 by the three North American leaders was a tentative step down this path. However, pursuing a strategy that so clearly ties the country closer to the United States economically and politically continues to be viewed by many Canadians as a highly risky and controversial choice. The Harper government's 2007 launching of a new Latin American strategy is a propitious moment to review Canada's position in the hemisphere. As discussed elsewhere in this volume, the strategies adopted by Canada and the United States have not been successful in promoting sustainable economic in the region. Canada could play a positive role by promoting bilateral, regional, and hemispheric initiatives that would counteract the existing asymmetries in the hemisphere, and by limiting the influence of big business actors and the U.S. government in the establishment of foreign policy initiatives.

Notes

I thank Arne Ruckert for his research assistance. I thank Arne Ruckert, Jean Daudelin, and the editors of this volume for their comments and suggestions. I also appreciate the financial support of the Social Sciences and Humanities Research Council of Canada (SSHRC).

1. In 2006, for example, Canadian exports to Latin America (without Mexico) were only C$5,768 million, compared to C$363,643 million to the NAFTA region.
2. Donald Mackay argued in 2002 that Mexico has apparently adopted a "spoiler" strategy because of its reliance on its status as the only low–labor cost manufacturing platform in Latin America with preferential access to the U.S. market; it has thus been "obstructionist and frequently unconstructive inside the negotiations" (Mackay, 2002: 12).
3. European functionalist theory was extremely influential in processes of regional integration promoted in Latin America by ECLA in the 1960s.
4. It is important to note that the Canadian government has played an active role not just in the inclusion of certain economic provisions, but has also advocated the reform of the FTAA negotiating process to

236   LAURA MACDONALD

incorporate a certain degree of civil society participation in the FTAA
process in response to widespread civil society discontent with the
FTAA. The results of this process, including the establishment of a
Committee of Government Representatives on the Participation of
Civil Society (CGR) and the so-called mailbox mechanism for public
inputs were, however, viewed as highly unsatisfactory by civil society
organizations (see Shamsie, 2003: 17–21).
5. The Brazilian ambassador to Canada says these are self-images shared
   by both Canadians and Brazilians (Leão Neto, 2004: 3).

References

Daudelin, J. (2003) "Foreign Policy at the Fringe: Canada and Latin
America," *International Journal*, 58 (4): 637–666.
Daudelin, J. and M. A. Molot (2000) "Canada and the FTAA: The
Hemispheric Bloc Temptation," *Policy Options* (March): 48–51.
Department of Foreign Affairs and International Trade (DFAIT) (2003)
"Multistakeholder Consultation: Canada and the Free Trade Area of
the Americas (FTAA) Report," available: http://www.dfait-maeci.gc.ca/
tna-nac/documents/Report.pdf, accessed April 4, 2006.
——— (2007) Foreign Direct Investment Statistics, Available: www.
dfait-maeci.gc.ca/eet/FDI-stock-outward-by-country-data-en.pdf,
accessed September 7, 2007.
Diez, T. (2001) "Speaking 'Europe': The Politics of Integration Discourse"
in *The Social Construction of Europe*, ed. T. Christiansen, K. E.
Jørgensen, and A. Wiener, London and Thousand Oaks, CA: Sage,
85–100.
Diez, T. and A. Wiener (2004) "Introducing the Mosaic of Integration
Theory," in A. Wiener and T. Diez (eds.) *European Integration Theory*,
Oxford: Oxford University Press, 1–22.
Duina, F. (2006) *The Social Construction of Free Trade: The European
Union, NAFTA, and MERCOSUR*, Princeton, NJ: Princeton University
Press.
FOCAL (2000) "The FTAA after Toronto and Seattle: Why It Still
Matters", FOCAL Policy Paper, available: www.focal.ca/pdf/ftaa2000.
pdf, accessed April 4, 2006.
Gabriel, C. and L. Macdonald (2007) "From the 49th Parallel to the
Río Grande: U.S. Homeland Security and North American Borders," in
Y. Abu-Laban, R. Jhappan, and F. Rocher (eds.) *Politics in North America:
Redefining Continental Relations*, Peterborough, ON: Broadview.
Gecelovsky, P. (2002) "Una gran familia: Le Canada et la ZLÉA," *Études
Internacionales*, 33 (4): 745–762.
Gilbert, E. (2005) "Inevitability of Integration? Neoliberal Discourse and
the Proposals for a New North American Economic Space after
September 1," *Annals of the Association of American Geographers*, 95 (1):
202–222.

Globe & Mail (2006) "How Canada Can Help Latin America Grow,"
    April 24, A14.
Goldfarb, D. (2004) "The FTAA Bulletin: Analysts Comment on Their
    Country and the Free Trade Area of the Americas," Toronto, Canada:
    C.D. Howe Institute, available: www.cdhowe.org/pdf/FTAABulletin.
    pdf, accessed April 4, 2006.
Goldstein, M. (2001) "Canada: Economic Development under NAFTA,
    Dominant Economic Player under FTAA," *NAFTA: Law and Business
    Review of the Americas,* 7 (1–2): 183–206.
Golob, S. R. (2002) *North America Beyond NAFTA? Sovereignty, Identity,
    and Security in Canada-US Relations,* Canadian-American Public Policy
    Occasional Papers, No. 52.
Hettne, B. (1997) "Europe in a World of Regions," in R. Falk and T. Szentes
    (eds.) *A New Europe in the Changing Global System* Tokyo, New York and
    Paris: United Nations University Press, 16–40.
Hurrell, A. (1995) "Regionalism in Theoretical Perspective," in L. Fawcett
    and A. Hurrell, eds., *Regionalism in World Politics: Regional
    Organization and International Order* (Oxford University Press, 1995),
    37–73.
Industry Canada (2007) "Strategis [*sic*] Trade Data Online," available:
    http://strategis.ic.gc.ca/sc_mrkti/tdst/engdoc/tr_homep.html, accessed
    July 9, 2007.
Katzenstein, P. J. (2005) *A World of Regions: Asia and Europe in the
    American Imperium,* Ithaca, NY: Cornell University Press.
Larner, W. and W. Walters (2002) "The Political Rationality of 'New
    Regionalism': Toward a Genealogy of the Region," *Theory and Society,*
    31: 391–432.
Leão Neto, V. C. (2004) *FOCAL Point,* Special edition (November):
    3–5.
Lofthouse, A. (2004) "Making Choices: Canadian Trade and Investment Policy
    in the 21st Century," *International Journal,* 59 (4): 815–828.
Macdonald, Laura (2004) "In the Shadow of the Hyperpower: Beyond
    Canada's Middle-Power Image," in G. Williams and M. Whittington
    (eds.) *Canadian Politics in the 21st Century,* Toronto, Canada: Thomson
    Nelson, 291–311.
Mace, G. (2007) "The FTAA Stalemate: Implications for Canadian Foreign
    Policy," in I. Studer and C. Wise, eds., *Requiem or Revival? The Promise
    of North American Integration,* Washington, DC: Brookings Institution
    Press, 108–123.
Mackay, D. R. (2002) "Challenges Confronting the Free Trade Area of the
    Americas," *FOCAL Policy Paper,* available: www.focal.ca/pdf/ftaa2002.
    pdf, accessed April 4, 2006.
———— (2003) "FTAA: The Common Tragedy of Losing the Single
    Undertaking," *FOCAL Point,* 2 (11): 10–11.
MacKay, P. (2007) "Expanding Trade and Foreign Relations in the
    Americas: Canada Counts," notes for an address to the Canadian Club

of Toronto, May 25, available at www.international.gc.ca, accessed February 20, 2008 .

Phillips, N. (2004) "U.S. Trade Strategies and the FTAA Process," *FOCAL Point,* 3 (1): 3–4.

Randall, S. J. (2002) "In Search of a Hemispheric Role: Canada and the Americas," in N. Hilmer and M. A. Molot (eds.) *Canada Among Nations 2002: A Fading Power,* Oxford: Oxford University Press, 233–255.

Rosamond, B. (2001) "Discourses of Globalization and European Identities," in T. Christiansen, K. E. Jørgensen, and A. Wiener (eds.) *The Social Construction of Europe,* London and Thousand Oaks, CA: Sage, 158–173.

Rugman, A. M. (2004) "Economic integration in North America: Implications for the Americas," in S. Weintraub, A. M. Rugman, and G. Boyd (eds.) *Free Trade in the Americas: Economic and Political Issues for Governments and Firms,* Cheltenham, UK and Northampton, MA: Edward Elgar, 90–106.

Shamsie, Y. (2003) "Mutual Misgivings: Civil Society Inclusion in the Americas," Ottawa, Canada: North-South Institute.

Stephanson, A. (1995) *Manifest Destiny: American Expansion and the Empire of Right,* New York: Hill and Wang.

Tittemore, B. (1995) "Canada and the OAS—the First Five Years," *Human Rights Brief,* 2 (3) (Spring), available at: www.wcl.american.edu/hrbrief/02/3tittemore.cfm, accessed April 28, 2006.

Wallace, W. (1994) *Regional Integration: The West European Experience,* Washington, DC: Brookings.

Wiener, A. and T. Diez (eds.) *European Integration Theory,* Oxford: Oxford University Press.

Chapter 10

Trade Negotiations and Development Politics: Caving In or Edging Up?

Diana Tussie

What are we waiting for, assembled in the forum?
The barbarians are to arrive today.
Why such inaction in the Senate?
Why do the Senators sit and pass no laws?
Constantine P. Cavafy (1904), *Waiting for the Barbarians*

Globalization is one of the most controversial topics of our times. Academic debates range from whether the results are good or bad and for whom, what the development implications are, how it is affecting policy process, and what the possible courses of action and reaction are. The main objective of this chapter is to analyze how globalization affects trade options and, more specifically, how the politics of trade are being played out in the region. How do trade demands affect in-country decision-making? How do they affect the potential for facing the developmental challenges that are the overall topic of the book?

The response to globalization in the Americas south of the Rio Grande is caught between two sets of closely related challenges: on one hand, rising mass mobilization, and, on the other, the general disarray of development strategies discredited by their failure to incorporate disenfranchised groups and promote more equitable patterns of income distribution. While commodity prices are soaring, in one country after another, trade and access to strategic resources have become bones of contention. Trade negotiations and their social implications are at the center of these challenges. These concerns are compounded by the new rules that are being written into the trade agreements, which restrict the rights of governments to intervene in the domestic economy, even for what would previously have been considered legitimate social purposes.

These dual challenges constitute the backdrop to the unsettling tensions that undermine development strategies, requiring a new balancing act that can address popular dissatisfaction and social equity as fully integrated issues.

Seen in the context of global trade negotiations, some definitional points are in order. Trade is an inherently distributive policy. It has a direct impact on consumption, production, fiscal revenues, and employment. The distribution of gains both among and within countries is a matter of serious contention. In this conjunction lies the question of the political limits that should be imposed on markets. Trade negotiations thus produce a particular form of political conflict and require taking advantage of political cooperation opportunities astutely. The processes of trade negotiations are themselves questionable. Negotiations have tended to be quite secretive and hardly accessible to governments and societies on the receiving end. Decisions are marked by a great deal of bilateral bargaining over reciprocal measures on commercially sensitive issues and there is little or no emphasis on plenary-based open negotiation. Private meetings and "flexible" decision-making processes are often a euphemism for a system of governance deeply flawed by lack of transparency and accountability. There are also high requirements for legal and economic expertise that heighten the challenge. These factors place a high premium on national political arenas and individual state-civil society complexes.

The processes and structures we describe are not of course static. In terms of the visibility of domestic repercussions, the late 1990s marked a turning point. By then the global South had abandoned most traces of the import substitution, a system that allowed substantive insulation of domestic trade politics from external pressures. Under high tariffs, business and labor had been able to fix a price structure that favored the Keynesian compact which brought together domestic firms and workers. The international distributional impact of trade was then concealed from sight; if and when it emerged, business and labor converged in favor of sustaining protection, wages, and domestic consumption. But when layer after layer of trade protection was shed, the international price structure became internalized. The international negotiations that resulted had immediate impact on prices and incomes.

In consequence, the domestic dynamics of trade relations have acquired unprecedented relevance. The requirement to grant reciprocity in negotiations whereby the gains of one external sector require one or more internal sectors to adjust to heightened import competition have increased domestic sensitivity to the adjustment process. Moreover, a foreign offer of market-access for a particular good or sector acts as bait by creating an in-country vested interest that will lobby the government. That lobby pushes to get its interest as exporters to the forefront against all other interests, even as many of these groups are seldom aware they also will be paying a cost by virtue of the principle of reciprocity in trade negotiations. The fact that trade negotiations have expanded their sway over so many aspects compounds the seriousness of this problem.

The weaving and articulation of interests in the trade policy process is a staggering task in Latin America today. One of the main problems that countries face is lack of influence in determining how the rules are set. Even the largest countries have little international clout, and what clout they do have is limited to a negative veto power rather than positive control of the agenda setting process. To magnify the weight of their options and boost their relative bargaining power, in a logic of utility maximization they have come together in groups that can enable positive influence over the rules of the game.

Bargaining power in trade negotiations (Drahos, 2003) depends on a mix of domestic and international capabilities. Among the latter are two dimensions in which countries have flexed their muscles. The first regards the accumulation of market power: to overcome the constraints of limited market power, countries have come together in regional groupings that can allow them to obtain a more favorable position in reciprocal trade negotiations. The second area of action regards coalition-building capacity: coalitions including both public and private actors to strengthen negotiating power in asymmetric settings.

Both these projects are efforts at the formation of clubs.[1] These two varieties of club formation—regionalism and coalition formation—are not usually analyzed as part of the same phenomena. However, they are closely linked in the strategic calculations of countries with impaired market power in trade negotiations, acting as revolving doors and mutual springboards. Experiences around the world have been uneven with outcomes proving different in ASEAN and Latin America.[2]

The problem of achieving collective action has attracted scholarly attention for decades (Olson, 1965). From realist approaches that focus on alliance formation without much hope of clubs to flourish, to neoliberal institutionalist theories that concentrate on logrolling and the possibilities of cooperation; and constructivist views which focus on ideas and identities, international relations theories have tried to provide understanding of why coalitions seem so difficult to maintain. None of the theories per se can explain this new plethora of strategies. An eclectic approach is merited where rationalist and neoliberal views explain one part of the story and constructivist lenses fill the gaps.

Each type of club offers different types of levers in specific settings. Regional trade agreements rely on the adoption of formal legal commitments by members. The pooling of market power is expected to increase leverage in reciprocal negotiations with third parties, under the premise that the more you have to give away, the more you can extract from others. This is the type of association that has received the most scrutiny in empirical and theoretical work. Coalition formation, in contrast, remains more elusive; it acts in informal decision-making processes, as an informal process itself that escapes prescribed institutionalization or legal commitments. These coalitions perform a role at the time of agenda setting, when rules, processes, and formulas for market access (but not market access per se) are shaped and settled. They are informal arrangements that materialize in order to have some bearing on highly informal but nonetheless highly determining and opaque processes.

In the following sections this chapter will recount the trajectory of these clubs, in order to draw contrasts between the current state of regional projects and coalition building within the World Trade Organization (WTO). The objective is to see how these clubs impinge on one another, to what extent they reinforce on each other or, replace each other? What is the gravitational pull of each and what are their developmental implications?

Act One: Region Building

For many countries in Latin America that had been silent bystanders in the General Agreement on Tariffs and Trade (GATT), regional arrangements of the North-South variety provided an opportunity to increase inward investment and to gain the market access they sought but had never really extracted from multilateral negotiations. Subregional arrangements of the South-South type were in part political calculation to allow "strategic bloc bargaining" and gain influence. As a "state- or states-led project to reconfigure space along defined economic and political lines" (Payne and Gamble, 1996: 2; Wyatt-Walter, 1995: 77), regional arrangements also allowed considerable export diversification. It is a well-known fact that manufactures are more important in intra-Latin American trade than they are in extra-regional trade. Some agreements served to integrate very specific and narrowly defined product markets, such as cars or car parts, with a bandwagon effect on other products—for example, Mexico and Argentina. Broader agreements were projects to allow economies of scale and to create a potential bargaining tool for further negotiations—for example, the Andean Community, the Central American Common Market, and Mercosur. In all three, and indeed in the Caribbean, the construction of customs unions and common markets encapsulated a development strategy of export diversification with externalities in the long run. In all four regions, manufactures total more than 80 percent of their intraregional trade, whereas the share of manufactures drops noticeably in trade with the rest of the world.

Despite the plethora of crisscrossing agreements (see table 10.1) the volume of intraregional trade remained rather small at 17 percent of total

Table 10.1 Latin American Trade Agreements

	Intra Latin America		Other than Latin America	
	Countries	Year	Countries	Year
Chile	Mexico	1992	Canada	1996
	Venezuela	1993	EU	2002
	Colombia	1994	US	2003
	Ecuador	1995	EFTA	2003
	MERCOSUR	1996	South Korea	2003
	CACM	2001	New Zealand–Singapore–Brunei	2005
	CAN	In the Pipeline[a]	China	2005
	Peru	2006[b]		
Mexico	Chile	1992	Canada–United States	1994
	Bolivia	1995	EU	1996
	Costa Rica	1995	EFTA	2000
	Colombia–Venezuela (G3)[c]	1995	Israel	2000
	Nicaragua	1998	Japan	2004
	El Salvador–Guatemala–Honduras	2001		
	MERCOSUR	2005		
Peru	MERCOSUR	2003	Thailand	2005
	Chile	2006	US	2006
Dominican Republic	CACM	1998		
	CARICOM	1998		
Colombia	Chile	1994	US	2006
	Mexico–Venezuela (G3)	1995		
Panama	CACM	2002	Taiwan	2003
			US	2006
Costa Rica	Mexico	1995	Canada	2001
ACN	Chile	In the pipeline	EU	In the Pipeline[d]
MERCOSUR	Chile	1996	EU	In the Pipeline[e]
	Bolivia	1996		
	Peru	2003		
	Colombia–Ecuador–Venezuela	2004		

Continued

Table 10.1 Continued

	Intra Latin America		Other than Latin America	
	Countries	Year	Countries	Year
	Mexico	2005		
	Venezuela	2005		
CARICOM	Dominican Republic	1998		
	Costa Rica	2004		
CACM	Dominican Republic	1998	United States	2004
	Panama	2002	EU	2006
			Canada Central America Four (Salvador, Guatemala, Honduras and Nicaragua)	Currently Under negotiation

Notes:
[a] ACN invited Chile to become an Associate Member (August 8, 2006).
[b] Replacing LAIA Economic Complementation Agreement No.38 of 1998.
[c] Venezuela pulled out of the G3 trade bloc (May 2006).
[d] The European Union (EU) has announced that it will wait for the ACN to come together again before opening negotiations.
[e] The EU expects that an agreement will be reached at the end of 2006, to make up for the deadlock of the Doha Round.
Source: OAS/SICE Foreign Trade Information System and www.bilaterals.org, accessed September 2006.

trade, (in contrast to intra-Asian trade that represents over a third). Reality has been unkind to expectations and many of these efforts have lost steam and seem errant. As Macdonald argues (this volume), hemispheric politics seems dominated by the configuration and reconfiguration of "porous regions" that are meant to simultaneously engage and offset U.S. power. The Free Trade Area of the Americas (FTAA) was trumpeted as a solution to the collective action and transaction costs problems that impede cooperation among large numbers of countries in multilateral negotiations. Not so long ago it was expected that an ever-widening processes of regionalism in the hemisphere would develop, as the net was cast over more and more nation-states to bring them into the spiral of expanding agreements. The FTAA was meant to be a clearing house for this patchwork collection of regional pacts. But the contested nature of the project took it down a winding road and this objective of the hemispheric enterprise has receded if not disappeared. The United States, frustrated both domestically and internationally with the FTAA process, changed course and turned to the pursuit of bilateral pacts. The change of course was not merely a means of favoring loyal allies and punishing indecisive friends. The promotion of the new trade agenda in a more docile environment appeared increasingly more productive than a continued struggle against a myriad obstacles (Bulmer-Thomas and Page, 1999: 89–90). One of the main reasons for U.S. interest in, first, the FTAA, and subsequently the bilateral deals that emerged, was the window of opportunity to advance a "new trade agenda," at a time when the progress of multilateral trade negotiations looks precarious, and when the ability of the United States to control the multilateral agenda seems uncertain (see, also, Phillips, this volume). For the United States, trade policy has never been just about trade, but also about setting the rules of the game with a view to broader global political interests.

With the fading of the FTAA card, the game switched to the policy of competitive liberalization, the opening of a race for access to the large U.S. market, thereby encouraging foreign countries to open their economies to U.S. companies and farmers. Competitive liberalization has been taken to describe a trade negotiating strategy containing a sequential logic linking negotiations, and therefore trade liberalization, across different levels (bilateral, regional, and multilateral). It is also the dynamic that is said to be created by that strategy (Bergsten, 1995; Phillips, this volume; Shadlen, 2008).

The strategic motivations behind the plethora of bilateral deals need to be understood in the context of the possibilities they provide for compensating the deficiencies of broader regional negotiations, identifying friends and enemies, creating more opening for piecemeal rule acceptance, and building on sequential negotiations as a means of generating "a spiral of precedents" (VanGrasstek, 1998: 169–170). The thrust of the new bilateral deals is toward implanting a range of disciplines in the region which reflect a set of extra-regional and global interests at least as much as they respond to regional priorities. (Phillips, 2003: 6) At the hemispheric level, the deals were part of the strategy to encircle Mercosur, and can be interpreted as a preventive gamble to avoid Brazilian leadership of a consolidated South America resulting from the linking of Mercosur with the Andean Community. Apprehension switched from competition with Brazil to concern about oil-rich *chavismo* and its regional outreach with the *Alternativa Bolivariana para las Americas* (comprising Venezuela, Bolivia, and Cuba). But the logic underlying the whole approach is to remain at the centre and encourage the adoption of U.S.-style market-friendly business laws and regulations, or at least the adoption of regulations that U.S. businesses can accommodate more easily.

Winners of the race are supposed to garner more foreign direct investment (FDI) and exports, both of which may well have been diverted from losers. The loss of trade shares is said to put pressure on the losers to participate in the contest more enthusiastically in the future (by offering to liberalize more). On this logic countries are concerned not just with their absolute position with respect to the U.S. market but also with their relative position vis-à-vis other U.S. trading partners. Business interests are prodded in one country after another, in one export sector after another. The race has put considerable weight on the inter-relationships between different levels of trade negotiation and reform (namely, the bilateral, regional, and multilateral levels). For countries on the receiving end of this policy, the developmental trade-offs have been formidable: they retain market access and opportunities for specialization in exchange for restricting their use of industrial policy instruments to create new productive capacities. This is especially evident in the management of inward investment (commitment to "investor-state"-type arrangements and the elimination of capital controls) and intellectual property protection (see Shadlen 2005; Abugattas and Paus, this volume; Van Harten, this volume).

Why do Latin American countries agree to such bilateral agreements that undermine their aspiration to increase bargaining power in the bygone FTAA and the WTO? A significant part of the answer is to be found in three trends of export specialization which can be identified in the Latin American region and the political dependence that these generate. First, there is integration in the North-South trade flows of manufactured goods mainly destined for the U.S. market and characterized by the off-shore processing industries of Mexico and some Central American and Caribbean countries. Second, South American countries are integrating into South-South trade flows. These countries have more diversified trade based on exports to regional markets. Even though basic product exports have been reduced in total regional trade, in Mercosur and the Andean Community exports of basic products and manufactured goods based on natural resources still represent a high percentage in the total external sales (58% Mercosur, 86% Andean Community). Third, in some Caribbean countries and Panama, the export of services, particularly those related to tourism, finance and transportation, are becoming very important. While this is a simplistic classification of export specialization, it sheds light on the potential interests of each group of countries in the collapse of the FTAA and the ensuing scramble for bilateral negotiations. In sum, except for Mercosur the rest of Latin America remains highly dependent on the United States as a destination for its exports and source of direct investment flows.[3] As of April 2007, the United States completed a trade agreement with Chile in 2004, with Dominican Republic-Central America Free Trade Agreement (DR-CAFTA) in 2006 and has negotiated three others in Latin America, with Colombia, Peru, and Panama. Motivations to live under the U.S. umbrella are varied. They are not only hostage to export interests. Particularly in the case of Colombia, security issues also prevail in the strategic calculations.

Another source of fear is the phase-out of nonreciprocal agreements which contain preferences granted on a discretional base. The most widespread is the General System of Preferences, which coexists with the Andean Trade Preferences and Drug Eradication Act and the Caribbean Basin Trade Partnership Act. By encouraging trade in sectors where there are rents, preferences induce specialization in those sectors. In addition, by raising returns, they have also created a powerful business interest that will lobby for the continuation of access (Shadlen, 2008). If preferences apply to highly protected sectors in donor countries, they will result in high rents for those able to export free of trade barriers. Hence the threat of phase out generates an immediate policy induced distress.

Bilateral trade agreements are a way of locking in benefits on a binding basis. But binding, in turn, is only granted so long as there is reciprocal give and take. Most important in the case of Central American and the Caribbean is the panic provoked by the phase out of the Multifibre Agreement at the end of 2005 leading to the elimination of quotas, which, restrictive as they might have been, guaranteed access levels to the U.S. market. The free-for-all with China's highly competitive industry would lead to the collapse of the rents associated with quota rights. Holders of rents are well aware of how they stand to lose. They are well organized and have considerable clout (Shadlen, 2008; Sánchez-Ancochea, this volume). Leading export sectors in many countries are either internationally integrated or have well-established links with buyers. In this context they have been able to exert powerful pressure on the conclusion of agreements. Other industrial sectors behind the agreement were the electronics industry (Intel in Costa Rica), medical equipments (Costa Rica), pharmaceuticals (Costa Rica, El Salvador, and Guatemala), chemicals and chemical by-products (El Salvador and Costa Rica), paper and paper by-products (El Salvador and Nicaragua) (Nowalski and Osterlof, 2004). Foodstuff producers such as fresh and preserved foods, including pineapples, melons, flowers, plants, cigars, vegetables and pulses, tubers and roots, traded by transnational enterprises such as Chiquita and Del Monte were also keen players.

Another broad segment of U.S. interests were satisfied with the elimination of duties on 80 percent of all industrial goods exported to

DR-CAFTA countries. The big winners of the agreement are information technology, construction equipment, chemicals, paper products, medical and scientific equipment. In addition, the agreement wipes out duties on U.S. (subsidized) farm exports, including cotton, rice, wheat, soybeans, as well as processed foods, fruits and vegetables and beef. DR-CAFTA also agreed to open markets to U.S. telecoms, banks, insurers, retailers, advertising agencies, express-delivery couriers, travel and transport firms. It also allows freer movement of professional services such as engineering and accounting (granting short and medium term visas). At the same time the deal will grant WTO-plus protection for patented drugs, copyrighted movies and software, internet domain names and other forms of intellectual property.

The crumbling of the Central America Common Market as a result of these pacts is, at the risk of belaboring it, an important development. Together with the Andean Community, both had been relatively successful in articulating a set of common negotiating objectives in the FTAA process, in good part because these objectives had been largely limited to the single issue of special and differential treatment for small economies (Phillips, 2003). In addition, the reduced clout of the smaller nations in the negotiations themselves allowed them to take a comfortable place in the back seat while the bigger players were left to fight the big battles. The Andean Community had been generally rather robust vis-à-vis the FTAA process. In part this owed to the presence of supranational institutional structures, and a certain devolution of authority which allowed some coordination amongst member countries. The pattern had been one in which different countries assumed leadership on different issues and at different times.[4] So there had been a (albeit timid) record of more success at executing common negotiating positions. Moreover, in the last quarter of 2002 members had reached an agreement over 62 percent of the lines in the common external tariff and had made a commitment to agree on the remaining 38 percent by December 15 (*El Comercio*, October 15, 2002). But the commitment was never honored: Colombia, Peru and Ecuador defected and opened up to negotiations with the United States. With neither the letter nor the spirit of this agreement to hold on to, Venezuela's President Hugo Chavez announced in late April 2006, that his country was pulling out of a hollowed Andean Community.[5]

In all subregions, but particularly in the Mercosur where hopes were highest (given the considerable power derived from market size and its commitment to deep integration), the discrepancy between initiatives to strengthen collective action and the results of such efforts is colossal. If a common market or indeed a customs union had been a remote prospect for the subregional blocs, wider hemispheric and global pull entices all countries in a centrifugal manner toward links with other regions and markets. The race for bilateral pacts has swept away the ground on which to cohere and move together.

In the case of Mercosur the lack of cohesion has long-standing causes. The inability to temper the divergent visions of the wider regionalist and subregionalist projects in member countries was never solved. Brazil has the most diversified trade structure of all both in terms of composition and in terms of destination. Because of the extent of its extra-regional trade Brazil favored the Doha Round of multilateral trade negotiations over the FTAA. The resistance of the government (and indeed a sizeable segment of Brazilian business[6]) to engage meaningfully in the FTAA can be explained in large part by the potential trade-off it represents with multilaterally-agreed liberalization provisions in the WTO. Large segments of industry fear the competition of American business not only at home but also in adjacent markets where the FTAA would lead to the erosion of intra-Latin American preferences. Brazilian policy is premised on the construction of subregional leadership as a means of steering the hemispheric process away from U.S. dominance (Phillips, 2000: 393–94). Negotiations with the EU assist in this direction, as they rest heavily on the notion of a relationship between blocs and hence Brazilian strategic interests remain tightly bound to the preservation of subregionalism (Hurrell, 2001: 201). Brazil had carved out for itself the role of intermediary between these regional processes. Until the arrival of Chavez on the scene, it represented the principal counterweight to the United States. But Brazil failed to anticipate the hike in oil prices and the new balance of power in commodity markets, and hence to articulate a clear alternative to the strengthened hand of Chavez—with a fresh ally in Evo Morales's Bolivia.

The Argentine vision of regionalism, by contrast, seems to sit at the intersection of the reliance on Mercosur and the need to offset Brazilian power. It veers from *bandwagoning* (seeking closer ties with Brazil) to *balancing* Brazil by searching for closer ties with other partners. Caught in the dilemma Argentina has consistently favored the extension of the Mercosur to other countries (Chile in the 1990s, Venezuela in the present) and the construction of wider regionalist arrangements, reflecting its relatively much greater reliance on regional markets. Uruguay, once expected to pull back from its keenness for a trade agreement with the United States when President Tabare Vazquez was sworn in in 2004, nonetheless continued to hold the line and indeed has become increasingly outspoken not only about closer relations with the United States but also about its utter and complete dissatisfaction with Mercosur. "Mercosur is more a problem than a solution for Uruguay," President Vazquez noted (as quoted in *The Economist*, May 11, 2006). All illusion lost, squeezed between negligible growth rates in Brazil (and hence no pull for its exports) and an unfavorable bilateral exchange with Argentina, mobilized by a controversy with Argentina over the location of paper and pulp firms on the bank of the shared Uruguay River, the Uruguayans seem to believe that a bilateral deal with the United States is their best option. The Paraguayans have also been eager to engage in an trade agreement with the United States to compensate for their marginalization within the Mercosur. In addition, the dominance of primary and agricultural exports in these countries shapes a rather different set of structural and negotiating imperatives from those of the Brazilian state and business sectors. Uruguay and Paraguay in particular have now found elbow room, fending off their big neighbors by becoming good friends both of the United States *and* Venezuela at the same time.

Mercosur was not overtaken as was widely expected by the materialization of the FTAA. True, it has been encircled, but, that is a factor of second order importance in relation to its own internal weaknesses. Together with rife political tensions over energy and the use of shared river resources, these divergent visions of regionalism had driven Mercosur to a virtual standstill. These rifts magnified and were themselves magnified by the peculiarities of the Mercosur process which, lacking even minimal supranational decision-making authority, relied on the passing of legislation at the national level to adopt collective decisions. By 2001 Paul Cammack (2001: 215) had held

> Mercosur . . . is an ineffective regional association with little remaining capacity to contribute to regional or global integration, and little capacity to promote other goals

Perhaps expectation had been too high, and even overly influenced by the European benchmark. Nonetheless, even confronted with declining effectiveness, institutions and rules can persist after the leader loses the capacity or will to lead (Keohane, 1984). Persistence in the case of Mercosur may be restricted to two dimensions. First, is the legacy of a decade of agreements and procedures, and the formal commitment to some common positions that result from a "meeting-by-meeting" basis. Because they do not reflect the prior formulation of a cohesive strategy in negotiations, it does not provide much sustenance to make significant contributions at a global level. Second, at the issue level, Mercosur not only accounts for a significant share of world agricultural exports (table 10.2); it has also attained the deepest and most complete liberalization worldwide in agriculture, and in fact much more than was afforded multilaterally. As such, the bloc is the regional initiative that has made the deepest strides in this area. The considerable regional liberalization in place means that there is no baggage to deal with (Diaz-Henderson, 2003) while it provides both a desire and a platform for becoming a

Table 10.2 Export Shares in Global Trade of Selected Foodstuffs (Percent, 2005)

Sector	Argentina	Brasil	Mercosur
Rice and wheat	13.4	0.1	15.4
Corn and other cereals	10.8	0.5	11.6
Vegetables and fruits	2.9	2.0	5.0
Soya	9.4	23.6	36.3
Oilseeds	8.2	0.1	8.4
Sugar	1.4	19.5	21.2
Coffee and tea	1.0	8.3	9.8
Cattle and animal products	2.7	4.3	8.1
Beef	6.4	6.0	17.8
Poultry	0.2	9.7	9.9
Dairy products	3.7	0.1	5.4

Source: Laens. Silvia and Terra María Inés. "Impacto de las Negociaciones del MERCOSUR en la OMC. ALCA y Unión Europea" http://www.iadb.org/intal/aplicaciones/uploads/ponencias/CURSO_BID-INTAL-OMC_2006_09_10_MARIAINESTERRA.ppt/.

global player. The bloc as the articulation of a "strategic trade objective" may have lost stamina but as a political and symbolic process it retains some value, to be capitalized elsewhere.

Thus, jockeying for a better position vis-à-vis other countries has been a pervasive theme and conducted all of the regional blocs to reach their limits of their usefulness as clubs to accumulate market power. Smaller countries in particular, sandwiched between the regional leader and the hemispheric strongman, suffer from stark asymmetries in all processes and hence succumb easily to the logic of competitive liberalization. The proliferation of regional and bilateral agreements is not likely to allow a positive result either in terms of promoting development (see Shadlen, 2005; Abugattas and Paus, this volume) or in curtailing U.S. power, but in the short term it serves to appease export interests, of sizeable importance in the smaller countries with a high concentration of exports in heavily regulated goods, such as sugar, bananas and garment exports. In the latter, the micro dimensions are especially important precisely because of the production methods that encourage the globalization of value chains (Sanchez Ancochea, this volume).

In sum, the phase out of historical preferences that gave life to specific patterns of trade and investment now pose demands on governments for locking in. Deprived of the regional power base, the politics of contestation are, however, restaged differently in the WTO clubs, where foodstuff exporters, and in particular Brazil, have flexed their muscle to become more strategic in their partnership practices.

Act Two: Coalition Building in the WTO

Bloc bargaining has run into a number of political, institutional and, indeed, economic obstacles within the subregions. But obstacles do not mean inaction and immobilization and there is still the possibility that external negotiations progressively constitute a catalyzer of another sort.

As a key actor in these intersecting blueprints, Brazil both shapes and is shaped by these projects. Its policies and preferences can reveal much about the complex dynamics of trade relations in the Americas, in particular in South America (see Bahadian and Carvalho Lyrio, this volume).

The Uruguayan and Paraguayan interest in breaking away from Mercosur by signing bilateral pacts with the United States, and thus contravene the common external tariff, is first and foremost a blow in the face to Brazil; it indicates a serious undermining of the regional platform on which it had relied to construct its rise to global power. The threat of break away reflects a failure of Brazilian leadership, attached as it is to a perception of the country's stature in the world and a paradigm which posits that Brazil must counter-balance U.S. hegemony in the Americas if it is to aspire to a global role (Soares de Lima, 2000). Moreover, this failure happens at the same time that Brazilian firms are making serious strides toward internationalization with outflows of FDI growing by about US$ 15 billion a year, amounting to a stock of $93 billion. The appreciation of the domestic currency (up by 18% in the course of 2006) provides firms with increased liquidity and fresh incentives to invest abroad. Against this backdrop, multilateral trade negotiations are of utmost importance for many competitive sectors in Brazil. It is at the global level where Brazil seeks access; there it can find sympathetic friends and powerful allies, such as India and South Africa.

In search for a place in the world Brazil's strategy was driven by a view in which the North-South axis acquired growing relevance. Brazil's leadership in the formation of the G-20 is perhaps the prime example of a new pro-Southern stance. The opportunity was found in the preparatory process leading up to the Cancun Ministerial in 2003 when developing countries engaged in several joint initiatives that involved an exchange of information as well as the formulation of joint proposals. Many of these already had a history in the preparations for the Doha Ministerial in 2001, if not earlier. Examples include the African Group, the African Caribbean Pacific Group, the Small and Vulnerable Economies (see table 10.3). None of these past coalitions had been issue-specific; rather, they were blocs that adapted their agenda according to the pressing needs of the day. Events at Cancun seemed to represent a symbol of the dissatisfaction with trade

Table 10.3 WTO Coalitions

G-20 Mission: Elimination of export subsidies, domestic support and liberalization of market access in agriculture

Members: Argentina, Bolivia, Brazil, Chile, China, Cuba, Ecuador, Egypt, Guatemala, India, Indonesia, Mexico, Nigeria, Pakistan, Paraguay, Philippines, South Africa, Thailand, Tanzania,Uruguay, Venezuela, Zimbabwe.

G-33 Mission: Food security and rural development

Antigua and Barbuda, Barbados, Belize, Benin, Botswana, China, Congo, Côte d'Ivoire, Cuba, Dominican Republic, Grenada, Guyana, Haiti, Honduras, India, Indonesia, Jamaica, Kenya, Rep. Korea, Mauritius, Madagascar, Mongolia, Mozambique, Nicaragua, Nigeria, Pakistan, Panama, Peru, Philippines, St. Kitts and Nevis, St. Lucia, St. Vincent and the Grenadines, Senegal, Sri Lanka, Suriname, Tanzania, Trinidad and Tobago, Turkey, Uganda, Venezuela, Zambia, and Zimbabwe.

SVEs Mission: Attention to small and vulnerable economies

Antigua and Barbuda, Barbados, Belize, Bolivia, Cuba, Dominica, Dominican Republic, El Salvador, Fiji, Grenada, Guatemala, Guyana, Honduras, Jamaica, Mauritius, Mongolia, Nicaragua, Paraguay, Papua New Guinea, Solomon Islands, St. Kitts and Nevis, St. Lucia, St. Vincent and the Grenadines, Trinidad and Tobago.

G-11 Mission: Full liberalization in tropical products

Bolivia, Colombia, Costa Rica, Ecuador, El Salvador, Guatemala, Honduras, Panama, Peru, Nicaragua, and Venezuela.

---

arrangements and indicated a greater willingness to act in pursuit of collective interests and against the developed world. In identifying and expressing collective dissatisfaction, Brazil took the lead and joined forces with other emerging powers of the developing world—China, India, South Africa—as well as with leading agricultural exporters in the Americas. The policies and positions of developing countries at, and around, the Cancun ministerial of the WTO seemed therefore to reveal an unexpected tendency toward reassertion and resistance by developing countries, both individually and collectively.

Many of these groups have some overlapping members. Despite the differences in the agenda of the various coalitions, a successful effort was made to coordinate their positions so that they did not enter into direct conflict with each other (Narlikar and Tussie, 2004), an effort that has continued successfully. Unlike some of the older coalitions involving developing countries, the new ones do not have a blocking agenda but a proactive one, which is typified in technically substantive proposals at each stage of the negotiations, one that is increasingly covering issues other than agriculture, the so called non-agricultural market access chapters in particular. Each one of these coalitions relied on considerable research to support its agenda and looked for windows of opportunity to move. As such, the strategy is a stark contrast against the weeping lamentations that developing countries had put up in their call for the new international economic order of the 1970s. Even more interesting is the permanent interaction between the coalitions. As a result of the differing priorities (and sometimes directly conflicting interests) of some of these coalitions, rifts are bound to appear from time to time. "Alliances of Sympathy" between coalitions build bridges and demonstrate efforts to coordinate positions and share information with other developing countries, and at the very least minimize overt contradictions when fuller coordination is not possible. Facilitated by overlapping membership, the bridges between the G-20 and the G-33, the first representing offensive agricultural interests and the latter, arguing for the respect of food security are a case in point.

The resilience of these coalitions and such innovative methods are surprising. These developments were greeted with considerable surprise in the scholarly as well as policy communities, not least because of scholars have for long placed an accent on binding and legal instruments and face difficulties in coming to grips with soft clubs.[7]

These informal coalitions however, survive in the face of agnostic theory, pessimistic diagnoses and negative precedents that show a history of developing country coalitions that have collapsed. A prominent place among them was taken by the G-20, a group created at the behest of Brazil to influence the agricultural negotiations. The G-20 combines a vast mix of developing countries, including small countries whose susceptibility to bilateral arm-twisting was high and whose ability to hold out against such pressures low. Even while focusing on the issue area of agriculture; it brought together countries with divergent positions on the issue of agricultural liberalization vs. protectionism. The apparent contradiction led to the impression that the group would crumble with ease. There was also the apprehension that Brazil, as leader of the G-20, would try to broaden the agenda or to incorporate other areas at stake in the round and hence undermine the staying power of the group. Despite these tensions the group has remained together, survived the ebbs and flows and is still active in the negotiations of the Doha Round. At the same time, it seems to have become clear that its concentration on agriculture, an area that brings together the collective interests of the Mercosur, the G-20 represents a relevant factor for the dynamics of regional relations.

Several currents led to the gestation and final advent of the group on the scene. It appeared formally on stage on August 20, 2003 when sixteen countries came together to table a paper with a proposal for negotiating modalities in agriculture. The proposal was a reaction to the initiatives of the European Union (EU) and the United States, considered to be unacceptable by developing countries with interests in the agricultural negotiations. In the immediate aftermath of the formal presentation, five other countries joined the group and prior to Cancun another four countries followed, then adding up to twenty-five. Cancun was a turning point. After the collapse of the meeting, the United States exerted consistent pressure over those that had earlier displayed signals of readiness to move negotiations in the FTAA and offered them fast track bilateral pacts on condition that they move out of the G-20. Colombia, El Salvador, Ecuador, Guatemala, Costa Rica, and Peru dropped out, but the latter two subsequently rejoined once the pacts had been firmly secured.[8] Such movements indicate one of the strengths of these soft bargaining arrangements. Dropouts are breaking no law and at the same time, rejoining (or repentant) members, pay no costs once the market deal has been seized and the incentive to stand in line neatly with U.S. foreign policies ceases. But a United States that came to see its interests in terms of developing special relationships with major regional powers on a "hub and spoke" model and that was prepared to offer real benefits to foster such relationships would present Brazil (and Argentina) with very difficult choices and that could well strain the strength, cohesion and the rhetoric of the coalition. At the same time, as suggested by the classical theory of clubs (Olson, 1965) if the benefits of belonging to these associations bear fruit, they may well move from casual groups to varying degrees of formalization; on this variant one may then expect some form of sanction to help bear the burdens and obtain the payoffs, however intangible these may be. A point will be reached when the movement in and out of the group may not be ignored and self-reinforcing disciplines will be required.

In essence the Group is an agenda-setting coalition focused on the terms for agricultural negotiations, but it is also seen as a club to bring together the interests of southern producers. Regardless of the current inclinations of President Lula's administration, there are strong bureaucratic and structural arguments supporting the embeddedness of these issues in countries with both strong export interests as well as broad domestic markets to defend, such as Brazil and to a lesser extent Argentina, an ardent activist in the Group. In 2002, under the Cardoso administration, the then Secretary of Production and Marketing of the Brazilian Ministry of Agriculture, Pedro de Camargo Neto, advocated the idea that Brazil needed to define an independent strategy for the agricultural negotiations in the WTO. According to Camargo Neto, "our interests as a large agricultural country and large consumer with great challenges for development make it an obligation for us to assume the leadership of negotiations in this sector. This means a South–South articulation, including India, China and others," (*Gazeta Mercantil*, November 18, 2002).

Learning from the experience of the G-20, tropical exporters in the Andean and Central American countries have followed suit and come together as the G-11 upholding the liberalization of tropical products.

Interestingly, this coalition is so far comprised solely Latin American members of the Andean Community and the Central American Common Market (Bolivia, Colombia, Costa Rica, Ecuador, El Salvador, Guatemala, Honduras, Panama, Peru, Nicaragua, and Venezuela). Coalitions have incorporated the key features of trade blocs. They are limited to the developing world, frequently come to operate across issues, and are bound by a collective idea that the developing world shares several problems and needs to address them collectively. "One of the strengths of the G-20 is its ability to combine a political stance with a focused approach to agricultural negotiations," (Brazilian negotiator quoted in Motta Veiga, 2005: 118). Coalitions have also attempted to institutional- ize greater coordination and information-sharing among themselves with the help of some external organizations. Coalitions have produced increased contacts at the level of the home governments and intensified consultation amongst delegations leading to soft and partial institution- alization through the Permanent Mission to the WTO with feedbacks to and from the national capitals. They have also adopted research-oriented strategies in order to flesh out alternatives to the points under discussion and pursue cooperative relations among different blocs.

As such, the challenge posed by these coalitions is based within the broad liberal paradigm of the 1990s. Unlike regional integration which espoused a development vision or the demand of the 1960s–1970s for a new international economic order, the challenge mounted by these coalitions has not been accompanied by a call to replace the WTO with an alternative organization. Their mission is to inject momentum when it is lacking and to advance proposals for negotiations (a stark difference to the attempt in the 1960s to establish the UNCTAD as a alternative to the GATT). They have not advanced an alternative vision of development to the liberal one; and the change that they have demanded is change within the WTO regime rather than a radical restructuring. In all these coalitions, memories of the failures of the old, third world-ism persist, and most members are quick to deny any ideological leanings or identity politics of the coalition. Instead, they emphasize the importance of interests and the production of knowledge. The tactics, nonetheless, still show a strong policy commitment to distilling the issues of development and social justice along North-South lines as the external face of the governments' domestic concerns.

There is final characteristic of these coalitions that merit attention and distinguishes them both from predecessor coalitions in global politics and regional coalitions in the hemispheric setting. This is the establishment of fertile associations with nongovernmental organizations (NGOs). The intellectual and public health group in the run-up to Doha demonstrated the importance of such links most visibly. Countries found influential allies in Southern based grassroots constituencies and in Northern NGOs that exercised considerable pressure on their governments to concede to the demands of the coalition and also reinforced the legitimacy of its demands (Odell and Sell, 2003). Similar transnational alliances have also grown between governments and certain NGOs. Some operated as think-tanks in supporting the agenda of developing countries such as Oxfam and the International Center for Trade and Sustainable Development. Others issued statements expressing political support for the demands of the G-20. The willingness of the developing world to engage with NGOs is fairly recent, and still evolving. Up to now most of the literature on the resistance to globalization has concentrated on social groups and the anti-globalization movement and has neglected the complex associations with major developing states. Here we have focused on the latter aspect although there is needed research to be done on the links between the two, following the path shown in the area of financial conditionality.[9] On the one hand, there is scope for mutual reinforcement, as in the way in which countries have helped to open up political and discursive spaces in international institutions that can be exploited by social movements and NGOs; or coalitional possibilities, as with Oxfam's cooperation with the G-20, or that of the International Center for Trade and Sustainable Development with the G-33. Although these are novel linkages, most of them are still based on a calculus of incentives rather than on new under-standings of what constitutes "good" processes. Should these partner-ships acquire staying power, one would see governments consulting actively and regularly with NGOs about development problems and solu-tions, joint design and implementation of development policies, programs and institutions and increasing formalization of these joint activities.

To summarize, clubs have been the chosen model of governance and participation in the WTO. Developed countries have plenty of accumulated experience at multilateral governance as founding architects of the present institutions. Multiple coalitions of developing countries are now making inroads in decision making and contributing to increase the bargaining power of such countries. Though nascent, the pattern has now become embedded within the trade system, changing the direction and also the shape of the agenda. Many interlocking games are at stake in a single act.

The Multiple Purposes of Clubbing

Having distilled the trajectory of two types of development-oriented clubs, questions emerge about the longer term impact of each and their respective implication in terms of development. Leaving aside the discussion of intrinsic features of each, it is clear that regional, subregional and multilat-eral clubs are in constant and revolving interaction in the Americas.

Good working relations within coalitions are extended to the remapping of regional trade agreements. Venezuela has moved out of

the Andean Community and joined Mercosur, indicating stronger
cooperation ties with countries that have not signed bilateral agreements
with the United States than with its previous partners. Mercosur and
India signed a preferential agreement in 2004 that became operational
in 2005, albeit covering a reduced number of goods. But there is also
talk of merging the Mercosur-India and the Mercosur–South African
Customs Union agreement. Despite the limited coverage of these first
steps they are not only important signals, but also opportunities for
agent interests and identities to be shaped through and during increased
interaction. Bargaining coalitions have potential for developing
countries, especially if they involve weak levels of actual or attempted
integration (Narlikar, 2003:191). This "weakness" turns into a "strength"
as coalitions get stronger and persist over time. Though leaky and fuzzy,
they are here to stay.

Table 10.4 MERCOSUR and G-20 in the WTO

	Mercosur	G-20
Agriculture	Two communications on food security and principles declaration (December 2001 and August 2003)	G-20 technical proposals and formulas for liberalization since September 2003.
TRIPs		Argentina, Brazil and India **: Communication on no infringement claim (October 2002) Brazil and India **: • Three communications/proposals on TRIPs and public health (June 2001, October 2001 and June 2002) • Two communications on TRIPs and biological diversity and traditional knowledge protection convention (before September 2003) Brazil and India: Five communications/ proposals on TRIPs and biodiversity (after September 2003)
Services	Two proposals on tourism and assessment issues (before September 2003)	Argentina, Brazil and India: Proposal on GATS Mode 4 (February 2005) Brazil and India: Two communications on procedures (March 2004 and September 2004)
TRIMs		Brazil and India**: Proposal on S+D (October 2002)

Note: ** Previous to the formal appearance of G-20 on stage.

The intersection of regional agreements with coalitions is a new phenomenon, and so far based on a limited range of experience. Table 10.4 shows the intersection of the G-20 with Brazil's regionally-based positions. There never had been much of an effort to a common Mercosur position taking in the WTO. The presence of the coalition has catalyzed some action, if albeit rather timid. For example, Indian cooperation in the agriculture negotiations has been reciprocated through support on the free movement of labor in the GATS mode 4 negotiations. Prior to the establishment of the G-20, Mercosur presented few proposals and distributed few communications; as G-20 matured in the course of the Doha Round, Mercosur's WTO agenda was catalyzed drop by drop, even in the intellectual property issues in which Argentina and Brazil had shown little inclination to rapprochement on their own.

Multiple games take place simultaneously; each level has an intrinsic value, but each also serves to enrich the other two indicating the essential impermanence of trading arrangements. Regional associations and trade coalitions intersect and spread out leading to a variety of mutual influence and market outcomes. But market outcomes need to be legitimized. Intense trade negotiations have to a large extent crippled and hollowed efforts of regionalism, at the same time that there is growing civil society discontent over the question of benefits from trade policy, who grows, whose market is at stake. Many government leaders are currently facing the realpolitik dilemmas of attempting to pacify powerful business interests and the electorates who voted them into power an accommodation of governments in power to take forward elements of the agendas articulated by popular movements. Morales, Chavez, Lula, Vazquez, Palacios, and Kirchner are perhaps feeling the full effect of these competing pressures most acutely. But the governments that materialized from elections in Peru and Mexico in 2006 will be in a similar position. What emerges from these trends is an interesting relationship between the use of mobilization and resistance, in which it is not always clear how governments will balance the risk adverse mindset of elites with the widespread disaffection of civil society to the results of neo-liberal reforms, and from that point respond to claim-making and mobilizing.

The stronger emphasis on South-South alliances is very much a response to this disaffection. The choreography now grapples with relatively loosely knit coalitions that take up specific issues and specific products on the global scene, thus reinvigorating South-South cooperation with a view to changing the rules of the game, opening new markets and negotiation of trade rules with major trading partners through introducing additional leverage.

How far loosely knit coalitions can go in terms of adopting formal language to structure membership and participation and to strengthen internal accountability mechanisms is uncertain. But in their current shape they do offer an institutional framework in which a learning process could take place. At the same time, acting as they do as the external face of the governments' concern with development and policy spaces (see Abugattas and Paus, this volume), they have been able to add some ingredients of legitimization to otherwise controversial trade negotiations with growing domestic economic and political impacts.[10] Technical preparation, intense coordination and ad hoc coordination with NGOs help build domestic consensus supporting a good deal of the official position in the negotiation. The G-20 as well as the G-33, together with new ones springing up, look set to become fixtures on the WTO scene. They will likely play a pivotal role in the core agricultural negotiations.

But coalitions are not a matter of principle. They are formed for specific contextual reasons, in this case, the need to open up and to an extent democratize the WTO decision-making process. In such settings coalitions play a major regulating role through movement as much as through being. They enhance participation and instill greater degrees of transparency and accountability. The loopholes and traps that have been left in some agreements also provide a room for the formation of coalitions.

Ultimately framing and defining problems, questions and issues does not translate neatly into a full development strategy. Such issue-specific trade alliances are restricted to the liberalization of certain products or, alternatively, to the concern not to give away policy space in exchange for market access. These are necessary, but not sufficient, conditions for development.

Notes

1. I use the term as defined by the *Oxford English Dictionary* to mean an association dedicated to a particular interest or activity. Both of the clubs abovementioned—regions and coalition—have different constitutive elements that will be described in this chapter. Narlikar (2003: 29) refers to a coalition as any group of decision-makers participating in . . . a negotiation and who agree to act in concert to achieve a common end.
2. For an extensive account on coalition formation and bargaining see Narlikar (2003).
3. See Shadlen (2008) for an elaboration of patterns of interest and the heuristic value of his political trade dependence indicator.
4. For example, in the FTAA negotiations Peru had taken the lead particularly on special and differential treatment for smaller countries and on indigenous rights (see Phillips, 2000).
5. Chile in contrast announced plans to rejoin the Andean Community after thirty years. The Andean Community hence will come to house all the countries on the Pacific Rim holding a bilateral pact with the United States.

6. This portion of Brazilian business refers principally to smaller domestic firms oriented largely toward the domestic markets. Nonetheless, recent research has demonstrated that large segments of Brazilian business are increasingly interested in global rather than regional markets. See Rios and Iglesias (2005).

7. Keohane and Nye (2003) have highlighted the obsolescence of the club approach to governance used by developed countries in the WTO. Inroads must now be made into the use of clubs as contestation platforms and thus reshaping decision-making processes.

8. The sixteen original members were Argentina, Bolivia, Brazil, Chile, China, Colombia, Costa Rica, Ecuador, Guatemala, India, Mexico, Paraguay, Peru, the Philippines, South Africa, and Thailand. The next five countries to join were Cuba, Egypt, El Salvador, Pakistan, and Venezuela. After August 2003, Indonesia, Nigeria, Tanzania, and Zimbabwe joined. Uruguay did so in March 2005 when the Tabare Vazquez government was sworn in and Ecuador jumped ship in September 2006 after the suspension of negotiations with the United States for a bilateral deal.

9. Both the World Bank and the IMF have shaped "soft" conditionalities that promote partnerships for government-NGO collaboration. Over time, professional collaboration in these institutional venues can induce a new common understanding of the "right" way to solve problems and to work together, as well as new realizations of interests, and this can lead to new preferences. Yet if NGOs and governments "learn" how to collaborate through a combination of professionalism and repeated interactions, the receptivity of governments varies not only according to political preferences but also over specific issues.

10. In Ecuador, social mobilization by the indigenous movement, unions and NGOs, central in ousting two presidents, has campaigned against the bilateral pact with the United States using the acronym in Spanish (TLC) for its dubbing into "Tratado de Ladrones Corruptos." Although the case of Ecuador may not be extrapolated elsewhere, it is, nonetheless, a stark indication of the new level of politicization whereby the legitimacy concerns of trade negotiations are manifest and hence consultations with society appear more pressing and simultaneously more risky to some governments.

References

Bergsten, C. F. (1995) *Competitive Liberalization and Global Free Trade: A Vision for the Early 21st Century*, Washington, DC: Institute for International Economics, (Working paper 96-15).

Bulmer-Thomas, V. and S. Page (1999) "Trade Relations in the Americas: Mercosur, the Free Trade Area of the Americas and the European Union," in J. Dunkerley and V. Bulmer-Thomas (eds.) *The United States and Latin*

262 DIANA TUSSIE

America: The New Agenda, Cambridge, MA: Harvard University Press.

Cammack, P. (2001) "Mercosur and Latin American Integration," in K. Radke and M. Wiesebron (eds.) *Competing for Integration: Japan, Europe and Latin America*, New York: M.E. Sharpe.

Diaz-Henderson, M. (2003) "The Negotiation on Agriculture: The Regional-Multilateral Relationship," in D. Tussie (ed.) *The Problems and Promise of Trade Negotiations in Latin America*, Basingstoke, UK: Palgrave.

Drahos, P. (2003) "When the Weak Bargain with the Strong: Negotiations in the World Trade Organization," *International Negotiation*, 8 (1): 79–109.

Hurrell, A. (2001) "The Politics of Regional Integration in MERCOSUR," in V. Bulmer-Thomas (ed.) *Regional Integration in Latin America and the Caribbean: The Political Economy of Open Regionalism*, London: Institute of Latin American Studies.

Keohane, R. (1984) *After Hegemony: Cooperation and Discord in the World Political Economy*, Princeton, NJ: Princeton University Press.

Keohane, R. and J. Nye (2003) "The Club Model of Multilateral Cooperation and the World Trade Organization: Problems of Democratic Legitimacy," Cambridge, MA: John F. Kennedy School of Government, Harvard University (Visions of Governance in the 21st Century, Working Paper no. 4).

Laens, S. and Terra, M.I. (2006) "Impacto de las Negociaciones del MERCOSUR en la OMC, ALCA y Unión Europea," paper presented at the *Seminario para académicos latinoamericanos: Las negociaciones en la OMC y los procesos de integración en América Latina*. Buenos Aires, September. Available: http://www.iadb.org/intal/aplicaciones/uploads/ponencias/CURSO_BID-INTAL-OMC_2006_09_10_MARIAINESTERRA.ppt/, accessed July 10, 2007.

Motta Veiga, P. (2005) "Brazil and the G20," available at http://www.latn.org.ar/, accessed July 12, 2007.

Narlikar, A. (2003) *International Trade and Developing Countries. Bargaining Coalitions in the GATT & WTO*, London: Routledge/RIPE Studies in Global Political Economy.

Narlikar, A. and D. Tussie (July 2004) "The G20 at the Cancun Ministerial: Developing Countries and their Evolving Coalitions in the WTO," *The World Economy*, 27 (7): 947–966.

Nowalski, J. and D. Osterlof (2004) *CAFTA/TLC Potencial Competitivo de los Sectores Productivos de Centroamérica*, San José, Costa Rica: CIDH (Colección Prospectiva # 7).

Odell, J. and S. Sell (2003) "Reframing the Issue: The Coalition on Intellectual Property and Public Health," in John Odell (ed.) *Negotiating Trade. Developing Countries in the WTO and NAFTA*, Cambridge: Cambridge University Press.

Olson, M. (1965) *The Logic of Collective Action: Public Goods and the Theory of Groups*, Cambridge, MA: Harvard University Press.

Payne, A. and A. Gamble (1996) "Introduction: The Political Economy of Regionalism and World Order," in A. Gamble and A. Payne (eds.) *Regionalism and World Order*, Basingstoke, UK: Macmillan.

Phillips, N. (2000) "Governance After Financial Crisis: South American Perspectives on the Reformulation of Regionalism," *New Political Economy*, 5 (3): 383–398.

―――― (2003) "Reconfiguring Subregionalism: The Politics of Hemispheric Regionalism in the Americas," *International Affairs*, 79 (2): 327–349.

Rios, S. and R. Iglesias (2005) "Anatomia do boom exportador E implicações para a agenda de negociações comerciais do brasil," LATN Working Paper 31 (July).

Shadlen, K. C. (2005) "Exchanging Development for Market Access? Deep Integration and Industrial Policy under Multilateral and Regional-Bilateral Trade Agreements," *Review of International Political Economy*, 12 (5) (December): 750–775.

―――― (2008) "Globalization, Power, and Economic Integration: The Political Economy of Regional and Bilateral Trade Agreements in the Americas," *Journal of Development Studies*, 44 (1) (January): 1–20.

Soares de Lima, Maria Regina (2000) "Instituiçoes democráticas e política exterior,", *Contexto Internacional*, 2 (June–December): 265–304.

VanGrasstek, C. (1998) "The Fast Track: Along a Winding Road", Caracas: Capítulos del SELA, junio, available at, http://www.sela.org/cgi-win/be_alex.exe?Acceso=T023600000095/4&Nombrebd=sela-pub&TiposDoc=s. last accessed February 18, 2008.

Wyatt-Walter, A. (1995) "Regionalism, Globalization and World Economic Order" in FAWCETT, L. and HURREL, A., eds. Regionalism and World Politics. Regional Organization and International Order. Oxford: Oxford University Press, 1995.

Periodicals, various issues

El Comercio
Gazeta Mercantil
The Economist

Contributors

Luis Abugattas is Senior Expert in the Trade Negotiations and Commercial Diplomacy Branch (TNCDB) of the UNCTAD Trade Division. Formerly he was Director of the Institute for Economic and Social Research of the National Society of Industries in Lima (Peru) and Advisor to the Peruvian Ministry of Trade and Tourism. He participated in the Peruvian trade negotiating team. He was a member of the Intellectual Property Tribunal at INDECOPI (Peru), worked for the Secretariat of the Andean Community and was faculty at the Economics Department in the Universidad del Pacifico in Lima.

Adhemar G. Bahadian represented Brazil during negotiations for the Free Trade Area of the Americas. From 2003 to 2006 he acted as Co-chair of the negotiations, on behalf of the Brazilian government. He is currently Brazil's Ambassador to Italy.

Mauricio Carvalho Lyrio is a diplomat with the Brazilian Ministry of Foreign Relations.

Enrique Dussel Peters is Professor at the Graduate School of Economics, Universidad Nacional Autónoma de México (UNAM), 1993 to present. He is a Consultant for several Mexican and international institutions with a B.A. and M.A. in Political Science from the Free University of Berlin, and a Ph.D. in Economics from the University of Notre Dame. Research topics of interest to him include: economic development, industrial organization, and trade theory; the North American Free Trade Agreement and the Central American Free Trade Agreement; evolution of industrial, trade, and regional patterns in Latin America and Mexico. He is the Coordinator of the Area of Political Economy at the Graduate School of Economics at UNAM and Coordinator of the Center for Chinese-Mexican Studies. His publications include *Polarizing Mexico: The Impact of Liberalization Strategy* (Boulder, CO: Lynne Rienner Publishers, 2000); *Claroscuros. Integración exitosa de las pequeñas y medianas empresas en México* (Mexico: CANACINTRA/CEPAL/JUS, 2001); with Luis Miguel Galindo and Eduardo Loría Díaz, *Condiciones y efectos de la* *inversión extranjera directa y del proceso de integración regional en México durante los noventa. Una perspectiva macro, meso y micro* (Mexico: Facultad de Economía/UNAM, Banco Interamericano de Desarrollo-INTAL, and Plaza y Valdés, 2003); with assistance from Liu Xue Dong, *Economic Opportunities and Challenges Posed by China for Mexico and Central America* (Bonn: German Development Institute, 2005).

Laura Macdonald is a Professor in the Department of Political Science and the Institute of Political Economy at Carleton University, and the Director of the Centre on North American Politics and Society. She has a Ph.D. from York and is the author of *Supporting Civil Society: The Political Impact of Non-Governmental Assistance to Central America* (London/New York: Macmillan/St. Martin's, 1997). She has published numerous articles in journals and edited collections on such issues as the role of nongovernmental organizations in development, global civil society, citizenship struggles in Latin America, Canadian development assistance and the political impact of the NAFTA on human rights and democracy in the three member states.

Michael Mortimore is the Director of the Unit on Investment and Corporate Strategies, at the United Nation's Economic Commission on Latin America and the Caribbean (ECLAC), Santiago, Chile. He has published extensively on the strategy and effects of transnational corporations in Latin America, including articles in *World Development, ECLAC Notes* and *CEPAL Review*, as well as numerous contributions to edited volumes.

Eva Paus is Professor of Economics and Director of the Center for Global Initiatives at Mount Holyoke College, MA. She has published widely on the impact of foreign investment and trade liberalization on technological change, productivity growth, and wage developments, particularly in Latin America. In October 2005, Palgrave Macmillan published her book *Foreign Investment, Development, and Globalization. Can Costa Rica Become Ireland?* The University of Costa Rica Press published a Spanish translation of the book in 2007. Paus is also editor of the book *Global Capitalism Unbound: Winners and Losers from Offshore Outsourcing* (New York, Palgrave Macmillan, 2007).

Nicola Phillips is Professor of Politics at the University of Manchester, UK. She is Managing Editor of *New Political Economy* and Co-editor of the *International Political Economy Yearbook* series. Among other visiting positions, she is an Associate Fellow of the Royal Institute of International Affairs (Chatham House) in London, and from October 2004 to March 2005 was Ford Foundation Visiting Fellow at the Centro de Estudios y Programas Interamericanos at the Instituto Tecnológico Autónomo de México (ITAM). Her most recent books are *The Southern Cone Model: The Political Economy of Regional Capitalist Development in*

Latin America (New York: Routledge, 2004) and, as editor, *Globalizing International Political Economy* (New York: Palgrave Macmillan, 2005).

Diego Sánchez-Ancochea is Senior Lecturer in Economics at the Institute for the Study of the Americas, University of London. His research concentrates on trade policy and on state-society interactions in small Latin American Countries (LAC). Recent publications include "Development Trajectories and New Comparative Advantages: Costa Rica and the Dominican Republic under Globalization," *World Development*, June 2006 and "Domestic capital, Civil Servants and the State: Costa Rica and the Dominican Republic under Globalization," *Journal of Latin American Studies*, November 2005.

Kenneth C. Shadlen is a Political Scientist in the Development Studies Institute (DESTIN) at the London School of Economics and Political Science (LSE). He is the author of *Democratization without Representation: The Politics of Small Industry in Mexico* (University Park: Pennsylvania State University Press, 2004). His current research addresses the politics of intellectual property (IP) and the politics of North-South economic integration. His work on IP and integration has appeared in *Global Governance, International Studies Quarterly, Journal of Development Studies, Journal of International Development, Latin American Research Review, Review of International Political Economy, Studies in Comparative International Development*, and *World Economy*. He is completing a book manuscript on the politics of IP in Latin America.

Diana Tussie directs the Latin American Trade Network (LATN). She wrote one of the first books on the experience of developing countries in the times of the General Agreement on Tariffs and Trade. She is now a Research Fellow at the Argentine campus of the Latin American School of Social Sciences. She has served as Under Secretary for Trade Negotiations and was a member of the board of the International Trade Commission in Argentina. Her recent books include *Trade Negotiations in Latin America: Problems and Prospects*, (New York: Palgrave Macmillan, 2003); *El ALCA y las Cumbres de las Américas:¿Una nueva relación público-privada?* (Buenos Aires, Argentina: Biblos, 2003). In 2005 she was selected to join the High Level External Panel for the Trade Assistance Evaluation of the World Bank.

Gus Van Harten is Assistant Professor at the Osgoode Hall Law School in York University. He was previously a Lecturer in Law at the LSE. His work on investment law has been published in the *European Journal of International Law*, the *Review of International Political Economy, Arbitration International*, and the *Yale Human Rights & Development Law Journal*. He is the author of *Investment Treaty Arbitration and Public Law* (Oxford: Oxford University Press, 2007). His current research addresses the historical position of LACs, and contemporary strategies, with respect to investment treaty arbitration.

Index